Jamaica: Preparing for the Twenty-First Century

Preparing for the Twenty-First Century

Papers from

Jamaica 30 Anniversary Symposium

6, 7, October 1992, Kingston, Jamaica

Jamaica

Preparing for the Twenty-First Century

Edited by

Patsy Lewis

Published for
The Planning Institute of Jamaica

by

Ian Randle Publishers
Kingston, Jamaica

First Published in 1994
by
Ian Randle Publishers Limited
206 Old Hope Road, Kingston 6, Jamaica
for
The Planning Institute of Jamaica

ISBN 976-8100-29-X
A catalogue record for this book is available
from the National Library of Jamaica

Book design by David Mcleod
Cover design by Michael Gordon
Printed by DATA REPRODUCTIONS CORPORATION
            Rochester Hills, Michigan, USA.

PART 1
Economic Strategies and Perspectives for the Future

PART II
The Jamaican Production Environment

FOREWORD

I am pleased to be associated with the publication of the papers presented at the Symposium on Preparing for the Twenty-first Century, which was jointly sponsored by the Ministry of Finance and the Planning Institute of Jamaica, in cooperation with the United Nations Development Programme, to mark the 30th Anniverary of Jamaica's Independence.

The symposium provided an excellent opportunity to review Jamaica's development experience over the past 30 years and to identify strategic options for ensuring the country's economic viability in the twenty-first century. The discussions which took place during the symposium benefitted from presentations from local as well as foreign scholars and produced an interesting exchange of experience and cross-fertilization of ideas on a range of development issues. This has provided an extremely useful basis for the identification of practical policy options. I am confident that this publication of the symposium papers will be of interest to scholars, development practitioners and the general public.

Dennis Benn
UNDP Representative to Jamaica
December 1993

CONTRIBUTORS

Omar Davies

Minister of Finance (1993).

(Director General, Planning Institute of Jamaica at the time of the symposium and Special Adviser to the Minister of Finance (1992.) Davies has written widely on Caribbean economics and broad developmental problems.

Donald J Harris

Professor of Economics, Stanford University.

Harris has published *Capital Accumulation and Income Distribution*, (translated in Japanese and Spanish), and numerous papers on capital theory, income distribution, growth theory, economic development, history of economic thought, economics of discrimination, US economy, Caribbean, Latin America and Asian economies.

Michael Hepburn Best

Professor of Economics, University of Massachusetts, Amherst.

Best has published *The New Competition: Institutions of Industrial Restructuring*, Cambridge: Harvard University Press; Cambridge, UK: Polity Press, 1990. *The Politicized Economy*, Lexington, MA; D.C. Heath, first edition, 1976; second edition, 1982 (with William E. Connolly).

Sung Sang Park

Adviser, Asia Pacific Institute. Former President, Korea Institute for Industrial Economics and Technology (KIET). Former Governor, Bank of Korea. Author of the first Five Year Plan for the Korean economy in 1961.

Trevor Munroe

Head of Department of Government and Reader in Government and Politics, University of the West Indies, Jamaica. President of the University and Allied Workers' Union and founding member of the New Beginning Movement.

Munroe is known for his work on constitutional development in Jamaica and the Jamaican left. His works include *The Politics of Constitutional Decolonization in Jamaica: 1844-1962; Jamaican Politics: a Marxist Perspective in Transition; the Cold War and the Jamaican Left.*

Carl Stone (OM)

Professor, Department of Government, University of the West Indies, Jamaica (died February 1993). He holds the Order of Merit from the Jamaican Government.

Stone pioneered the use of survey research methods to study voting behaviour and public opinion in Jamaica. He has written eight books, including *Democracy and Clientilism; Class State and Democracy in Jamaica, Power in the Caribbean Basin,* and coedited four others; has published three monographs and more than 50 articles in books and academic journals.

Gladstone G Bonnick

Economist, World Bank. Former Deputy Governor, Bank of Jamaica, and former Director of National Planning Agency, Jamaica.

Maxine Henry-Wilson

Minister of State in the Ministry of Finance. (At the time of the symposium she was Minister of State in the Office of the Prime Minister.)

Henry-Wilson has published on women and public policy and institution building and policy implementation.

Beverley Anderson-Manley

Host of a respected Jamaican radio programme, 'The Breakfast Club', Jamaica's representative to the United Nations Commission on the Status of Women and Vice-President of the Third World Foundation, and a consultant on third world development issues and issues of communications and gender.

Arnoldo K Ventura

Special Adviser to the Prime Minister of Jamaica with responsibility for upgrading Jamaica's science and technology system.

Norman Girvan

Professor and Director of the Consortium Graduate School of the Social Sciences, University of the West Indies (UWI) and University of Guyana.

Girvan's work on the Jamaican bauxite/alumina industry, technology, the IMF, and Third World development issues, is well known. His publications include *Copper in Chile* and *Foreign Capital and Underdevelopment in Jamaica.*

Alfred M W Sangster

President, College of Arts Science and Technology.

Sangster holds the following distinctions: Commander of the Order of Distinction (Government of Jamaica); Musgrave Gold Medal (Institute of Jamaica); Hon LLD (UWI); Distinguished Service Award (CAST); Daily Gleaner Honour Award for 1989.

Richard Bernal

Jamaica's Ambassador to Washington and Permanent Representative to the United States of America.

Bernal, who lectured in economics at the UWI, Jamaica, has written widely on the debt problem, economic adjustment in developing countries, North-South issues, US/Jamaica relations and trade policy.

Sir Allster McIntyre

Vice-Chancellor of the University of the West Indies. Among his distinctions are: The Order of Merit and Commander of the Order of Distinction (Government of Jamaica) and the Cacique's Crown of Honour (Government of Guyana).

McIntyre has written extensively on regional integration, trade issues and development, relations between the Commonwealth Caribbean and North America and Europe, and the New International Economic Order.

ABBREVIATIONS

CARIBCAN *Caribbean Canadian Agreement*
CARICOM *Caribbean Community*
CAST *College of Arts Science and Technology*
CBI *Caribbean Basin Initiative*
CFTC *Commonwealth Fund for Technical Cooperation*
CNN *Cable News Network*
EAI *Enterprise for the Americas Initiative*
EEC *European Economic Community*
EES *European Economic Space*
EFF *Extended Fund Facility*
EFTA *European Free Trade Area*
EX-IM *Export-Import Bank*
FTA *Framework Agreement on Trade and Investment*
GATT *General Agreement on Trade and Tariffs*
GDP *Gross Domestic Product*
GMC *Gender Monitoring Checklist*
GNP *Gross National Product*
IDB *Inter-America Development Bank*
ILO *International Labour Organization*
IMF *International Monetary Fund*
ITC *International Trade Commission*
JAS *Jamaica Agricultural Society*

JDF *Jamaica Defense Force*
JIT *Just-in-Time*
JLP *Jamaica Labour Party*
JPSCO *Jamaica Public Service Company*
MITI *Ministry of Trade and Industry (Japan)*
NHT *National Housing Trust*
NIC *Newly Industrializing Countries*
NIR *Net International Reserves*
OECD *Organization for Economic Cooperation and Development*
OECS *Organization of Eastern Caribbean States*
PIOJ *Planning Institute of Jamaica*
PNP *People's National Party*
PRU *Policy Review Unit*
R&D *Research and Development*
SDC *Social Development Commission*
SPRU *Science Policy Research Unit (University of Sussex)*
SRC *Scientific Research Council*
TNC *Transnational Corporation*
UNDP *United Nations Development Programme*
USAID *United States Agency for International Development*
UWI *University of the West Indies*
XGS *Export of Goods and Services*

INTRODUCTION

Jamaica: Preparing for the twenty-first century brings together papers presented at a symposium held to mark Jamaica's thirtieth year of independence. It represents an attempt, three decades after the promise of independence, to reflect on the development strategies followed so far and their relevance for the future. The approach of the twenty-first century provides an appropriate focus for developing new strategies to tackle old problems. In doing this, the symposium avoided the tendency to equate development with economics, presenting instead, a wide menu covering, *inter alia,* the economy, technology, international trends, education, women's affairs, the political culture and violence.

Although its focus was on Jamaica, the symposium sought to provide a more international context for discussing problems, and this was achieved by the breadth of the presentations as well as the professional spread of the presenters. There were deliberate attempts to draw on lessons from the Newly Industrializing Countries of Southeast Asia, particularly South Korea as was evident in the presentation by Dr Sung Sang Park, the architect of South Korea's development plan. Michael Best and Robert Forrant sought to show the relevance of the concepts of just-in-time' production and 'flexible specialization' to Jamaican industry, and Ambassador Richard Bernal and Sir Alister McIntyre

brought their considerable knowledge of the international community
to show how movements on the world stage affected Jamaica.

The Symposium was the brainchild of then Minister of Finance,
Hugh Small, who, on assuming his position as Finance Minister, was
interested in having a long-term perspective on Jamaica's problems to
assist in defining policy; and was executed by the Planning Institute of
Jamaica (PIOJ), then headed by current Finance Minister Omar Davies.
Although presentations were made primarily by practising academics,
the symposium sought to widen the scope by extending invitations to
a wide cross section of political groups, private sector and trade union
Organizations, public servants, and service groups. It was given the
financial support of the UNDP in Jamaica, headed by Denis Benn, who
was a keen supporter of the project.

This book is divided into four sections which group together articles reflecting a broad theme. Part I includes articles which analyse
Jamaica's economic performance and suggest directions for the future. Davies, Best, Forrant and Harris all present a broad historic sweep
examining the performance of the Jamaican economy, while providing
an in-depth analysis of the periods which perhaps are of greatest
interest — the 1970s and 1980s. They all go beyond an analysis of the
recent past and suggest prescriptions for the future. Best and Forrant
argues that though different policies were pursued in both periods,
the effect was the same: to worsen the economic conditions of most
Jamaicans. This was because neither addressed the fundamental issue
of production. They present a 'third' production-led alternative. The
final article, by Sung Sang Park, takes the experience of South Korea
and the other Southeast Asian NICs as its point of departure to suggest
an economic model suitable for small developing countries, specifically Jamaica.

The articles in Part II seek to describe the environment within
which production must occur. Munroe analyses the industrial relations
climate, a key consideration when a development path emphasising
foreign investment is advocated. His perspective is historical, seeking
to identify the different social and political influences in order to
explain industrial relations today. Stone, with his focus on the political
culture, examines what is perhaps the most important element in any
development strategy: it is impossible to appreciate either the character of the Jamaican economy or the environment for economic development, without an understanding of the dynamics of the political
culture. Stone's article, one of his last, is an important contribution to
his legacy of defining and explaining the inner-workings of Jamaican

society. Bonnick singles out a particular aspect of that culture — the endemic violence in the society. He makes a strong correlation between economic development and a peaceful, relatively crime-free environment. He argues that it is difficult for the best laid economic plans to succeed where the crime rate actively discourages investment. Thus, Jamaica's priority must be the creation of a stable climate for economic development, and he prescribes some drastic and controversial measures for achieving this.

Anderson-Manley and Wilson both highlight sectors, often neglected, which, nevertheless, have an important role in defining the development process. Both emphasise the need to empower people to make them full participants in their own development. Anderson-Manley examines this from the perspective of women — the neglected majority. She argues for a gender-specific agenda which puts the concerns of women at the forefront of policy. Henry-Wilson takes the perspective of empowerment at the community level. She recognizes the key role the community has to play in development. In a period when the community is practically non-existent in many impoverished areas, hers is a timely and urgent call for a refocusing on the strength of the community as a forum for involving ordinary people in defining and addressing their needs.

Part III looks at technology and education. The two articles on technology, by Ventura and Girvan, speak to an oft-neglected aspect of the development process. We are reminded that technology is, more than ever, an instrumental aspect of any development strategy. Girvan argues for a shift away from natural commodity exports to a strategy which has technological advancements and human resources as its focus. Ventura looks generally at the importance of technology globally, and urges the more effective utilisation of existing technology in the development process. Alfred Sangster also looks at a further critical aspect of the role of education in the development process, arguing that education was in crisis. He called for increased financial commitment to education and argued that it needed to be made more relevant.

The articles by Richard Bernal and Alister McIntyre, in Part IV, both bring their authors' international perspective to bear on the problem: McIntyre, from his long relationship with regional and international bureaucracies, and Richard Bernal from his experience as Jamaica's ambassador to Washington, discuss the effects of changes in the world economy on development. Bernal's focus is Jamaica, while McIntyre's is more broadly on the member countries of the Caribbean

Community. This difference in focus only serves to highlight the commonality of the issues raised by the globalization of the world economy. Indeed, to ask what effects these changes have on Jamaica, is to ask the same question for the entire English-speaking Caribbean.

Although the book focuses on the academic presentations, it tries to present a broader picture of the actual conference itself in appendices at the end. Appendix 1 presents the main speeches made at the opening ceremony which provide some idea of why such a symposium was thought important. Appendix 2 summarises the reports of discussants on the papers as well as discussions from the floor. Finally, appendix 3 summarises the panel discussion held at the end of the symposium.

Patsy Lewis

PART I

Economic Strategies and Perspectives for the Future

CHAPTER 1

The Jamaican Economy since Independence:
Agenda for the Future

Omar Davies

Introduction

In reflecting on the possible approach to this challenging topic, it occurred to me that there were several ways in which the discussion could be handled, each with some degree of relevance and validity. One could identify certain key economic variables and, presumably, it should not be difficult to agree on a set of such indicators and track the changes over the 30 year period. One could use these same indicators and examine the performance of different political regimes. Another approach would be to focus on the influence of external institutions on policy decisions and by implication on domestic economic performance. This latter approach is separate and apart from, but complementary to, assessing the impact of international developments, both economic and political, on the domestic economy. Finally, there is need to assess the effects of domestic developments, however broadly these are defined, on the economy.

If I have learnt anything over the past three and a half years, it is that all the factors listed above must be taken into account in making decisions, whether on a broad policy issue or on some specific issue of taxation. Hence, I have decided that the paper will attempt to incorporate all these factors into the analysis of the past 30 years. Whilst we should have no difficulty identifying exactly what the numbers say in terms of each variable, there will undoubtedly be differences in the relative importance of each causal factor. In fact, it is to be expected that there will be disagreements about causation.

The paper will review the main economic trends over this period; discuss the influence of external factors and the policy dictates of the international financial institutions; speak to the lessons from the past which should guide the future agenda; and, finally, make a statement on the perceived future role of the state in the economy.

Review of Economic Performance

Jamaica's economic performance during the first decade after independence was directly affected by the post World War II economic boom of the 1950s. During the 1960s, real Gross Domestic Product rose at an annual average rate of 5.5 per cent. Apart from the output from the traditional agricultural sectors, the economy had grown during the 1950s as a result of the rapid expansion in the mining, tourism, and manufacturing sectors facilitated by very generous incentive legislation. During the 1960s, the expansion in these sectors continued and there were the expected changes in the structure of the economy, with agriculture's percentage contribution to GDP declining, and manufacturing's increasing.

These positive global figures masked certain worrying underlying factors which clearly indicated the fragility of the economy. One such worrying feature was that the external accounts showed persistent current account deficits which were offset by direct foreign investments in bauxite/alumina, tourism, and manufacturing. Hence, much of the growth which took place during this period was highly dependent on the availability of external investment capital as well as on the buoyancy of international export markets. However, in terms of real sector performance, there were also worrying signs. In agriculture, particularly in the sugar industry, decline had set in. In manufacturing, there had always been questions concerning the 'quality' of investments which had been attracted. Most of the investments were highly import-dependent, not only, as would be expected, for capital goods, but also for raw material inputs. In fact, many of these entities were simply repackaging operations, benefitting from the low wages which obtained in Jamaica as well as the high tariff regime.

There were also social indicators which demonstrated quite clearly that the majority of the population had reaped little of the benefits from the record levels of economic growth. Despite the investment inflows and continued high levels of emigration, primarily to England, unemployment remained a major problem. Furthermore, income distribution remained badly skewed, with the top 20 per cent of households commandeering approximately 50 per cent of national income.

During the second decade of independence the high rate of growth which had characterised the previous 15-20 years came to an end. There was a sharp reduction in the rate of capital inflows, which affected investment levels, and the negative results of the shortcomings of the manufacturing and agriculture sectors, which were noted above, came dramatically to the fore. There was a sharp decline in agricultural output, particularly in export agriculture. Similarly, there was a decline in output from manufacturing which had reached its peak in the early 1970s.

The balance of payments situation worsened, with a significant decline in net international reserves. Several factors contributed to this deterioration. Perhaps most significant were the increases in the price of oil which quadrupled during the decade. These increases affected the economy directly in two ways. In the first place, it increased the import bill and, in the second, the recession which followed the first round of increases compressed international demand for exports. In 1977 the oil bill accounted for 30 per cent of the value of imports. By this time, the large foreign investment inflows which had characterised the earlier period had dried up. The balance of payments problem was partially addressed by increased external borrowing. This dependence on resources borrowed externally would lead to serious negative repercussions in the following decade.

Furthermore, the major investments in the bauxite/alumina sector came to an end during the decade. Production from Jamaica reached a peak in the mid 1970s (which has never been attained subsequently) and then started to decline, partly as a result of the decision of the international companies to locate new investments in countries with cheaper power sources.

Whilst the negative effects of the external developments were significant enough, there were movements on the domestic front which also contributed to the deteriorating economic situation. It is fair to say that there was mutual distrust between the governing party and the private sector. This mutual lack of confidence led to massive capital flight which, although still not precisely quantified, is known to have been of significant proportions. This capital flight contributed to a worsening balance of payments situation.

The government/private sector relationship had a negative impact on other areas of the economy and, in certain instances, led to government actions which were not originally part of any articulated policy position. A specific example relates to the government's increased role in tourism. This was a reaction to widespread private sector withdrawal and what could have led to a collapse of a sector that had by then emerged as the largest gross earner of foreign exchange.

In addition to its direct involvement in economic sectors, the government attempted to use the fiscal budget to address some of the socio-economic problems that it faced. Given the overall economic downturn, increased government expenditure translated into a larger fiscal deficit. Although the increase in the fiscal deficit represented an incorrect policy decision, the mistake was compounded by a characteristic of the government's capital budget which still remains today: this is, that a significant portion of what is included in the 'Capital ' budget is nothing more than recurrent expenditure. Perhaps, more importantly, is the fact that most capital projects were inefficiently implemented. Hence, whilst increased government capital expenditure could be defended in light of reduced private sector investments, given the inefficient manner in which the state's capital projects were implemented, much of the hoped-for expansion in economic activity had not materialized.

In addition to its own direct efforts to stimulate the economy, the government in the 1970s adopted various policy positions aimed at eliciting positive reactions from the private sector. Although the need to increase export earnings was identified as the priority, and there were several special incentives reserved for exporters, a summary assessment of the policies showed that they were inward-looking and protectionist. The most prominent of these were import restrictions, foreign exchange rationing, and price controls. Some benefits resulted initially from these policies: the most notable being the expansion in the output of the domestic agriculture sector. However, in general, the government's increased regulatory stance elicited little support from those it was meant to encourage and led to widespread uncertainty about government's future role in the economy.

An integral part of the economy's performance during the latter part of the 1970s was the interaction between the government and the International Monetary Fund (IMF). During that period the government entered into two agreements with the Fund, a Standby, which came into effect in June 1977 and was terminated in December of the same year, and an Extended Fund Facility (EFF), which began in May 1978 and ended in December 1979. Both agreements were terminated before their scheduled completion dates. In retrospect, this was inevitable as the attainment of the standard IMF 'targets' could have been viewed as being mutually exclusive to many of the government's own policy initiatives.

The coming to office of a JLP Administration in late 1980 ostensibly eliminated the contradictions in policy which obtained during the latter part of the PNP's term in office. As such, the new EFF negotiated in early 1981 was very mild, in terms of adjustments required. In particular, the government was able to maintain the value of the Jamaican currency at the existing level, even while liberalizing import controls. This EFF agreement was part of a major financial support package which was put together for Jamaica and it was justified on the basis of an expected major turn around in the economy over a three-year period.

Whilst positive growth was recorded during the initial years of the decade, this was due more to the level of external financing which had become available, than to any fundamental changes in the real economy. The failure of the real sectors to respond and increase output, as was projected, was not surprising as there had been very little substantive change in economic policy. As happened in the latter part of the 1970s, there was a premature termination of the EFF, followed by a two-year period of sharp adjustment measures. These included systematic devaluation of the currency, cuts in public sector employment, reductions in the fiscal deficit as a percentage of GDP, the removal of several price and import controls and of most subsidies on items such as basic foods. This period of adjustment also coincided with a sharp downturn in the bauxite/alumina industry resulting from the worldwide economic recession.

Not surprisingly, during this period the economy experienced negative growth and high levels of inflation. Furthermore, the effort to reduce the fiscal deficits resulted in significant increases in the prices of goods and services produced by state enterprises such as the Jamaica Public Service Company (JPSCO). Added to all the above, the rapid changes in the value of the Jamaican currency contributed to an unstable business environment.

The latter half of the decade was far more positive. A major contributory factor was the fall in world oil prices which, because it was not passed on to domestic consumers, simultaneously assisted in

reducing the external trade deficit and in bolstering the fiscal accounts. The stabilization of the exchange rate was another positive
factor which contributed to a reduction in the rate of inflation.

To a large extent the period 1986 to the present, although covering
two political regimes, has been marked by a continuation of economic
policies. There have been a few significant departures, the most important of which was the PNP administration's decision to totally liberalize
the foreign exchange regime. This decision partly contributed to the
record levels of inflation recorded in both calendar 1991 and fiscal year
1991/92. However, there are certain clear positive results which can be
identified; the most critical is that the economy has recorded positive
growth for six consecutive years (1986-1991) —the longest period of
sustained growth in two decades. There was a systematic decrease in
unemployment levels over the same period, despite the reduction in
employment by the state. There is the obvious question as to the
'quality' of the new jobs being created and this deserves further
analysis. Nonetheless, the trend is encouraging.

One feature of the Jamaican economy which continues to be of
concern is the size of the country's external debt. The stock of debt
doubled during the 1980s, passing the US$4,000 million mark. Al-
though there has been a reduction in this total resulting from the
write-offs by the US and Canada, the country's debt servicing requirements remain one of the major handicaps to sustained growth in the
economy. Most analysts focus on the implications for external accounts, and these are obvious and important. However, it may be
argued that the fiscal implications may be even more important from
a developmental point of view, when such a large percentage of government expenditure is accounted for by debt servicing.

The Effects of External Factors and Institutions

During the 30-year period under review, one fact which has been
consistently evident is the extent to which our economy is subject to
developments in the wider world. The shock of the oil price increases
in the early 1970s brought the lesson home very sharply and made us
appreciate, in retrospect, the benefits of the relative stability of the
international economy during the 1960s. Similarly, the bauxite/alu-
mina companies' decision to redirect new investments during the
1970s, did not only have an impact on the growth of the domestic
industry, but also brought into sharp focus the extent to which the

investment inflows had served to 'paper over' some of the critical defects in the domestic economy. The memory of the consequences of the oil price increases in the 1970s gave more than adequate reason for concern during the most recent military engagement in the Middle East. The sad truth is that the economy is no less open to the negative effects of a major increase in the price of oil in 1992 than it was 20 years ago. Nor has there been any progress to speak of in the development of energy conservation measures. In this particular example, because of the direct involvement of the US, there were also negative repercussions for the tourist industry.

More recently, the dissolution of the former Soviet Union has affected our earnings from bauxite exports. This disruption, although negative, has not been devastating because exports to this market represents only a small percentage of total bauxite exports. Apart from external factors, the Jamaican economy, especially in the last 15 years or so, has been affected by the policy dictates of the major international financial institutions from which we borrow, as well as by those of our major bilateral creditors. Whilst it is impossible to establish definitive dates to mark the beginning of particular periods of influence, there can be no doubt that the decade of the 1980s, dominated by the trans-Atlantic Reagan-Thatcher alliance, was such a period. Their leadership, and the policies which they articulated, did not only dominate their domestic agendas but also had a profound influence on the policies of international financial institutions. Whilst these institutions had always explicitly supported the primacy of the market in the allocation of resources, they became increasingly aggressive in their policy demands.

Furthermore, although the official stance required continued denial of the existence of 'cross conditionalities', in reality, the increasing complementarity of loan requirements amounted to nothing less than this. There was once something of an unofficial division of 'territory' between institutions, with matters related to exchange rate, monetary and fiscal policy being seen as the exclusive preserve of the IMF. The World Bank's area of responsibility covered projects and adjustment loans, whilst the IDB was restricted to project loans on the grounds that it did not possess the technical support to analyse the kinds of issues involved in IMF-type programmes or adjustment loans.

In recent years, there have been significant changes in this arrangement of areas of responsibility with a blurring of 'boundaries' of operations. These changes have not necessarily been to the benefit of borrowing countries. In Jamaica's experience, the blurring of responsibilities between the multilaterals first started when the IDB took the decision to begin cofinancing adjustment loans with the World Bank. Jamaica was one of the first countries to be considered for a loan cofinanced by the two institutions and we entered into the negotiations on the assumption that there would be a common set of conditions and that once negotiations with one were completed, disbursements from both would follow automatically. This turned out not to be the case as the IDB demanded significant additional conditions once the negotiations with the World Bank were completed. Hence, in reality, the expected major benefit of cofinancing to the borrowing country, whereby resources from two institutions would be linked to the same set of conditionalities — as had been originally promoted — never materialised.

The negative effect of this change was two-fold. In the first place, there had to be a new assessment of the implications of the new adjustment measures which were added. However, since the expected inflows from the new loan had already been counted in the projected balance of payments within the context of the existing IMF programme, any delay in agreeing to the additional conditionalities simply translated into a greater probability of failure to meet the quarterly IMF target for the country's Net International Reserves (NIR).

The IDB's decision that it now had the capacity to make adjustment loans on its own simply formalised what was already the practice. However, this means that at any moment, any or all of the three major multilateral financial institutions from which we borrow can have a say in determining critical policy issues. It may be argued that there are potential benefits to be reaped if the three institutions were to take a unified position but our experience to date has shown that the blurring of areas of influence has been to our detriment. The situation becomes a little more complicated if we add the intervention of the United States Agency for International Development (USAID), which itself has begun to attach macro-economic policy conditionalities to some of its support. In fact, USAID preceded the multilaterals in terms of its strong advocacy for privatization.

Lessons Which Should Have Been Learnt

In reflecting on Jamaica's experience over the 30-year period, it is stating the obvious to say that the developments in economic performance, as well as the changes in economic policy have been many. At first it seems a daunting task to try to extract from the experiences of the period a small number of lessons which should help us to formulate our policy agenda for the future.

The first lesson which should have been learnt is that economic growth is best facilitated within an environment of stability and predictable policy direction. If we go even slightly beyond the period under review to the 1950s, it seems clear that the periods of sustained economic growth — the decades of the 1950s and 1960s and the more recent and shorter period, 1986 to present — have been characterized by, if not a national consensus, then by something close to general agreement on broad economic policy. These periods can be contrasted with the mid to late 1970s and the mid 1980s when there were rapid shifts in policies, resulting in general uncertainty about economic direction. This should not be interpreted as advocating an acceptance of the *status quo*, or inflexibility in the face of changing circumstances (external or domestic). However, the need for clear, unambiguous policy directions remains paramount.

Within the more general framework of stability outlined above, there are more specific objectives to be pursued. The first is a tight fiscal policy. It is all too easy for a country to slip into a situation where its fiscal deficit begins to grow rapidly. Halting this growth and reversing the trend becomes much more difficult the longer the wait to address the problem. As the fiscal deficit grows, there are inevitable negative consequences in terms of the need for increased borrowing and/or price and exchange rate instability.

One of the results of lax fiscal policy which has had the most devastating effect on the economy has been the need to borrow extensively from overseas sources. Although there has been some improvement in the overall debt indicators in recent years, the burden of servicing the external debt will remain a major constraint to our growth potential for the medium term. When the effects of a large debt servicing obligation are combined with those of devaluations of the order experienced during the past 15 years, the result is a government with an extremely limited capacity to address urgent problems. This is the situation which characterises Jamaica today.

This then leads to the next lesson that should have been learnt: the need to make price stability a priority. Rates of inflation which are significantly above those of your major trading partners, or those of your major competitors must invariably lead to exchange rate adjustments.

As regards this latter issue, the lesson which we should have learnt from the period is that instability in the exchange rate market is a major contributor to uncertainty. As such, the recommendations concerning adherence to policies in order to ensure tight fiscal management and stable prices are indirectly related to the desire to achieve stable exchange rates, relative to our major trading partners. However, if these efforts fail for whatever reasons, and it becomes evident that the currency is overvalued, it is counterproductive to try to defend it under such circumstances, even if the country has the foreign exchange reserves to attempt such a defence. In Jamaica's case, this is simply a hypothetical situation. In the absence of such reserves the methods which we have used — import controls and controls on foreign exchange transactions — were not only unsuccessful in the past, but are doomed to become less and less relevant in the future with the ever increasing facility for the movement of capital internationally.

Future Role of the State

The role of the state in the economy has changed drastically over the period under review. Some of the most important changes have taken place in the last five years and they mirror similar adjustments elsewhere in the world. By and large, these changes have been carried out in an ad hoc manner with decisions taken on a case-by-case basis and it is only in recent years that there has been an attempt to define a clear set of guidelines for the state's role. Specifically, the state is in the process of divesting most of the economic entities which it once owned, which produced goods and services for sale on a commercial basis.

What of the state's role in the future? Responsibility for designing and implementing fiscal, monetary, and external trade policies will still remain the exclusive domain of government. In other areas, even in circumstances where privatization has taken place, there is need for the establishment and maintenance of a regulatory framework. The privatization of the telecommunications company and the planned divestment of other monopolies provide adequate examples of the need for a clearly defined framework within which these entities should operate when ownership is transferred to private hands.

In terms of the social services, the state's responsibility will remain dominant for the foreseeable future. This is not only necessary to maintain standards but also to ensure that those who are economically disadvantaged have access to adequate educational opportunities and basic health services. However, a critical task which has to be addressed is that of recovering as much of the cost of providing these services from those who are able to pay. A specific example relates to the provision of tertiary education. The simple fact is that unless cost recovery becomes a central objective, the existing scarcity of resources will imply either a severe curtailment of the number of individuals who can benefit from education at this level, or a serious erosion of the quality of training provided. The converse to the problem of cost recovery is improved targeting to ensure that those who are at the bottom of the economic ladder are the ones who first benefit from those resources which are available. A great deal of work must be done in this regard.

The question must be posed as to whether there is any role for direct state intervention in economic activity. The answer is yes. Certain specific examples come to mind: the first relates to the housing sector. For the foreseeable future the state, through the National Housing Trust (NHT), will represent the major source of finance for this sector. Furthermore, any intervention on behalf of those who are unable to afford a conventional unit will of necessity be the responsibility of the state. A second area where direct intervention by the state must continue is in the agricultural sector. This sector is critical, not only in terms of economic output, but also because of its impact on stabilizing rural population and addressing the rural/urban imbalance in the distribution of services and economic opportunities. More generally, the state will have to retain the right to intervene to stimulate production in specific geographical zones where, for a variety of reasons, reliance on the market will not bring about desired economic activity.

In addition to the above, the state must reserve the right to intervene, in the national interest, in key sectors of the economy and either initiate development or support an existing investment. A concrete example of this is the bauxite/alumina industry. The decision of the government in the eighties to keep the Halse Hall alumina plant in production and subsequently to become joint owners with Alcoa was courageous and correct. The state must reserve the right to carry out similar acts in the future.

Conclusion

The paper has sought to review, briefly, the major developments in the economy over the past three decades, identifying changes due to external factors as opposed to domestic policy decisions. It has sought to pin-point some lessons which should have been learnt from the period and with it an implied agenda for future policy direction and a role for the state. It is hoped that our major focus will be on the question of the way forward.

CHAPTER 2

The Jamaican Economy in the Twenty-first Century:
Challenges to Development and Requirements of a Response

Donald Harris

The Problem

As I look back through our history, from the beginnings in slave society to the present, I see an economy characterized by an enormous potential for growth embodied in the labouring and learning and survival capacity of our people and in the richness of our natural resources. And, yet, this potential has failed to be realized in cumulative and sustained growth in the economy as a whole. Therein lies an apparent contradiction that continues to challenge our collective intellect and imagination. It also forces us to ask ourselves: in what sense, if any, have we made headway, at least in terms of economic growth, and perhaps also in terms of 'progress'.

It is not that the economy has not experienced growth in one form or another. In fact, there have been episodes of significant economic expansion in the past. Looking broadly at the historical record, I would identify four such major episodes. First, in chronological order, is the heyday of sugar and slave economy at the end of the eighteenth century. Second is the period of rapid emergence of bananas as the leading export product in the late nineteenth century. Third is the interwar period of export boom in agricultural products leading up to the Great Depression. Fourth, and most recent, is the Golden Age of the 1950s and sixties, associated with bauxite-alumina and tourism.

But, inasmuch as these were all boom periods (at least one, in my judgement, deserves the title of Golden Age), their striking feature is that, in each and every case, as if by an inexorable logic, the momentum petered out and the economy fell back into a mode of stagnation or decline.

The growth, when it did come, has therefore been spasmodic. Moreover, it has always been highly concentrated in one or a few sectors of the economy, oftentimes at the expense of growth in other sectors. Furthermore, if output levels have selectively increased, productivity levels throughout the economy have tended to be sluggish. And, perhaps most markedly, growth of employment has failed to keep pace with the labour force, so that there has been chronic unemployment, open and disguised, of the working population throughout much of this century.

These generalisations are supported by careful and detailed study of the historical record by many scholars.[1] Some pieces of the evidence concerning the most recent episode are also presented here, though it is not my purpose to do more than highlight a few relevant features.

Rather, the main purpose of this paper is to suggest that there is a definite economic logic underlying this long-standing pattern of economic performance. It is the logic of a particular kind of economic process: a process that is characterized by an internal, built-in mechanism of persistent drag or *inertia*. The understanding of this process and the adoption of effective measures to counter its present-day sources of drag or inertia are necessary requirements for our ability to progress as we advance into the twenty-first century. In particular, if we want to achieve real progress, we have to find ways of breaking out of the old mould and shifting over to a different and new way of doing things. Some indications are given here, in broad outline, of the crucial requirements of an effective new way.

The task of making this transition is made doubly difficult, however, by the fact that the world we now see emerging around us is fundamentally different in important respects from the world in which we managed to experience the booms of the past. It therefore calls for us to exercise our reserves of creativity and drive and fresh, new, enterprising initiatives, as never before in our history.

This paper also has another purpose. It has been customary, among many of us, to point the finger at 'outside forces' and to claim that they are responsible for the ills that affect us. I suppose I would have to agree that in a certain specific sense that claim may have some validity, the exact sense remaining to be shown. But, the purpose of this paper is to explore a rather different approach. Specifically, I want to try to identify the levers that we ourselves control that may possibly be internal sources of our problems. This is in the belief that at some point we have to take responsibility for change in our condition and, to that end, we have to begin with those levers that we ourselves control.

A Case in Point: The Recent Golden Age and its Aftermath.

In order to break into the problematic identified above, I choose as an example the episode that is fresh in our minds and has the most readily available historical records, namely, the Golden Age that the Jamaican economy has just passed through in the last 40 years or so.

This episode is a truly remarkable and distinctive one in our history. Though the detailed comparative work going back through previous episodes has not yet been done, I would hazard the guess that it is the period of the greatest quantitative expansion in our history and of the most significant and broadly based structural transformation. If this is granted, then, it is all the more remarkable that this expansion phase, like previous ones, was followed also by a contraction phase of corresponding dimensions, involving sharp declines in production and living standards and widespread dislocation and retrenchment throughout the whole economy and society. If the expansion phase was spectacular (and it certainly was), the contraction phase was a disaster of equal proportions. It took the form, for instance, of a fall in per capita income from its peak in 1975 (which was only slightly higher than in 1972) back to a level in 1986 equal to that of 1969. Thus, one could say, it set us back at least 17 years (and the setback may turn out to be 20 years or more when the figures are all in). Remarkably, too, this latter phase was not accompanied by the deep social upheavals that occurred in previous episodes.

It could be argued, and some observers suggested at the time, that the Jamaican economy was poised for 'take-off' in the late sixties and early seventies. Certainly, it appeared that many of the relevant conditions were then in place. But, instead, it is now clear that the economy very soon after this went into a nose-dive, with long term consequences from which the country is only now beginning to recover, and that very weakly. In the light of this performance, it seems now that the take-off theorists should be made to eat their words!

What happened to bring about this rupture, that is, to knock the economy off the Golden Age path and throw it into a tail-spin with the consequences that we observe till today?

A full answer to this question is no doubt complex, and requires systematic and detailed analysis. No one, to my knowledge, has yet developed a comprehensive analysis of the whole episode. In two earlier papers, I tried my hand at this analysis. The first (Harris, 1970) gives a detailed econometric analysis of the growth pattern prevailing during the period 1950-1966, with projections forward to 1975 that are, in retrospect, amazingly robust (up to 1973, but not after).[2] The second (Harris, 1990) develops a macroeconomic model as a frame-work for analysis of the more recent experience and presents initial results of an empirical analysis of data for the period 1969-1989. Further work remains to be done along these lines, so as to uncover thereby the deeper levels of the story.

But, meanwhile, it is possible to identify some broad patterns. For this purpose, I have assembled in the Appendix of this paper some tables and graphs summarising these patterns as they appear from the data. For analysis, I divide this historical episode into two periods: 1950-1965, for which the data and results are taken from the 1970 paper, and 1969-1989, with data and results from the 1990 paper as well as some new calculations made for the present paper.

For ease of reference, let me simply quote here the main findings from the 1990 paper (pp. 31-33):

(a) The period of 1950 to the early 1970s was a kind of 'golden age' of growth in the Jamaican economy, as measured by all of the relevant indices of economic performance. A summary measure of this per-formance is represented by an average annual growth rate of GDP equal to 6.5 per cent for the whole period.

(b) In the subsequent period up to 1989, there has been a dramatic change in economic performance. One might date the transition or turning point from, say, 1973. A sharp reversal of trend evidently occurred during 1974-1980. There was virtual stagnation during 1981-1985. The economy picked up again during 1986-1989. The entire period of 1969-1989 is marked by an absolute decline in GDP at an average annual rate of 0.24 per cent and in all the major components of GDP on the expenditure side, except for government consumption, exports, and imports.

(c) The period 1969-1989 has a number of striking features, some of which may be regarded as indicating significant change in the underlying structure of the economy. For comparative purposes, it is useful to take as a reference point the corresponding data for the 1950-1965 period.

(d) The most obvious and commonly noted feature of the 1969-1989 period is the sharp increase in the role of foreign indebtedness. This change has converted the economy into what one might properly call a 'debt-propelled economy'.

(e) Along with the increase in foreign indebtedness has come a significant decrease in the role of net direct investment from abroad.

(f) But what is equally, if not more, striking is that these changes have been accompanied by a transformation in the relations of consumption, saving, and investment as well as the role of exports in the Jamaican economy.

(g) Net saving declined from an average of 11 percent of national income in the earlier period to 7 per cent in the later period. The saving ratio actually turned negative in 1976-1977, 1981-1982, and 1985. Most of the dissaving occurred in the government and household sectors.

(h) Gross fixed capital formation as a proportion of GDP was on average higher in the later period, but the level of gross investment declined during this period at an annual average rate of 1.45 per cent.

(i) The share of private consumption in GDP fell from 75 to 65 per cent. The share of government consumption rose from 10 to 17 per cent.

(j) There is a definite inverse relation between government consumption and gross investment in the later period.

(k) Both exports and imports have risen as a share of GDP, indicating that the economy has become more 'open' in this sense. Estimated income and price elasticities of export demand are both low, respectively 0.52 and -0.34. Import demand has high income elasticity of 1.11 and low price elasticity of -0.29. These elasticity estimates cast doubt on the stability of the balance of payments adjustment mechanism.

(l) In the earlier period, export growth was highly and positively correlated with growth of GDP (with correlation coefficient of 0.96). In the later period, the correlation of exports and GDP is low and negative at -0.26.

(m) The wage share rose markedly during 1969-1977 and has been declining ever since.

All of these trends and changes, taken individually, are quite remarkable and dramatic. Taken together, they constitute the central elements of the problematic requiring to be analysed in order to understand the recent history of the Jamaican economy and the prospects for the future.

For present purposes, I wish to focus only on a few key points that are relevant to the argument of this paper. The first concerns the substantial decline in the export growth rate from an average annual rate of 9.3 per cent in 1950-1965 to 2.39 per cent in 1969-1989. Insofar as exports constitute a major driving force in the growth of the economy, this decline could be considered a significant factor in the downturn. But, even so, it is not sufficient to explain what happened. This is because the actual export growth rate in the later period was a positive and quite respectable 2.39 per cent per annum while, on the other hand, GDP declined at an average rate of -0.24 per cent during the same period. This indicates that something must have happened to break the strong positive correlation between exports and GDP established in the previous period. It means, certainly, that the mechanisms which would normally transmit the impetus from growth of exports to expansion of GDP were not at work in this period. Therefore, factors other than the decline in export growth must be introduced to explain this striking structural discontinuity. This is a key finding of this research. It also helps to reveal the crucial role of internal factors.

There was also a significant decline in the level of investment during the later period, in part attributable to reductions in the level of net foreign direct investment. Again, this may help to explain the downturn, but only partially. For, though foreign direct investment declined, there were large capital inflows in the form of official loans and grants from multilateral and bilateral sources during 1975-1985. It is also notable that during the 1969-1989 period the average share of investment in GDP was higher compared with the earlier period 1950-1965.

What is of crucial significance is that, in this context of decreased growth of exports and decline in foreign direct investment, there was a sharp rise in the level of government consumption, sharp enough to push up its share of GDP from 10 per cent in the earlier period to 17 per cent on average in the later period, reaching a high of 20-22 per cent during all the years 1976-1983. This increase in consumption was certainly at the expense of public investment, and must also have helped to induce cutbacks in private investment to the extent that the latter is led by the former.

As to the level of private consumption (excluding transfer payments), that actually fell at an average rate of -0.22 per cent over the later period and its average share fell from 75 to 65.3 per cent between the two periods. But, like government consumption, the share of private consumption also rose significantly within the later period, from a low of about 60 per cent in 1970 to a high of near 70 per cent in 1981-1985.

To complete this picture one would have to take account of the actual composition of saving and investment in the later period. For this, relevant quantitative data are not readily available, but the evidence suggests that much of the activity underlying the numbers in this area took the form of the flight of capital out of the country and an internal shift to investment and speculation in real estate.

There is an evident question here of how one explains the causal factors at work in this situation. In this connection, there has been a notable tendency in existing discussions to point to the role of 'external causes'. The decreased growth rate of exports and fall in foreign investment would presumably be put in this category. However, this idea itself begs another question, namely, to what extent were those supposed 'external' factors strictly autonomous and independent or, instead, induced by *internal* developments within the economy? This would require more detailed study. But even if those factors are shown to be autonomous, independent, and significant (and there is no gainsaying that they were to some extent), that result would simply beg a further question, namely: *Why did internal factors not respond to compensate, at least in part, for adverse external circumstances?* I consider this to be a key issue that has to be faced.

As regards this particular issue, what this analysis shows is that there were *internal* causal factors at work as well. Primary among these was the collapse of saving and investment in the government and household sectors. The other side of this collapse is what can fairly be called a *consumption binge*, taking the form of the observed sharp increase in the share of consumption in GDP by both the government and private sector. Evidently, the increased consumption was financed by foreign borrowing to a large extent, and by dissaving. The consequence of this, in turn, has been to create a heavy overhang of debt payments that continues to plague the economy and to hamper possibilities of a recovery.

The private sector also played its part in this process in ways that contributed to the collapse of saving and investment. For instance, it is evident that many of the actors in this sector simply 'ran for cover', so to speak, seeking safe shelters for their saving and capital, and that served to drain away the potential for productive investment.

It does not help matters to say that this consumption binge was necessary in order to maintain the standard of living of the poor. On the contrary, from close examination of the actual tax and expenditure flows involved, the evidence shows that, at least in part, the increased consumption took place *at the expense of the poor*, because of redistributive effects across different income groups.[3]

Besides, even if one discounts the magnitude of these redistributive effects, there is still the key issue of the intertemporal tradeoff involved, which cannot be ignored. It arises from the fact that the consumption binge of today imposes a necessity to cut back consumption tomorrow as a cost on tomorrow's consumers. Since the cost cumulates over time, it may turn out to be quite high.[4]

I have tried to examine this issue analytically by performing the following simple exercise. Take the actual level of per capita consumption in 1970 as the starting point. Assume that, from 1970 on, consumption grows at the observed average growth rate of exports equal to 2.39 per cent per annum for the period 1969-1989. This assumption is equivalent to supposing a steady state process with exports as the driving force. Call the time path of per capita consumption generated in this way the path of 'potential consumption'. It is the path of consumption that would be sustainable if the normal structural relations that feed back from the growth of exports to the growth of consumption continued to hold. Now, compare this path with the actual path of per capita consumption, and compute the ratio of the two. The result is shown in Table 7 and in Figure 1.

It turns out from this exercise that the actual path rises above the potential path for a while, from 1971 to 1976, by an average of about 6 per cent per annum. But after 1976 there is a precipitous fall of the actual below the potential path, down to a ratio of the two of 63 per cent in 1987 when the process runs out of data.

Thus, in this exercise, the intertemporal tradeoff is between (a) a temporary gain in consumption of 6 per cent per annum for six years and (b) recurrent losses thereafter growing to 37 per cent in the last year of the recorded accounts. This last year might only be the bottom of a process that perhaps continues indefinitely or, at best, until actual consumption rises sufficiently to catch up with potential consumption in the distant future. I am not able to compute the implicit rate of return involved in this tradeoff because of its open-endedness in time (and the catch-up, if it ever comes, may take a long time in coming).

Table 7

PER CAPITA CONSUMPTION, ACTUAL AND POTENTIAL
(1980 J$)

YEAR	PER CAPITA CONSUMPTION		RATIO OF ACTUAL POTENTIAL
	ACTUAL	POTENTIAL	
1968	1,777.8	..	..
1969	1,828.5	..	..
1970	2,041.7	2,041.7	1.00
1971	2,149.3	2,090.5	1.03
1972	2,480.4	2,140.5	1.16
1973	2,204.6	2,191.6	1.01
1974	2,399.0	2,244.0	1.07
1975	2,504.6	2,297.6	1.09
1976	2,387.1	2,352.5	1.02
1977	2,324.9	2,408.8	.97
1978	2,154.4	2,466.3	.87
1979	1,978.6	2,525.3	.78
1980	1,887.7	2,585.6	.73
1981	1,837.5	2,647.4	.69
1982	1,951.5	2,710.7	.72
1983	1,938.2	2,775.5	.70
1984	1,965.6	2,841.8	.69
1985	1,902.2	2,909.7	.65
1986	1,848.1	2,979.3	.62
1987	1,919.7	3,050.5	.63
1988	..	..	..
1989	..	..	..

Figure 1. Time Paths of Actual and Potential Consumption per Capita (in 1980 J$)

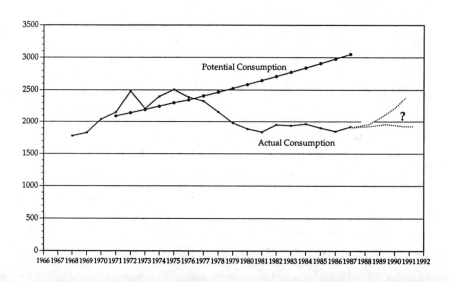

But it seems obvious that it is highly negative and, hence, this should be considered a disastrously unprofitable transaction by any standard. Clearly, it would have turned out much better if, for instance, the funds that financed the initial gain in consumption had simply been deposited in a pass-book account in the savings bank! This alternative, even at the terribly low rates then actually prevailing on pass-book accounts, would certainly have sustained an indefinitely continuing stream of extra consumption.

There are some who would view this overall economic performance as a disaster of public mismanagement and private disarray. Others would say it was an inevitable consequence of external shocks. There may be something to the arguments on both sides, and the truth perhaps lies somewhere in the middle. But I believe it would serve no useful purpose at this stage to engage in pointing the finger and allocating blame. The proper goal must be to learn the appropriate lessons from this experience and find constructive ways forward.

It is in this spirit that I turn now to try to develop a constructive analytical perspective on the problem. The aim is to make some sense and gain some deeper understanding of where we have been in our history and where we are now, so that we can, hopefully, better determine where we ought to be going in the future.

Model of an Economic Process with Inertia

It will help to fix ideas and sharpen our perception of reality if we think in terms of a simple, abstract, analytical model. To this end, consider the process schematically described in Figure 2. It begins with the entry of inputs into the process. These inputs are identified as finance, investment, and technology. As an economic process, these can be readily recognised to be key ingredients for starting up the process and keeping it going. Another such ingredient, of course, is labour, but that is assumed to be readily available without limit. Lying in the background, also, are natural resources ready to be used. It is an essential characteristic of the process that the inputs, other than labour and resources, enter from outside the process or, so to speak, 'from abroad', supplied by external agents.

The inputs pass into a production phase where they are transformed into products. The production phase is a fully specified box of given and known dimensions, and unchangeable except to the extent

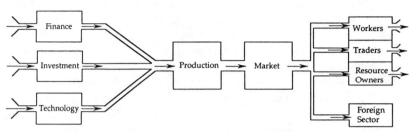

Figure 2. An Open System with Inertia

that the input suppliers or others in charge care to change it. But the suppliers, being external, and basing their economic calculations on a larger circuit, may have no incentive to introduce change. Others may, for their own reasons, be indifferent.

The products, in turn, pass into a market phase where they are sold. Like production, the market is a fully specified box, known and unchangeable except by external factors. It is simply there, sheltered and fully protected, as a guaranteed outlet for the products.

Finally, sale of the products yields revenues from which various groups draw incomes. Some of these groups, namely, workers, traders, and resource owners, are an internal part of the process. Another sizeable group, the foreign sector, consists in part of the input suppliers, but may also consist of an external state to which tribute is paid by requirement of a 'colonial rule'.

It is also an essential characteristic of this process that it terminates in the phase of withdrawal of revenues and, thus, is 'open' at its end point, as at its starting point. Some groups may grow rich from the amounts of revenue which they withdraw. Others remain poor. The openness in this phase is associated with leakages from the process. One such leakage is that part of the revenues goes directly to the foreign sector. Another part also leaks out because of the behavioural propensities of the different internal groups, namely, (a) their high propensity to consume, (b) their high propensity to spend on imported objects of consumption, (c) their preference for investment and speculation in real estate, and (d) their tendency to shelter their income and capital by shipping it abroad.

Considered as a whole, then, the essential and defining feature of this process is that there is no organic linkage that binds together the withdrawal of the revenues at the end of the process and the inflow of inputs at the start. In this respect, *it is a process without feedback.*

To the extent that this organic linkage is missing, the process as a whole cannot therefore be self-sustaining. Moreover, to the extent that there are significant leakages from it, the process must necessarily tend to stagnation operating by itself. If there is growth, it must come from the continued inflow of inputs from outside. But since that inflow, governed as it is by external factors, is necessarily intermittent and discontinuous, the growth itself must also operate by fits and starts.

I call this *an economic process with inertia*, where the sources of inertia (at least some of them) are visibly internal to the process. These internal sources are many, some more obvious than others. The more obvious ones I have already mentioned. They come from the behaviour pattern of the different social groups, in terms of the way they dispose of their revenues in each case. But the sources also show up in the spheres of production and marketing of products, in terms of the decision making structures affecting the process all along the line beginning with the external structures that start the process. And, as we have already seen from the concrete case studied in the previous section, the sources may also include specific policies and actions of the government.

It is important to note that this process is not inconsistent with change. In fact, we could write a history of this process showing marked structural changes. For instance, these could take the form of the unfolding of new production sectors (new products) and relative decline of old sectors (old products). Given the logic of the process, such changes would have to be seen, in large part, as results of the intermittent stimulus produced from outside.

The mechanism by which such changes work themselves through the process is interesting in and of itself, as well as for what it tells us about the possibilities for the emergence of new social groups (as new centers of decision making) conditional on these changes. A fundamental question would be: to what extent, if at all, are these new groups able and willing to act to change the basic form of the process.

Without going into these matters in detail, let me simply sketch the following dynamic of change. Structural change would take the form initially of a *primary stimulus* produced by the introduction of a new product (sector), say, sugar, bananas, bauxite, alumina, tourism. This would be followed by a *secondary wave* derived from the *spillover effects* produced by the primary stimulus on other sectors. These 'spillovers' would be both negative and positive, the net effect depending on the special conditions of each case. Another kind of secondary wave would arise from intermittent booms and declines in old products, depending on the state of the external market. The primary stimulus and secondary wave together will have the effect of stimulating expansion of the domestic market. This, in turn, creates room for the emergence of new forms of domestic production, say, in manufacturing, construction, and services, as well as new social groups associated with them. But it must be emphasized that this is essentially a *derivative effect*. That is to say, it is derived from the primary stimulus and secondary wave as a passive form of adjustment to those stimuli, and does not in itself represent a transformation in the basic process. It could, however, represent the seeds of such a transformation if and when the emerging centres of economic power begin to exercise appropriate entrepreneurial initiatives on their own.

This process is also not inconsistent with change in the *political* sphere. In fact, we could write a corresponding political history showing changes in the form of government, leading up through universal adult suffrage, constitutional self-government and, finally, to political independence. These developments would be associated with a growing share of government in economic activity, becoming in the last phase highly significant in quantitative terms. Here, again, as in the economic sphere, a fundamental question would be: to what extent, if at all, is the government able and willing to transform the basic dynamic of this process. It is possible that the government could act, in its own way, to strengthen the hold of the process by contributing significantly to the sources of inertia.

Perhaps the practical relevance of this history to the specific circumstances of Jamaica may become more transparent if we attach names and dates to these changes and the particular events associated with them. I leave those details to the historians as they are better experts at this. But, for illustration, I refer to Figure 3 where some of the main contours of the actual history can be traced out schematically. In particular, the diagram suggests that each phase of this history is

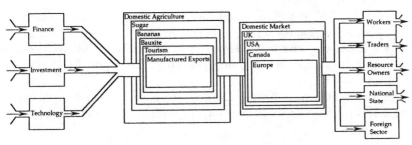

Figure 3. History of an Open System with Inertia

associated with the introduction of a new production sector, each forming an incremental layer in the production box and subsequently pursuing a life-cycle of its own. In the market box, these transitions are accompanied by differentiation of market outlets and, in the political sphere, by emergence of the national state.

The key point that this diagram emphasises is that all of these historical transitions take place within the context of an ongoing economic process, but without the economic process itself becoming transformed. That economic process, intrinsically characterised by inertia, remains essentially intact.

We would have to conclude from this history, then, that this process has a high degree of durability and that, indeed, it is deeply entrenched in the workings of the society. It is therefore to be expected that, whatever the momentum gained in each period of transition, that momentum would be, to a considerable extent, dissipated.

This is certainly the prediction that falls out of the model of the economic process that I have presented here. And, as we have seen, that prediction is confirmed in the case of the most recent episode of a Golden Age. The evidence for this is presented in the previous section.

It would also be interesting and useful to examine the actual workings of this process by going back to earlier historical episodes. But that task is much beyond my present scope. It is work that certainly deserves to be done and I leave it to others to do it.

Model of an Endogenous Process of Cumulative Growth

Now, let me go on to consider how, if at all, it is possible to alter this process and its intrinsic dynamic of persistent inertia. This is the problem that must be addressed if we are interested in improving the performance of the economy in terms of its capacity to sustain the momentum of growth.

Thinking of it simply as a process with leakages, one might be tempted to say that the answer is perfectly simple and straightforward: why not just stop the leaks? However, upon further thought, it turns out that the matter is not quite so simple. This is for the following reasons.

First of all, it would require some further analysis and experiment to determine the most effective ways of stopping the leaks. Since there is some history to go on, it may be possible to rule out some ways as having proved themselves in practice to be useless. But there may be many other alternatives that, for one reason or another, have not yet been tried.

Second, it is not 'just' a matter of leaks, but also of decisions affecting the whole process from start to finish, specifically in terms of finance, investment, technology, production, markets, and distribution. So, the overall scope of the problem is quite large.

Third, there is the deeper problem that the existing leaks and decisions governing the process may be the result of learned and adaptive patterns of behaviour that are a 'rational' and conditioned response to the incentives and disincentives produced historically by the prevailing socio-economic and political environment. In that case, change is inconceivable without altering the structure of incentives, without some 'unlearning' by those who have already adapted, and/or without waiting upon the emergence of a new generation that has learned in a different environment.

Finally, there is the problem of 'agency', namely: Who or what group is to act to implement and carry forward the changes once they have been decided upon and compatible structures designed? And, what are the strategic mechanisms of control that these actors have for performing this task?

For all of these reasons, and more, we have to recognize from the start that we are dealing here with a rather complex problem that is not capable of being solved by any simple and readily available formula. Moreover, there is the fact of history itself, which does make a difference, certainly in terms of what solutions might be workable in the particular 'initial conditions' that history imposes.

Yet it is possible, if we try, to make some headway towards an operational solution. As a contribution to that effort I have some ideas that I now wish to present. These ideas may appear, at first sight, quite complex and abstract. But I am confident that they have very concrete and practical implications, as I show in the next sections. Moreover, if we do get down to work out their implications, we might even come to accept that they are worth pursuing in practice.

Thinking of the problem abstractly in the first instance, in terms of the model presented in the previous section, it seems sharply clear what the overall objective must be. Specifically, the objective must be the following: *to close the loop of the economic process by building in feedback mechanisms and organic linkages, and thereby endogenizing the process of growth.*

This degree of clarity of the objective must in itself be regarded as a step forward. As an aside, note also that this objective, as stated, may on the surface evoke familiar sounds from slogans of the past, like 'self-sufficiency', 'indigenous development,' 'producing basic goods for basic needs', 'getting rid of dependency', among others. I want to warn the reader that the idea involved here is fundamentally different. The differences will become more transparent as I go along.

Once the overall objective is clearly defined, it becomes, next, a matter of identifying the appropriate feedback mechanisms and organic linkages necessary to close the loop. Here, I wish to propose that there are two essential components of an effective strategy for closing the loop and, then, go on to consider each of them in turn. For short, I call them: (1) the incentive system, (2) entrepreneurship.

It will help to show, first of all, how they fit as distinct elements in the conception of the overall economic process. This is shown schematically in Figure 4.

It can be seen immediately from Figure 4 that, once these components are in place and working effectively, we have an entirely different process from that of the first model. The essential difference is that this process has a built-in capacity for maintaining its momentum because there exists a regular and recurrent feedback of energy into the process. That feedback exists because, first, the various social groups are induced to engage in it, each in its own way, by the appropriate system of incentives, represented in Figure 4 by the column on the right. Second, it exists because there is a network of active decision making units, represented by the column on the left, capable of exercising a special quality of entrepreneurship that systematically channels the energy fed back into the process into specific activities, namely, finance, investment, and technology. These are the activities which, as we have seen in the first model, constitute the necessary inputs into production. But in the case of this process, the difference is that these activities are guided and directed by agents having a definite place as an integral part of the process and having, as well, the capacity and drive to restructure and enhance the process in all of its phases of production, marketing, and distribution.

I call this process, when it is duly constituted as such, *an endogenous process of cumulative growth.* The model of this process serves two didactic purposes. The first, the negative and backward-looking purpose, is that in comparison with the previous model this model tells us what is missing from the previous process that makes it a process with inertia. The second, the positive and forward-looking purpose, is that it tells

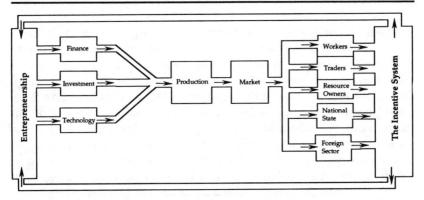

Figure 4. A Closed-Loop System with Cumulative Growth

us what are the specific elements that have to be instituted in the economy, as a matter of priority, if it is to change over to a process of cumulative growth. The model serves thereby to help us get the priorities right.

This is, of course, only a 'model', which is to say that it necessarily has a certain abstract and idealized character. That character is strictly necessary to give it usefulness for didactic purposes. But even so, if the model is to have operational value, there remains an important question of how to give a concrete and practical meaning to its elements. In this regard, what needs to be considered here are the two key elements: the incentive system and entrepreneurship. In the following sections, I try to give them concrete substance and bring out their practical meaning.

The Incentive System

The incentive system is one of the most profoundly important, and yet commonly misunderstood elements of the economic process. Psychologists, educational experts, industrial sociologists, and other behavioural social scientists, as well as shop-floor supervisors in manufacturing plants have for some time understood its unique significance. But, sad to say, economists are only now catching on to the problem (see, for instance, the new 'incentive compatibility theory'). The break up of the East European systems is also forcing us to recognise the importance of this element, not only for 'those' systems (which never quite managed to get it right), but for 'ours' as well which are far from being perfect in this respect.

Thinking of it in purely economic terms, many of us here in Jamaica would probably immediately associate the idea of an incentive system with the old investment-incentives law, which is indeed one relevant form of such a system. This form was mostly aimed at attracting foreign investors using as a model the example of FOMENTO in Puerto Rico. That programme has long been derisively dismissed by many of our economists as 'industrialization by invitation' because of its documented failures in our own context. I do not wish to go over the arguments that have already been made, pro and con. They are part of the history from which we have to learn for the future. But even if we can point to the failure of one set of incentives, that provides no reason whatever for us to dismiss or ignore the need for an incentive system as such, one that would not only relate to the foreign investor but also to local investors as well, and to other national groups, including workers, traders, resource owners, and state bureaucrats.

Now, considering first the matter of investment incentives, it seems to me that, as a set of investment incentives, the old system was bound to yield poor results. This is because, among other reasons, it was essentially based on what I would call the 'fishing net approach' (or, if you wish, the 'shotgun approach'); that is, cast your net widely enough and hope that some fish will be caught! With this approach, some of the fish you catch will undoubtedly turn out to be bad fish. But what if one went about it in a more systematic way, carefully selecting and targeting the prey, stalking him, and taking special measures and steps to make sure that he is caught?

This metaphor is intended to be taken seriously. What we learn from the earlier experience is, not that investment incentives sometimes do not work or produce a mix of good and bad results (that, after all, seems fairly obvious), but that to get meaningful and constructive results (a) the correct incentives must be designed and (b) they must form an integral part of a strategy of investment targeting. Such a strategy has long been successfully practiced in many of the Asian Newly Industrializing Countries (NIC) (South Korea, Taiwan, Hong Kong, Singapore) and elsewhere (India, Turkey), and much earlier in Japan. One element of that success is clearly the incentive system that was designed to go with the overall strategy. I propose that the experience of those countries in this area deserves our careful study.[5]

So far as specific targets of such an investment strategy are concerned, there are many reasons to suppose, and I wish to propose also, that Jamaica could develop a strong competitive advantage in a number of areas, some existing, some new. Among these, let me simply suggest the following list (based on my own preliminary effort at researching the problem):

(1) as an international financial center, catering to the needs of the wider Caribbean market and to the North American market as well (for instance, by linking up initially with immigrant communities there);

(2) in manufacturing industry: textiles, household gadgets and equipment, chemicals for household use, small machinery and machine parts, tools;

(3) in agro-industry: horticulture, scientific stock-breeding, all using modern advances in bio-technology;

(4) in the application of computer-systems software and control devices to service local production in all sectors including the government (and possibly export), for upgrading existing production techniques and meeting the needs of new industry.

All of the items on this list could serve well the goal of export diversification which is a necessary basis, not only for preserving the momentum of economic growth, but also for building into the economy resilience and resistance to external shocks. I need not go into the specifics of each case here. But the case can be made. Give me a team of technical experts and, together, we could make the most marvelous case. Others may have a similar or competing list, and a case too for their list. The difficulty is not in compiling the list or in making the case, but in implementing the strategy and keeping it going once it has been agreed upon. Here is where the issue of an appropriate system of incentives consistent with and coordinated with an overall strategy of investment targeting comes in.

But, quite apart from investment incentives as such, the consideration of an incentive system has to be extended to include, in an integrated manner, incentive structures affecting all national groups across the board: not only the 'economic groups' of workers, traders, resource owners, and entrepreneurs, in their capacity both as producers and consumers, but also state bureaucrats, and the so-called 'social sectors' (teachers, health workers, *et al*). Even environmentalists have to be brought on the bandwagon. The obviously wide range of interests involved among these different groups should give us a sense of the complexity of the problem we are dealing with here. It is further complicated once we recognise that not all incentives are economic. But this complexity should not cause us to shrink from dealing with it.

There is another side to the incentive system that cannot be ignored, namely, it can also be a system of *disincentives*. The burgeoning literature on the economics of planning systems in Eastern Europe has shown us sharply the perverse features of this other side (e.g. 'soft budget constraints', 'false signalling', 'queuing,' etc.).[6]   These disincentives can wreak havoc at the level of the factory, the farm, the consumer, and within the state bureaucracy at the highest levels. There is much that we could learn from studying that literature, insofar as it is relevant to our own conditions, for instance, to the functioning of our government bureaucracy and some of our private firms.

But we should also see that there is a positive and necessary role for disincentives. In this role they are really to be considered *penalties*. In the context of the business firm, bankruptcy is clearly one such penalty. Here, the firm is penalized for poor performance. In general, we cannot afford to tolerate poor performance. There must be built-in penalties that are explicit, clearly stated, and even-handedly applied. Examples of these penalties are: losing out on the bid for the contract, getting the line of credit cut off, missing the next pay raise, losing one's place in line for promotion, and so on. Here again a list can be drawn up of rules and laws in this case, but it would have to be done with the active involvement of all participants to ensure acceptance and compliance.

The system of penalties would also be far more effective if there are *rewards* built into it. Just as much as we cannot tolerate poor performance, good performance must be adequately rewarded. A pat on the back is sometimes all that is needed, but in most instances that is not enough and, if that is all there is, the really sharp people will begin to see through it and dismiss it as paternalism. The rewards must be ample and proportionate to the achievement. This means that we have to come to accept *inequality of rewards*. Equally, we cannot continue to reward mediocrity and incompetence.

I have to add to all of this another aspect of the incentive/disincentive system that we know very well from our own experience. This is the distortionary effect that an existing set of powerful incentives can produce on the overall structure of incentives, acting like a kind of 'Dutch disease' to weaken and perhaps nullify the other incentives. To give it a local name, I call it the 'ganja disease'. In Jamaica, this particular disease takes the form of a large part of a whole youthful generation of bright, energetic, and highly motivated people being drawn into the ganja industry by the incentive of quick and large gains to be made from growing and selling and providing security for this product. They, thereby, become lost to the possibility of pursuing other, more constructive, socially productive, stable, long term, opportunities. Others not directly or indirectly involved in that industry are themselves distracted by the large gains and fancy lifestyles they perceive in it, from seeing the prospects for a lower but safe and steady rate of return from alternative investments in existing or new lines of production. I suspect that the far-reaching economic consequences of this disease, especially in the sphere of economic incentives for agricultural production and, more generally, in the expectations-vs.-reality syndrome of a wide cross-section of our people, may still be with us.

Finally, we have to face the difficult problem of the appropriate incentives, economic and noneconomic, for getting a constant stream of innovation and new ideas, not only in the university and laboratories, but also in the top levels of public administration, in the control centres of the corporation, and in the workplace.

One of the best forms of incentive is freedom of entry and of access to the top. This proposition holds generally for industries, markets, business firms, bureaucracies, and other social institutions. But barriers to entry, such as custom and tradition, social privilege and prejudice, may get in the way of this incentive and prevent it from working. The tendency to hang on to 'status', aggravated in small societies by the absence of lateral mobility, may also help to block it. And in a class and race-conscious society, with a history of slavery, these barriers abound. They serve to inhibit the exercise of talent and initiative. At worst, they cause some of the most talented and motivated among us to move to more hospitable environments abroad where they can and do flourish, so that the country thereby loses some of 'the brightest and the best' while the status seekers continue to vegetate in their status positions. We cannot miss the opportunity to remove these barriers wherever they are to be found.

Broadly speaking, the problem of incentives requires finding a way to energise people to act in a manner wholly consistent with their own individually perceived needs and goals (in this sense, 'rationally'), so that their actions may also correspond to particular and commonly accepted social goals and needs. A solution to that problem does not presume that we have to go about trying to change people's perception of their own needs and goals. If that change does occur, and in the right directions, it would be a bonus. But who is to do it and how is it to be done? It is simpler, at least in the short run, to work on the incentive system. As I have argued here, this problem should not be posed too narrowly; it is complex and profoundly important. A solution should be a key element in the strategy that we adopt for dealing with the next century.

I do not consider here the related question of resource constraints. This is not because it is not important, but because I think it is strictly subsidiary to the question of incentives.

Entrepreneurship

Consider next the element of entrepreneurship. In seeking to concretise this element it is necessary to get away from old fashioned concepts and outmoded thinking that are the source of much confusion on the matter and an obstacle to moving forward.

The old idea is that entrepreneurship is a personal and innate quality of the individual as entrepreneur. There is perhaps something to this idea, insofar as we do know that there are many successful individuals whom we can point to as having this quality. There are many books and even scholarly journals dedicated to celebrating the lives and exploits of the most rich and famous of them. As some would say: 'You know one when you see one, and that's enough'.

If there is something to this idea, and to the degree that there is, then what I am about to say could be interpreted to mean that what we need in Jamaica is a new breed of entrepreneur different from the ones that we are accustomed to see and know here. However, to me, that interpretation would not be enough and, in any case, would amount to trivializing the problem. For instance, it may be possible, and some have argued, that the old breed (the so-called merchant capitalists) could be induced to change their ways by a change in the incentive structure that they face. There is no certainty of this result in my view, and the experiences of history here and elsewhere may be against it. There is perhaps greater hope for their children, and some of them do appear to be able to carry the ball. But, whatever one views as the likely outcome, this argument does point us usefully and constructively to consider the role of incentives in influencing economic behaviour and, hence, what changes in the incentives might produce better results.

I propose that what we need is not just any entrepreneur of common or garden variety, new breed or old, but entrepreneurs possessed with very special qualities. Moreover, and equally important if not more so, what we need is a structure of relations and interconnections among such entrepreneurs that makes them more effective as entrepreneurs.

The nature of these special qualities I shall come to in a moment. But a brief word on the need for such a structure seems appropriate before we get further into it. Specifically, the need for this structure can be shown straightforwardly on the basis of elementary economics (or business) principles and knowledge of one of the qualities that we are looking for. In particular, one of the qualities that we would all agree to be necessary is surely the capacity for long range planning of productive investment — a capacity that would enable 'sticking-to-it' instead of running for cover when the going gets rough or settling for quick profits. To develop this long range planning, it would seem necessary to have a structured framework in which individual entre-preneurs can take decisions and act, knowing that the actions of others will be consistent and predictable, and that they can thereby minimise the risks involved. Here is a role for a structure, not just of relations among the entrepreneurs, but including the state as well.

If it is also accepted that we have to pursue a long term strategy of 'investment targeting' worked out among the entrepreneurs and the state, as discussed above, then the existence of some such structure would be a necessary precondition to get this strategy to work effec-tively. The problem of course is to design the right structure and, for this, there is no simple formula. But, as I shall show in a moment, there are many models available from which we could learn.

Now, the way to cut through the fog on this issue is to break down by analysis the activity of the entrepreneur within the specific environ-ment in which he or she acts and to try to discover, thereby, the essential character of the actions involved and the attributes that they entail. When that is done, it will be found, to put it simply, generally, and briefly, that: entrepreneurship is a set of particular organizational capabilities and skills for doing things in a team, where the size of the team may be large or small depending on identifiable factors such as the nature of the task (or undertaking or enterprise) to be done and the environment in which it is done.

This is the analytical conception now being developed by scholars who have carefully studied the matter. They are typically in the business schools and not too many in economics. There is a great deal that we can all learn from the results of their studies.[7]

For present purposes, I would need to specify further this concep-tion by adding that: entrepreneurship is the capacity to coordinate finance, investment, and technology, for carrying out production and marketing of products, while also bearing the risks involved in so doing.

This conception is general enough to encompass the old idea of a one-man (the 'great man') operation, because that is simply the special case of a team of one. But it is more general because it focuses on the team rather than on the man. Such teams exist in all capitalist countries at the 'executive level' of firms where each such firm has a certain legal and institutional identity based on property rights. The team may be large or small in size, ranging from the large conglomerate and the joint-stock company, to the limited liability partnership, to the one-man operation inventing gadgets in the basement of his house.

By broadening our view of capitalism from the rather narrow one that takes as its paradigm the special case of the US, it becomes possible to see that the team as a unit of entrepreneurship may extend far beyond the individual enterprise, firm, or conglomerate, and across industries and sectors of the economy, to become a network of teams. Call this network the *Group*. And, what is even more striking, when we look at the evidence, is that the Group may incorporate the state in intimate and integral ways, formal and informal, constituting what we may call a partnership between the state and private sector.

Such Groups exist in many countries. They are typically found in Asia, so much so that we could think of them as 'the Asian Model'. But they are also found elsewhere closer to home, as in Mexico for instance, where they are in fact referred to as 'los grupos' (e.g. el grupo Monterrey). The particular form of the Group would vary somewhat from one country to another, the difference being marked by the specific role that the state plays in each.

To bring the matter even closer to home, the interesting fact, commonly recognised but not well understood, is that such Groups exist in Jamaica too, and have done so for a long time. They have developed historically within closely knit family units. They have also, certainly, not lacked close ties with the Jamaican state. I propose that we should now be searching for practical ways of extending that system outward beyond the family by allowing new entrepreneurial entrants and installing it on better modern institutional foundations as part of a new network of entrepreneurship based on a new partnership between the state and private sector. Continued extension and deepening of the capital market, for both stocks and new issues, are important steps in this direction, and there are other measures we should be considering.

In more general terms, my proposal is that we should be searching for a new model of entrepreneurship, starting with what we already have, and looking far and wide to find the best model suited to our own conditions.

Looking farther afield, we can identify another relevant model which moves towards the pole opposite to the Asian Model. The paradigm case of this is the French Model of Indicative Planning. It is a looser system of linkages between the state and private sector in which, to simplify a bit, the state sets the national targets for production and investment, exhorts the private sector firms to go along with the targets, and meets regularly with them to monitor how well they are doing.

Another case altogether is the Scandinavian Model, with its welfare state features and strong trade unions playing a much greater role than in the other models. But that model, it seems, is now beginning to fall apart.

Then, there is of course the American model which, for many, is the paradigm case of a 'free market economy'. What needs to be recognised is that this model is farthest out at the opposite pole. Even so, to understand that model correctly, it is necessary to distinguish between the ideology of it and the reality of it. For instance, it is clear from closer examination that in such industries as aerospace, electronics, and biotechnology, which are on the leading edge of modern technology and international competition, the government of the US, at all levels — federal, state and local — exercises a high degree of state intervention. The same is true, perhaps more so, of agriculture where, historically, private firms and government have worked hand in hand in all areas, from prices, subsidies, and export strategy to technology, irrigation, finance, education, and land grants. There is also evidence that the US may now be moving more and more away from the pole that the ideology presupposes, and may have to do so simply as a necessary requirement of being able to keep up with the increasing competition from economies at or near the other pole.

The 'Puerto Rican Model' is another special case which, in the past, we in Jamaica have tried to copy, failing to see that it is indeed a very special case not replicable under different conditions.

The politico-economic systems of 'the East' are now in such a state of turmoil that it is not clear what model they now represent, or to what model they are heading, although it seems quite clear that there is no going back exactly to the old model. Therefore, nothing more needs to be said about it here. In any case, after the experience of Grenada, many of us in the English-speaking Caribbean would have a hard time convincing ourselves that there is anything to be gained from trying now to take that route. The Cubans, on the other hand, did take it and are still trying to cope with its manifold problems.

So far as Jamaica is concerned, now that the old ideologies are breaking down on both sides, we should be in a better position to evaluate the available alternatives in a more careful, rational, and systematic way and, in the process, come up with our own model, instead of slavishly copying or imitating one or another of them.

If we do seriously attempt to move forward in this area, and perhaps move more towards the Asian Model (that is evidently an open question at this point), then it seems to me that there are four prime and related issues, among many others, that will have to be faced. One is the question of the most efficient scale and intersectoral reach of each Group, including in this the role and extent of participation by foreign firms in so-called joint ventures. Two is the need for an explicit system of rules and regulations, properly enforced, that will ensure competition in the sense of freedom of entry. Three, is the question of what is the role of the trade unions, since it is clear from our history and present-day institutions that they must have a role. Four, is the question of what is the specific role for the state in the Group and in mediating among Groups and trade unions, recognising fully and honestly that the state does have a necessary and indispensable role to play.

In other words, we have to open for systematic examination the whole question of what is usually called in popular discussion, 'industrial policy' or, in the textbooks 'industrial organization'. We might better call it, given the way the question is posed in this paper, a question of the model of entrepreneurship. Unfortunately, not enough of this sort of analysis is being done here right now among both our social scientists and policy makers, and in this respect we are far behind others in the game. Perhaps this is because we are still, in one degree or another, caught up in debating the mistaken ideologies of the past which supposed, on the one hand, that the state could substitute for the private sector, and, on the other, that the private sector could do without the state.

Converting the Economic Process from Inertia to Cumulative Growth

Knowing what are the necessary elements to be put in place in order to improve the performance of the economy does not mean that we are home free. There are many other difficulties that still must be faced if it is decided to go forward with the changeover to a new mode of operation. In general terms, the problem to be faced is one of transition; that is, the adjustment process involved in converting the economy from one with built-in inertia to one of cumulative growth.

It helps to be able to anticipate what the difficulties are and to think how we might best deal with them. Honesty requires, however, that it be recognized from the start that the transition will be rough. For dealing with the difficulties, I have no blueprint to offer (who does?). But here is a short list, with suggestions, of some of the things that we have to think seriously about and open for discussion.

The Problem of Initial Conditions

We have to start from where we are at any given time, and the reality that we start with may be very different from the ideal world of the model. That reality imposes constraints on what we can do to begin to make the changes necessary to get where we want to go.

Then, we have to be pragmatic: work with what we have and build on this, but with a definite goal and purpose in view. We can also seek to find ways of relieving some of the constraints. Debt relief is an obvious candidate. Another is, bargaining as hard as we can for better loan terms and more loans, provided that the loans are put to productive uses so that they can be paid back. For that provison to be met, we have to monitor ourselves carefully to ensure that the people responsible for spending the money don't blow it away again in another consumption binge.

The Contemporary World Economic Environment

The contemporary world environment may be very unfavourable at the time when we begin to move. In fact, we could not be starting at a worse time than the present. The 'engine of growth' has slowed down in the world as a whole. Protectionism and the formation of trade blocs are getting in the way to prevent the international transmission mechanism from spreading around the benefits of growth. There are many other countries at our own level 20 years ago that have already succeeded in moving far ahead of us, and we now have to compete with them in all areas. Countries that were out of the race before (the countries of 'the East') have now, all of a sudden, entered the race and so intensified the competition among all the participants. The technological requirements of competition are now very much different from what they used to be when we were successful as 'hewers of wood and drawers of water'. Investment capital is becoming more scarce. And there is more, but I need not go on.

We have no alternative but to stay in the race and try as hard as we can at least to keep up with the rest while aiming to catch up and even to get ahead. We also have to strengthen existing alliances that will help us to deal with the competition, while being courageous enough to opt out or act independently of those alliances that are holding us back. And we have to seek to build new alliances wherever there is an opportunity for mutual benefit, in the north, south, east, and west.

The Costs of Adjustment

It is inevitable that there will be costs (the no-free-lunch principle). But if we learn from the mistakes of the past and the correct strategy is pursued this time around, the payoff may make it worthwhile to incur the costs. The real problem is the distribution of the costs among all concerned, in both present and future generations. Among the present generation nobody wants to lose, and the losers can become upset enough to seek to put a halt to the process. Future generations have no voice so they tend to be ignored.

To get it all to work, given the inherent distributional conflict, there has to be a 'workable truce' between the different groups and a 'social pact' that allows for a fair distribution of the costs and benefits. This is not an easy thing to work out in a contentious parliamentary democracy such as we have, which differentiates us very much from many of the other 'successful' models that we see around us. It takes strong and wise leadership and a willingness on the part of all to try to find a pact that all can agree on. However, there is no guarantee of being able to get agreement or that any agreement, once reached, will hold for long. This may be a constant source of instability along the way.

The Environmental Consequences

Like future generations, the environment has no voice. But the costs that it bears may wreak havoc on both present and future generations. It is inherently difficult to measure those costs. But we have to find a way to pay back the environment. We have to remember also that 'the people' are part of 'the environment' and not get trapped into thinking that we can save the environment without saving the people. And, if the people are able to get together to speak for themselves and the environment, then we would have made some headway in dealing with this problem.

Conclusion

The twenty-first century is almost upon us, and we still have a far way to go in order to start it off on a good footing. We have an even farther way to go, once we start it off, to be able simply to cope with what lies ahead and keep our footing.

But all is not lost. The past we always have with us as our history. The present consists of the tentative steps that we take into a dark unknown. Perhaps we can better negotiate those steps if we have some pointers from our history to hang on to so as not to fall off into the abyss or back to where we started.

The main point of this paper is to suggest that we should learn from our history. If, in addition, we keep our eyes, our ears, and our minds open to learn from others around us near and far, we will be able to make much headway in terms of economic growth. As to whether we make progress in so doing, I leave that question to the philosophers.

References

Amsden, A., *Asia's Next Giant. South Korea and Late Industrialization*, New York: Oxford University Press, 1989.

Chandler, A. D., 'Organizational Capabilities and the Economic History of the Industrial Enterprise,' *Journal of Economic Perspectives, 6, Summer 1992*, 79-100.

Danielson, A., 'Surplus and Stagnation in Jamaica: Further Notes,' *Social and Economic Studies*, 41, March 1992, 45-66.

Eisner, G., *Jamaica, 1830-1930*, Manchester: The University Press, 1961.

Gereffi, G and Wyman, D. L., eds., *Manufacturing Miracles: Paths of Industrialization in Latin America and East Asia*, Princeton: Princeton University Press, 1990.

Harris, D. J., 'Capital Accumulation and Resource Allocation in an Import-Constrained Economy: A Framework for Analysis of Recent Experience and Current Trends in the Jamaican Economy,' presented to National Symposium on the Jamaican Economy, PIOJ, Kingston, June 25-26, 1990.

Harris, D. J., 'Saving and Foreign Trade as Constraints in Economic Growth: A Study of Jamaica,' *Social and Economic Studies*, 19, 2, June 1970, 147-77.

Jefferson, O., *The Post-War Economic Development of Jamaica*, Jamaica: ISER, 1972.

Kornai, J., *The Socialist System*, Princeton: Princeton University Press, 1992.

Nelson, R. R., 'Why Firms Differ, and How Does It Matter?' *Strategic Management Journal*, 12, Winter 1991, 61-74.

Thorne, A. P., 'Size, Structure and Growth of the Economy of Jamaica,' *Social and Economic Studies*, 4, 4, Supplement, 1955.

Wade, R., *Governing the Market: Economic Theory and the Role of Government in East Asian Industrialization*, Princeton: Princeton University Press, 1990.

Williamson, O. E., *The Economic Institutions of Capitalism: Firms, Markets, and Relational Contracting*, New York: Free Press, 1985.

Yusuf, S. and R. K. Peters, 'Capital Accumulation and Economic Growth, the Korean Paradigm,' *World Bank Staff Working Papers*, No. 712, 1985.

Notes

1.For studies of the overall economic record up to 1969, the best references are Thorne (1955), Eisner (1961), and Jefferson (1972).

2.In Harris (1970), the projections ended in 1975, ten years from the base period. This was by design, and conservative in relation to other modellers who seek courageously to project for up to fifty years or even more! But this conservatism paid off because of the subsequent turnaround in the economy that we now know started around 1973-4. As I can now rigorously document (part of the documentation is presented here), there was a sharp structural break that came into play afterwards which the econometric model of the earlier period obviously could not have captured because its parameter estimates were based on the economic structure prevailing in the expansion phase. The art of economic modelling,k as the practitioners know very well, is an iterative process of learning after the fact.

3.For a detailed accounting on this issue, see for instance Danielson (1992).

4.On this, see Harris (1990, p. 16). The reasoning is straightforward. Today's consumption must be financed by reducing saving from current income, by dissaving (i.e. consuming some capital assets) or, by borrowing (which is a claim on future income). Every dollar taken from saving or capital assets yields just one extra dollar of present consumption but reduces future income and consumption by a much greater amount, perhaps two or three times, depending on the size of the capital-output ratio. Insofar as today's consumption is financed by external borrowing, the buildup of foreign debt increases future liabilities for debt service and, unless the debt is used productively so as to increase future capacity to pay, payments for debt service must be met by reducing future consumption.

5.See, for instance, Amsden (1989), Yusuf & Peters (1985).

6.On this, see Kornai (1992).

7.I am referring here to works such as Williamson (1985), Nelson (1991), and Chandler (1992), among others.

Graph 1. Ratios of Government Consumption to GDP and Gross Fixed Capital Formation to GDP, 1950-1965

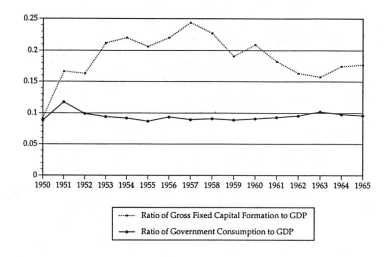

Graph 2. Ratios of Government Consumption to GDP and Gross Fixed Capital Formation to GDP, 1969-1989

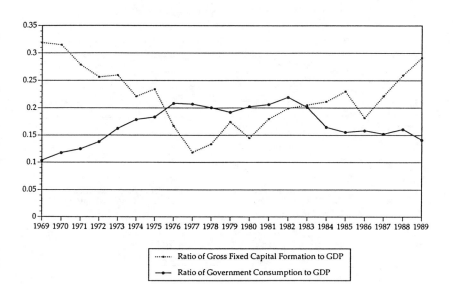

Graph 3.   Ratios of Total Consumption to GDP and Private Consumption to GDP, 1950-1965

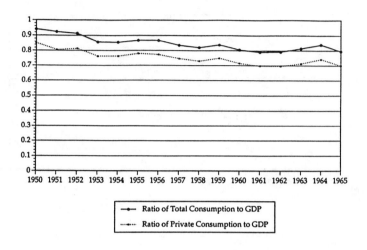

Graph 4.   Ratios of Total Consumption to GDP and Private Consumption to GDP, 1969-1989

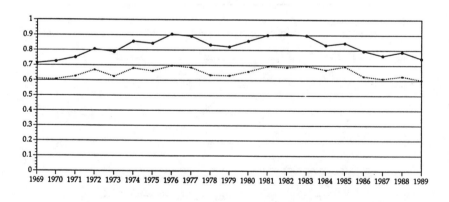

Graph 5. Ratio of Net Domestic Saving to Net National Income, 1950-1965

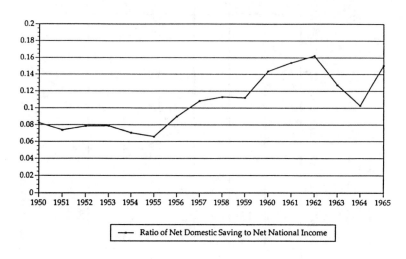

──── Ratio of Net Domestic Saving to Net National Income

Graph 6. Ratio of Net Domestic Saving to Net National Income, 1969-1989

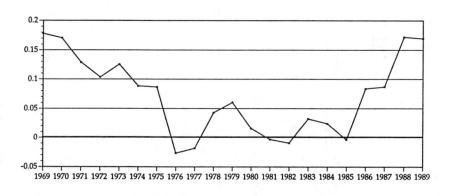

──── Ratio of Net Domestic Saving to Net National Income

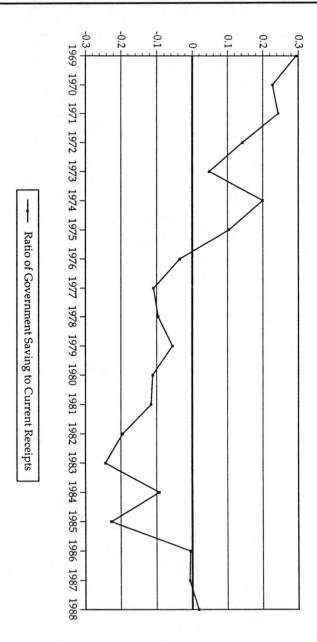

Graph 7. Ratio of Government Saving to Current Receipts, 1969-1988

Graph 8.   Ratios of Exports of Goods and Services to GDP and Imports of Goods and Services to GDP, 1950-1965

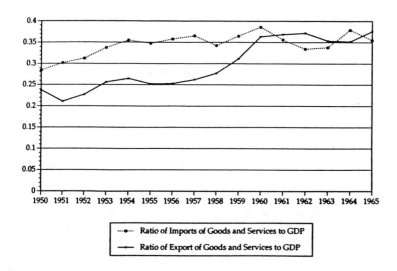

Graph 9.   Ratios of Exports of Goods and Services to GDP and Imports of Goods and Services to GDP, 1969-1989

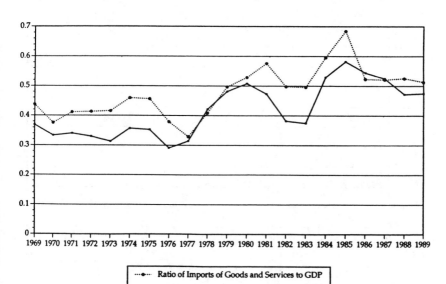

Graph 10. Ratio of Total External Debt to GDP, 1970-1988

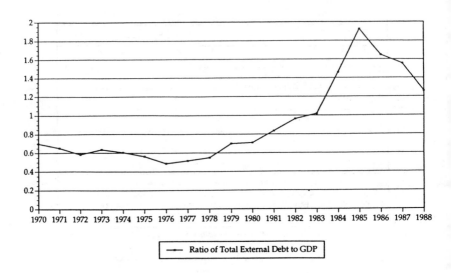

Graph 11. Ratio of Debt Service Payments to Exports of Goods and Services, 1970-1988

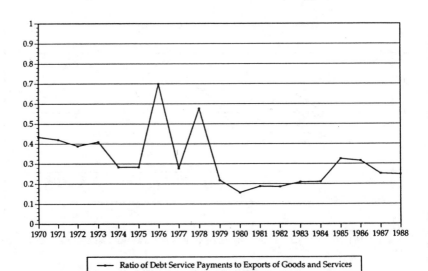

Table 1

SHARES AND GROWTH RATES OF GDP COMPONENTS
(at Constant Prices)

1950-1965, 1969-1989

GDP COMPONENTS	1950 - 1965		1969 - 1989	
	SHARES % (mean)	GROWTH RATES %	SHARES % (mean)	GROWTH RATES %
Final Consumption	85	5.5	82.3	-0.04
Government	10	6.4	17.0	0.82
Private	75	5.4	65.3	-0.22
Total Capital Formation	20	7.4	23.7	-1.45
Gross Fixed Capital	19	7.3	21.9	-1.16
Increase in Stocks	1		1.8	-4.86
Exports of Goods & Services	22*	9.3*	41.8	2.39
Imports of Goods & Services	30*	6.3*	47.8	1.69
GDP	100.0	6.5	100.0	-0.26

*Excludes Services

Table 2

SAVING PROPENSITIES

1950-1965, 1969-1988

SAVING SECTORS	1950 -1965	1969 - 1988	
	Average Propensity	Average Propensity	Marginal Propensity
National	0.11	0.07	0.34
Non-Financial Enterprises		0.35	0.98
Financial Institutions		0.09	-0.06
Households & Unincorporated Business		-0.04	0.51
Government		-0.10	-0.28

Table 3

COMPOSITION OF GROSS SAVING

1950-1965, 1969-1989

SAVING COMPONENTS	1950 - 1965	1969 - 1989
	MEAN %	MEAN %
Net Saving	46.2	23.6
Consumption of Fixed Capital	35.7	41.2
Net Capital Transfers from Abroad		2.3
Net Borrowing from Abroad	18.1	32.9

Table 4

SHARES AND GROWTH RATES OF PRODUCTION SECTORS
(at Constant Prices)

1950-1965, 1969-1989

PRODUCTION SECTORS	1950 - 1965		1969 - 1989	
	SHARE OF GDP %	GROWTH RATES %	SHARE OF GDP %	GROWTH RATES %
Agricultural Sector	17.5	0.5	7.9	0.49
Industrial Sector	30.2		33.1	-1.81
Mining & Quarrying	5.1	14.7	6.9	-1.76
Manufacture	13.4	6.3	16.9	-0.98
Construction	10.7	5.8	8.1	-4.21
Electricity & Water	1.0	11.2	1.2	3.32
Service Sector	51.4		63.5	0.53
Distribution	16.6	4.1	18.4	-1.42
Transportation	7.3	6.6	6.8	1.83
Finance & Insurance		6.4	5.4	2.22
Imputed Bank Charges			3.7	5.53
Real Estate & Business	4.0	2.3	11.1	1.48
Government	6.7	6.5	15.1	3.43
Household & Non-Profit			1.3	-2.44
Miscellaneous			5.4	0.04
GDP	100.0	5.3	100.0	-0.26

Table 5

GROWTH RATES OF PRODUCTION SECTORS BY SUB-PERIODS
(at Constant Prices)

1969 - 1989

PRODUCTION SECTORS	1969-1973	1974-1980	1981-1985	1986-1989	1969-1989
Agricultural Sector	3.42	0.50	2.59	-1.90	0.49
Industrial Sector	5.21	-5.88	-1.72	7.53	-1.81
Mining & Quarrying	11.64	-1.82	-10.83	9.16	-1.76
Manufacture	5.35	-5.47	0.82	4.35	-0.98
Construction	0.61	-12.04	0.96	14.68	-4.21
Electricity & Water	10.05	0.70	3.75	4.30	3.32
Service Sector	6.92	-1.05	0.01	2.47	0.53
Distribution	5.77	-5.60	-1.21	-0.75	-1.42
Transportation	5.91	-2.01	2.97	3.70	1.83
Finance & Insurance	10.30	1.00	2.12	1.98	2.22
Imputed Bank Charges	4.30	4.32	-4.16	14.97	5.53
Real Estate & Business	3.99	0.65	0.45	3.64	1.48
Government	11.60	6.20	-1.86	0.42	3.43
Household & Non-Profit	12.93	-11.90	2.79	1.15	-2.44
Miscellaneous	7.58	-3.94	3.08	2.50	0.04
GDP	6.03	-2.59	0.25	3.71	-0.26

Table 6

GROWTH RATES OF PRODUCTION SUB-SECTORS BY SUB-PERIODS

1970 - 1989

	1970-1973	1974-1980	1981-1985	1986-1989
TOTAL AGRICULTURE	2.95	0.73	1.64	-1.65
Export Agriculture	-3.90	-4.09	-0.68	0.90
Sugar	-2.28	-3.33	-3.76	1.50
Other Exports	-5.97	-2.72	4.94	1.90
Domestic Agriculture	12.24	2.48	2.90	-5.50
TOTAL MANUFACTURE	5.23	-4.84	1.30	4.43
Food (excl. Sugar)	3.40	-4.04	3.59	4.50
Sugar, Molasses & Rum	-3.37	-3.87	0.06	-0.25
Alcoholic Beverages	11.05	2.60	-2.92	
Non-Alcoholic Beverages	4.43	-2.40	-2.01	
Tobacco & Tobacco Products	6.60	1.49	0.48	-0.60
Textiles & Wearing Apparel	3.58	-8.90	5.48	13.55
Leather & Leather Products	-17.15	26.00	14.86	
Footwear	-2.34	-9.03	0.98	
Wood, Wood & Cork	2.28	1.74	1.12	
Furniture & Fixtures	15.25	-15.30	7.28	
Paper & Printing	11.05	-4.08	0.18	
Petroleum Refining	3.48	-5.47	5.14	1.70
Rubber & Plastic Products	13.01	-6.09	4.22	
Non-Metallic Products	1.40	-11.24	11.27	
Machinery & Equipment	5.11	-10.16	2.64	
Other Manufacturing Industries	-0.30	-6.36	7.40	
TOTAL MISCELLANEOUS SERVICES	7.75	-4.57	3.12	3.83
Hotels, Restaurants, Clubs	5.18	-3.50	5.76	4.95

CHAPTER 3

Production in Jamaica
Transforming Industrial Enterprises

Michael Best and Robert Forrant

I. Introduction: The Production Crisis

The World

These are turbulent times for the world economy: while regions in a few newly industrializing countries are growing rapidly, much of the world economy is in prolonged recession. In the West, people seem pessimistic with respect to future prospects. This, in part, stems from a lack of vision as to where to go, and what to do. The old visions that gave hope in the long run and shaped economic policy are less compelling. For example, central planning combined with state ownership of production facilities died with the Eastern European authoritarian regimes. The monetarist, supply side policies of the United Kingdom and the United States pursued throughout the eighties have not countered industrial decline. The United States has shifted from being the world's biggest creditor country to it's biggest debtor. The Scandinavian social democracy welfare states are also under pressure from high unemployment and budget deficits. Finally, the Keynesian inspired policies of the Carter years are remembered as the years of stagflation, not a popular period in the public mind.

The story is different in the Pacific Rim. The success of South Korea, Taiwan, Hong Kong and Singapore spawned a new term: the NIC's or Newly Industrialized Countries. Their growth rates have been spectacular. Korea and Taiwan, for example, went from per capita incomes that were only a fraction of Jamaica's in the 1960s, to 5 to 7 times higher by the end of the 1980s. The success stories, however, are not readily explained in terms of conventional economic theories of economic development. Conventional theories, and the policies derived from them, share a common assumption: production will take care of itself as long as the macro-economic conditions are right. This assumption is false for any country that does not enjoy industrial leadership.

The present economic crisis in the West is rooted in a revolution in the principles of production and organization, a revolution as profound as the coming of mass production and big business were at the turn of the last century. Today industrial leadership is contested as never before. It certainly is not the preserve of the United States or Western Europe as it was when the conventional, market based macro-economic theories were established. Blindly, economists and policy-makers continue to debate about proper macro-economic conditions as if matters of production did not take priority. In fact, in our public discourse we lack a set of terms for even engaging in debate over production issues. This is, in part, because none of the economic perspectives of the past have been grounded in a theory of production.[2]

Jamaica

The situation is considerably more perilous for small, less industrialized countries that lack a counterweight of successful growth sectors to sustain national income. Jamaica, for example, has suffered a decline in per capita income of roughly one third from the peak in 1972. The decline in output and income in Jamaica cannot be attributed to a lack of attention from international aid agencies. As a recipient of $4 billion in foreign aid and eight IMF adjustment programmes since the mid-1970s, Jamaica's increased indebtedness figures have rates of growth nearly as impressive as the output growth rates of the NICs. While a full explanation of Jamaica's economic dilemma is not available, a part of the story rests with the visions of industrial development that have informed policy making.

Jamaican economic policy-making in the declining decades has been guided by two radically different visions. The Michael Manley government of 1972-80 began office with a 'non-IMF path' based upon dependency theory. State planning, nationalization, bureaucratic regulation of external and internal trade, and government production were pursued as means of achieving economic independence. However, by the mid-seventies, foreign exchange and fiscal deficits, inflation, and devaluation were manifestations of a deteriorating economic base which led the Manley government to negotiate the first Standby Agreement with the IMF in 1977.

Ironically, the rhetoric of a 'non-IMF' path led to dependency on the IMF by the end of the first Manley government. Foreign official debt increased by two and one half times between 1975 and 1980. Economic policy-making had to be consistent with the conditions required to gain access to the extended fund facility of the IMF. The IMF, not the elected officials, was directing economic policy-making before the Edward Seaga government was elected in 1980.

But after 15 years of IMF intervention, the results have not been any better. Neither the 'non-IMF' nor the IMF paths have stopped the Jamaican economy from the continuing decline. Today, the situation is much worse than in 1973 because of the huge debt servicing that diverts funds away from the social services that Jamaicans enjoyed in the late sixties. Education and health as a per centage of public expenditure have declined from 27 in 1973-75 to 17 in 1985-87 (Levitt, Table 7). Interest rates of 35-40 per cent make productive investment prohibitive, and the massive exodus of skilled labour has deeply eroded the human resource base of the economy.

The first Manley government pursued an industrial policy like that of Eastern Europe: state planning and public ownership were perceived as the means of industrial growth. Here the task was one of replacing the market with the plan. The IMF years have sought to replace the plan with the market.

Both industrial policies have worsened economic conditions for most Jamaicans because neither addressed the fundamental issue of production. Both free market and state ownership visions offer the illusion of a fast track to industrial development by government decrees, such as nationalizing or denationalizing property, announcing or denouncing free markets, regulating or deregulating prices. Lacking a concept of production, both visions obscure the related concepts of industrial restructuring and industrial policy.

Industry in Jamaica is primarily based on cheap labour, foreign based multinational corporations interested in the extraction of primary products and the importation of raw materials, technology, machinery and equipment, requiring large amounts of foreign exchange. Many imported manufactured items could be produced domestically through a concerted effort to assist firms in upgrading their manufacturing capabilities and the development of an industrial research and development programme for Jamaica, saving much of this foreign exchange. This shift requires the development and implementation of a production-led industrial policy.

II. Production Visions: From Mass Production to Flexible Specialization[3]

Before we turn to the contours of a production-led, strategic industrial policy to fit the specific Jamaican situation an important detour is necessary. A strategic analysis must begin with an assessment of the revolution in production methods forcing restructuring in all manufacturing sectors worldwide.

Mass Production: Economies of Time versus Size

Surprizingly, the industrial engineering principles of mass production are not widely understood in many parts of the world. The first principle, interchangeability of parts, was established decades before mass production became a vision of modern industrialization. The American system of manufacturing, as the British labeled it, was based on interchangeability. First applied at the Springfield Armory in Springfield, Massachusetts in 1817, interchangeability revolutionized production. The concept of interchangeability is as relevant today as it ever was. Before interchangeability each drawer in a desk was hand fit, each firing pin on a rifle was hand filed. The idea is simple but it is rarely deployed in the non-industrialized world today. It is not common in Jamaica's furniture industry, for example. Just as armies in pre-interchangeability times had to include an army of hand fitters to repair arms; furniture firms need a department of hand sanders to assemble pieces. Designing a production system around the concept of interchangeability means breaking with the craft tradition and developing a range of specialist machines. The stock of a gun at the Springfield

Armory, the process to which the concept was first applied, was made by a bank of 14 specialist lathes. After each operation, the result was checked with a precision gauge, not by the feel of a craftsman.

The revolution was not only in the development of a machining and tooling industry to supply specialist machines, equally important was the emergence of product engineering. The new activity meant deconstruction of a product into its constituent pieces and each piece into its constituent operations and an analysis of each operation for simplification according to the principle of interchangeability.

The application of interchangeability involved a revolution in production methods in that specialist machines run by machine operators replaced hand tools used by craftsmen. Before interchangeability of parts every product had to be constructed and assembled by hand fitting. In this production method, every product was slightly different and none could be made without fitting which, in turn, required skilled labour. Application of the principle also led to the redefinition of the product in terms of machining operations each of which met certain tolerance limits which enabled the product to be assembled without altering any of the constituent parts.

Interchangeability, however, does not define mass production; instead, it is a precondition to mass production. Efforts to do mass production which do not take into account the requirements of interchangeability are bound to fail. For without interchangeability, economies of time, the defining feature of mass production, cannot be achieved. Ford's assembly line can be used to illustrate.

Henry Ford described mass production as production without hand fitters. He was only partly right, for production without fitters had a long history before mass production appeared. Henry Ford's plants were organized according to a second constituent principle of mass production and this is what made Ford famous. Mass production is the application of the principle of flow to the production of a *single product*.

The idea was to maximize the rate of throughput in the production process beginning with raw materials and ending with delivery to the customer. The primary focus, however, was on the production stage. The goal was to increase throughput or reduce the time required per unit output. The means was to rearrange machining and manual activities into the order of the operations required for the production of the product. Thus, instead of organizing a plant according to machining operations in which the lathes would be in one department, the drills in a second, the planers in a third, the machines were ordered according to the operations required to produce the product. Whereas under the pre-mass production system, batches of intermediate or semi-finished products were shipped from department to department, under mass production batches were eliminated; in principle, no two products were ever at the same state of production.

The vision of a flowline concentrated the attention of engineers on barriers to throughput. A barrier, or bottleneck, occurred wherever a machining operation could not process material at the same pace as the previous operation. Inventories indicated the existence of a production bottleneck. The pace of the machining operation that had the largest inventory before it determined the rate of throughput of the entire production process. The bottleneck machine was the activity that constrained not only the throughput at that machine but of the production system as a whole. Increasing the pace of work on any other machining activity could not increase output, only inventory. Thus the idea behind the principle of flow was to *synchronize* production activities so that each operation could process material without producing to inventory. Production for any non-bottleneck activity should be limited to the pace of the bottleneck activity. Production beyond this pace would only be producing to inventory, it could not increase the rate of throughput.

Henry Ford created a large plant to achieve synchronized production for two reasons. The first was because he produced in enormous volume. The second was because a supplier base did not exist at the time that could deliver parts and components in the volume and with the dependability of delivery times that was required to produce without machining bottlenecks. For the latter reason Ford was forced to vertically integrate; it was a means of attacking bottlenecks for the first mass producer in an industry.

The failure to comprehend the real competitive advantage of mass production misled many industrialists and industrial policy makers to establish large scale plants. Large plants failed for two reasons. The first, already noted, was the confusion of economies of time for economies of size. Size without synchronization of productive activities will generate greater diseconomies than economies of size. The second was due to a failure to observe an organizational principle of successful big enterprises: the decentralization of operations and the centralization of coordination, the defining principle of the multidivisional organizational form.[4]

The multidivisional plant involved the pinpointing of power and responsibility at the divisional manager level. The major strength of the multidivisional was that it enabled big business to expand but without diffusing operational decision making; the major weakness was that power and responsibility were not pushed down to the shop floor. Consequently, a Taylorized division of labour emerged which separated thinking, done by managers, from doing, done by workers. This system has proven incapable of responding to the New Competition which has pushed power and responsibility across the divide between managers and workers and enabled the emergence of organizations committed to continuous improvement.

Realizing the principles of mass production did not always lead to huge managerial organizations. In the Baden-Wurttemberg region of Germany, production was often synchronized, not by building huge vertically integrated plants, but by networked groups of small specialized firms. As we shall see below, decentralization of production into groups of small and medium sized firms has made the transition to the new production principles considerably easier than in vertically integrated enterprises. But we must first examine the weaknesses of mass production that emerged in practice and which were exposed by the development of a new set of production principles, commonly referred to as just-in-time methods.

Just-in-time: The Principle of Flow Applied to Multiple Products

The decades of the 1970s and eighties witnessed a revolution in production organization which began in the Japanese automobile and consumer electronics industries. The age of mass production is yielding to a new age of flexible production commonly referred to as just-in-time (JIT) production. The new production methods enable firms to gain a competitive edge on the basis of product-led as opposed to price-led competition. The winners are firms that can offer higher quality and shorter lead, delivery, and new product development times; the losers are still seeking to compete on the basis of lower prices alone. What went wrong with mass production?

Mass production worked well as long as the plant made one product. Problems emerged with the need to produce multiple products *in the same facilities*. The fundamental weakness of mass production was the inflexibility of the production activities. The drive to increase throughput led process engineers to design ever more specialized and dedicated equipment. Too often the machines were linked in ways that made it impossible to use them for the production of any product except for those for which the machine had been specially designed. In other cases it was possible to produce more than one product on a machine but only after a time consuming take-down and set-up procedure was undertaken.

The result was that inventories crept back into the system as engineers sought to reduce set-up costs per unit output by producing long runs. Mass production and multiple products meant a reversion to batch production. The insight of the link between synchronized production, no inventories and high throughput was lost. The principle of flow holds that throughput can only be increased by relieving the system constraining bottleneck; this bottleneck was all too often hidden from view by the buildup of inventories at every stage in production. (This is a significant problem in virtually all Jamaican firms visited.) The result was that management focused its attention on increasing the productivity of each machine and each worker. Management accounting came to focus attention on individual factor productivity levels not on barriers to throughput. Not surprisingly, no matter how many machines were purchased or new control systems developed, throughput was unaffected unless they tackled the single bottleneck that regulated output.

The idea of JIT is to apply the principle of flow not to a single product but to a mixed range of products using the same production facilities. Mass production is about driving down the throughput time required to produce a single product; JIT is about driving down the (production and new product development) time required to produce a range of products. In this sense, moving from mass production to JIT production does not involve a revolution in the underlying principle of production; both are based on the principle of flow. The transition involves the application of the principle of flow to the production not of a single product but multiple products on the same production line. But this small step involves a revolution in the organization of production including management structure, work organization, and supplier relations. Successful JIT production means reduced lead times, shorter runs, higher fixed and working capital turns, lower inventories, lower changeover times, and increased space productivities.

Too often, the difference between the two production perspectives is considered simply in terms of inventories. For mass production, inventories were produced to reduce changeover costs and to ensure that production was not interrupted by the lack of materials. For JIT, inventories are a sign of waste. Whereas the mass producers produced inventory to deny changeover bottlenecks; the flexible producers attack bottlenecks by eliminating inventory.

What distinguishes the JIT plant is the capability to produce a range of products on the same machines without producing to inventory. This is a major challenge in Jamaica since most small manufacturers cannot afford to purchase new machinery if and when they begin to diversify their product range. It demands the capability of minimal changeover times which, in turn, leads to new demands placed on workers and managers. Workers must be capable of operating, setting up, and maintaining a range of machines, not simply operating a single machine as in the mass production plant. Thus while the difference between the two production systems can be measured in terms of inventories, the real bottlenecks to JIT production are organizational: throughput cannot be increased without a revolution in the social practices of production.

For JIT, the production to inventory is a waste. It is better for resources to remain idle than to build up inventory. It is not simply that inventories add to working capital needs and increase financial costs. Inventories are costly in other ways: they have to be handled, transported, stored, counted, inspected; they take up space, they can be damaged and they hide defects. The goal of the JIT producer is one of inventory less production. To produce a range of products with a minimum of inventory leads to a drastic downsizing in the length of production runs; such a downsizing has also created new opportunities for small scale, flexibly specialized producers to compete in the marketplace. It is at this precise point that opportunities exist for Jamaican firms willing to invest in changing their existing production practices.

The New Competition

World class competitors in the 1990s tend to be organized according to JIT principles. But JIT is only part of the story. To understand industrially successful regions and countries we have to locate JIT within a broader four part institutional configuration which encompasses but goes beyond the industrial engineering issues we have examined so far to those of business and industrial organization. To describe the new vision of industry as flexible specialization, as opposed to flexible production, is to emphasize that the unit of industrial organization is not the factory or even the firm but a matrix of four interrelated institutions which combine to engender continuous improvement in production capabilities, or JIT production engineering principles. Together the new principles of production and organization constitute a New Competition.

1. Entrepreneurial firm. The entrepreneurial firm is one committed to continuous improvement in product, process, technology, and organization. Furthermore it is a problem solving firm which seeks to build world class capabilities in a specific, precisely defined production activity. The entrepreneurial firm denies the separation between thinking and doing associated with Taylorism and 'scientific management' and seeks to build an organization in which teamwork and learning are given high priority. It develops the problem solving skills of everyone in the organization and seeks new ideas not only from managers, workers, and professional specialists who are stakeholders within the firm but outside from customers, suppliers, joint venturers, research and development agencies, and educational institutions.

The hierarchical firm, in contrast, does not delegate authority and responsibility below the managerial ranks; it cannot for workers have not been trained in problem solving skills and are not consulted as team members. The entrepreneurial firm, by choosing to compete over product, as distinct from price, has attacked the hierarchical firm where it is weakest: the lack of flexibility and commitment on the shopfloor caused by the sharp separation between thinking and doing and the lack of teamwork between manager and worker, producer and seller, designer and machine maker caused by the fragmentation of tasks.

2. Consultative supplier relations. In the past, productive activities along the production chain have been coordinated by either plan or market. Coordination by plan means vertical integration within a single managerial hierarchy, coordination by market means impersonal relations mediated by price. Under the New Competition a third form of coordination, networking, has become widespread. Networking refers to long term, consultative relations amongst independently owned but mutually interdependent enterprises in which each firm specializes on one link in the production chain and trades with other specialist enterprises along the same and related production chains.

Specialization, combined with flexible production methods, is what explains the fact that the most successful new competitor nations are also nations with the highest proportion of small industrial firms. But these firms can best be described in terms of networked groups of small firms, for they tend to have long term, mutually interdependent relations with other firms. From this perspective, the bottleneck to hierarchical firms is a lack of problem solving suppliers capable not only of delivering just-in-time but in enabling the group of firms to pursue product-led competition.

3. Cooperative inter-firm infrastructure. Success in international competition can be enhanced by inter-firm cooperation, particularly in the collective provision of services with large economies of scale or that have a public good feature. Joint marketing is an example of the first and vocational training of the second. Often ignored, however, is a third form of inter-firm cooperation that can have a powerful impact on shaping the internal organization of production: the specific rules of competition. Price-led competition, for example, generates a pressure for worker deskilling; product-led competition, to the contrary, generates pressures for flexible production and multi-skilled workers.

4. Strategic industrial policy. A reactive industrial policy is one that attempts to save firms that are losing in the market. A strategic industrial policy is one that seeks to develop a sector strategy based upon a competitor analysis of the strengths and weaknesses of foreign and domestic firms. The sector strategy will facilitate shaping the inter-firm infrastructure, long term financial decision making, the visions of individual firms and promoting a coherent set of governmental services to firms.

Seen from a production oriented economic perspective, Jamaica's fragile industrial base is under attack from two forces. The first is the emergence of international competitors based upon new principles of production and organization. The second is the set of neoliberal economic policies being pursued in Jamaica while in other parts of the world, governments are quietly promoting the establishment of an industrial infra-structure that facilitates the transformation of old and creation of new industrial enterprises organized according to the new principles. Governments which give priority to production transformation and support an industrial infra-structure geared to implementing that transformation can be referred to as Developmental States.

III. Production in Jamaica

What would it take to dramatically increase output per person in Jamaica over the next three or four decades? Unless economic policy is guided by an awareness of the fundamental principles of production and organization, it is highly unlikely that Jamaica will escape the low productivity trap that immiserates much of her population. For what is required is a transformation in industrial enterprises according to entirely new principles. A number of enterprises are struggling hard to make this transformation. Unfortunately, they cannot do it alone.

Most Jamaican factories are organized in a hybrid production system that combines elements of craft/workshop and batch production. Craft production means traditional designs, hand held tools, and no systematic product engineering. Workshop methods refers to processes that have not been organized according to either process or product logics. Instead, the factory is more akin to an extended personal workshop. In the case of furniture, for example, individual or small teams of workers subcontract to make furniture with the owner of the company. Each of the small groups makes its way through the machines as they make the required components. The owner makes his/her profit on the difference between the making and selling price; profitability comes from the sales margin which, in turn, is greater the lower the wages. The methods and time of production are entirely controlled by the work team: in effect, the team does the design and the product engineering as well as the production. Dependability of delivery promises and quality are virtually impossible to control which creates considerable tension between the owners and the workers. As noted, the worker and even the supervisor work without the aid of any systematic product or process engineering; they are expected to produce to output and quality levels without training in production methods.

If the goal is to increase production with minimal increases in costs, the first task in a great majority of Jamaican factories is to introduce product engineering. This can lead to dramatic increases in productivity and quality with minimal financial costs. Briefly, product engineering entails each of the following activities:

1. assigning materials to balance function, cost, and aesthetics with company capabilities;
2. specifying construction methods for ease of manufacturability and enhancement of quality (for example: deciding between dowell or mortis and tenon joining techniques);
3. estimating product costs (different methods yield different results);
4. drafting blueprints for each piece part (computer aided drafting and, later, computer aided design capabilities are important here);
5. specifying routing sheets for each piece part (the routing sheets include details which specify machine, machine operations, proper jig, attachments and fixtures);

6. making worksheets (here the step by step standards for each piece part operation are made user friendly;
7. constructing jigs, attachments, and samples for each operation.

A number of Jamaican manufacturers have introduced product engineering. The challenge to them is to design an efficient or low cost production system. This involves developing production scheduling methods. The problem is that scheduling production even for simple products is complex. Each product has a number of parts and each part goes through a series of common machining processes. The times required on different machines vary widely as do the times required to changeover from making one to making a different part. A specific machine, for example, can easily take one and one half hours to set up but only seconds to do an operation. To economize on set up times the companies seek to run large batches through the machines with long setup times. Other machining activities, however, require only minimum setup times. This creates a lack of balance which tends to be solved by establishing batch sizes for all machining activities of the size required by the machine with the longest setup time.

Different machining operation times creates another problem: some machines are idle. Two solutions to this problem of imbalance are possible. First, all of the machining activities can be synchronized in a way that ensures that all of the piece parts are being constructed in the same time cycle. Here the assembly schedule would act like the clock to which all component production would be synchronized. It would not mean that all machining activities had the same operating times but that slower operating times were compensated for by more machines. This was the solution of Henry Ford who established the first mass production system based upon the principle of synchronizing machining activities to minimize production lead time.

A second solution is mass batch production, the organization of the factory into machining departments and coordinate across a range of products so that different cycle times are balanced over the total production scheduling period. As the range of products proliferates, management seeks to gain better control by organizing the factory into departments by machining function.

In Jamaica, as the world over, large or mass batch production methods emerge as a response to long changeover times and different operation times. Mass batch, however, has a dynamics of its own that leads to a number of unforeseen problems. The first is long production lead times caused by large lot sizes. The second is the emergence of

hidden bottlenecks. The subject of how to identify hidden bottlenecks
has been the topic of a number of our workshops in Jamaica.

The result of batch production methods is the same everywhere .
Working capital productivity is woefully low because of the high finance charges built into financing inventory. In most Jamaican factories, financial costs are 2 or 3 times greater than direct labour costs as a
proportion of product costs. Mass batch is also wasteful in that it is
virtually always associated with low quality, lengthy production and new
product development times, and little product or process improvement and innovation. In short, it is the old competition of today. In
certain industries –packaging is one– many Jamaican manufacturers
have sought to avoid the problems of batch production by purchasing
continuous process machines. But even in materials conducive to
continuous process machines such as glass making, pulp and paper
making, and plastics conversion, the production processes are mass
batch as distinct from multi-product flow. The reason, as we shall see,
is not because of the lack of the latest technology. It is because of the
organization of production. Fortunately, developing a flexible specialization production system does not, in most cases, depend upon the
importation of high technology machinery. It does require a revolution in the organization of production, both within and across firms.

IV. Transforming Production in Jamaican Enterprises

The New Competition has created a number of opportunities for
upgrading production capabilities in poor countries. Firm size is not
the relevant variable. In the Third Italy, the Baden Wurttember region
of Germany, and in Western Denmark industrial districts or networked
groups of small firms are internationally competitive in a variety of
sectors including machine tools, furniture, garments, footwear, food
processing, ceramic tiles. The requirement is not that a firm be big but
that it specialize, apply the principle of flow, and network or cooperate
with other firms to collectively offer the whole range of productive
activities. Cooperation amongst individuals or teams across firms or
within firms is required if high throughput specialization is to be
established. Firms compete in groups, not individually.

One close, consultative relationship cuts across every manufacturing sector: every manufacturer must have a problem solving relationship with repair, maintenance, and tooling shops. Then networking

can be substituted for machine importing. This is a superior method of applying the principles of interchangeability and flow. Capital accumulation is about developing and altering simple machines with jigs, fixtures, and attachments to accomplish the goal of multi-product flow. All too often industrial development has been perceived in terms of technology importation. Imported technology can be highly useful, but unless it is integrated into a problem-solving repair, maintance and tooling network it will not generate sustainable production.

The Jamaican government in its most recent economic development five year plan articulated the following longterm objectives: to establish a coherent and consistent policy for technological change; to improve the structure of research and development with support from the private sector; and to achieve and maintain international competitiveness. The strategy, the plan states, 'requires the adoption of general purpose machines and production methods which allow rapid change-over times from one product to another. It can be applied to product design, production, inventory management and quality control.' [5]

The foundation is being laid to develop a production-centred development policy. It is essential that the kind of detailed analysis which follows of the furniture, plastics and packaging and metal-working sectors be carried out across every manufacturing sector in the country as part of this process. Well over 100 enterprises were visited during late 1991 and 1992 and interviews conducted with managers and workers to assess the capabilities of firms in the furniture, plastics and packaging and metal-working sectors. A similar analysis has been done in the garment sector.

Furniture

Sector Analysis

A Jamaican woodworking sector analysis informed by plant visits to 20 firms revealed that the Jamaican furniture industry suffers from a low level of productivity for every productive input. Output per direct labour is about J$60-75 thousand which, given 50 per cent material costs and a 20 per cent overhead charge leaves only J$18-22.5 thousand (US$2300-2850) annual income per worker, a level roughly one/tenth that of a US furniture worker.

Working capital productivity is extremely low with work-in-process turns of two being commonplace. One of the most efficient Jamaican furniture firms (certainly one of the few with detailed factor cost accounts) has an interest charge of nearly 80 per cent of its wage bill. This is because of first, a work-in-process total of over one half annual sales; second, a 36 per cent interest charge on an overdraft facility that matches the work-in-process magnitude (this company is exceptional in that it has been able to receive European finance at 11.5 per cent on highly collateralized debt); and third, the slow pace of pre-and post-factory material flow caused by an inefficient customs and transportation infrastructure.

Fixed capital productivity is also low. The problem here is not the existence of excess capacity. Rather it is the poor working performance of machines and tools that are not properly maintained, that lack accessories, that are being used for purposes other than that for which they were designed. It is common, for example, to find tenons being made with boring machines; to find workers wrestling with six foot clamps where a six inch clamp would do the job more effectively; to find a bottleneck at sanding because sanding is being done labouriously by hand *after* assembly instead of with the aid of a simple machine *before* assembly.

Organizational productivity is low because of the lack of specialization. Consequently, most firms seek to make a wide range of products in the same plant making it virtually impossible to standardize or modularize anywhere along the product chain. The lack of specialization contributes to poor quality as no one firm develops a distinctive competence in one or a limited number of activities such as turning, finishing, or veneering. Instead of developing an array of machines capable of producing many variations of specialist activities to high degrees of accuracy, each company has the same range of machines none of which is capable of achieving high degrees of accuracy. The spontaneous adjustment to apparent market opportunities has resulted, not in specialization and coordination, but imitation and excess capacity.

Establishing a Restructuring Vision.

The sector analysis should feed into a vision that can guide restructuring efforts. The vision must emerge from the international competitor analysis specific to the sector. In the case of the Jamaican woodworking industry, a flexible specialization vision is being elaborated. The goal is to increase the rate of throughput; only with greater throughput can incomes increase.

The primary barrier to increased throughput in most companies was identified as the limited application of the three production principles of interchangeability, (standardization), flow, and flexibility. Interchangeability demands that machines and procedures be established that can produce the same unit to narrow tolerance limits so that the output can be assembled without being handfitted. Interchangeability is a prerequisite to increasing the rate of throughput for any one part or product. Flexibility demands that setups on the machines take minutes as opposed to hours but without compromising either interchangeability or (multiple product) flow time.

While idle machines are considered a sin according to the postulates of batch production, wasteful production is the no-no for flexible specialization. Under batch production, output per machine was an index of productivity. Not so under flexible specialization where it is far better to have idle machines than machines producing ill-suited or unwanted products. The goal is not to increase the productivity of machines but the rate of throughput. Machine or labour activity that produces to inventory or that does not increase the flow out of the factory gate is wasteful activity.

Application of flexible specialization methods can be illustrated by a comparison of the unproductive methods that both companies now use to make drawers and panel doors with specialized, flexible and cellular production arrangements. At present, all three principles are violated. The first problem is that the same machines are used for both products. The way ahead is to set up separate product lines, one for drawers and another for doors.

Drawers can be cut and assembled in less than one minute using three simple, heavy duty, precision cutting, non-electronic router machines which together can make corner cuts, bottom grooves and mortise and tenon joints.[6] Together the three routers, run on independent three horsepower motors and equipped with cutters and clip-on, color coded guide fences and plates can do all the operations required to make and assemble drawers in a manner that is solid, high quality, and quick. Changeovers to drawers of different depths of cut can be made in 10 seconds. One machine expert quoted a price of $1500 for such a three machine configuration. It can be easily demonstrated that the multiple specialist machine construction method proposed here will substantially increase quality. The drawer is firm without nails or clamps. With glue it will provide a solid drawer for years of normal use.

A similar machine specialization arrangement can be established for shaping panel doors. Small scale but durable machines designed for short set-up times without electronics are available at low prices here as well.

The economical use of these machines does not depend upon their utilization rates unless the making of drawers or panel doors is the bottleneck which limits throughput. Whether or not they should be operated depends upon the relationship between throughput and operating expenses. If they do not increase throughput, don't run them because they will only add to operating expenses.[7] The same applies to labour once piece rates are abandoned.

Under flexible specialization, labour, not machines, is the fixed factor of production. Labour is also the main source of flexibility in the wood processing industry, unlike processes that can work with materials that flow.[8] For these reasons, it is important to utilize labour effectively. The key to effective utilization of labour is to make it multi-skilled so that the worker can do set-ups and maintenance as well as operate a machine, and so that he/she can operate multiple machines. In our example, if the worker can shift from producing drawers to doors then the goal of increasing throughput can be realized. For then the whole product or range of products can be produced to demand and not to stock. The result will be shorter and more dependable lead times and lower working capital requirements.

Under flexible specialization labour produces more but does not work harder. Present methods demand much harder work particularly in hand sanding, fitting, and assembling than is required with properly functioning machines. Skills are not less but they are different: instead of being a wizard at fitting irregular drawers into irregular spaces, the worker must be able to read routing sheets and set up machines to do a variety of operations on a range of products. A critical precondition to establishing the new methods is that workers not fear that jobs will be lost. It is for this reason that the owner/manager has a problem-solving as opposed to a neo-plantation mentality which is not compat-ible with making the transition to flexible specialization production methods.

Making the transition requires the technical skills of a machine engineer. His/her job is to redefine how the products are produced consistently with the principles of interchangeability, flow, and flexibil-ity, to layout machines according to the new principles, to develop route sheets for each product, and to demonstrate how to do the new methods to the workers involved. The provision of such targeted technical services to small firms by an industrial policy agency is an example of a 'real' service.[9] In conjunction, the training departments within the appropriate governmental and educational institutions can be called upon to conduct group training sessions on the new methods. And, before and after practices should be recorded by video to demonstrate the transition for purposes of showing in other Jamaican plants.

Workshops and pilot projects

The next step is to conduct workshops on the new production methods which include several individuals from each participating firm. The purpose of the workshop is twofold: to better understand the principles of production and organization and to go back to the companies and develop a pilot project. The idea of the pilot project is to illustrate one theme which in turn captures a key element in the flexible specialization vision. For example, a team may illustrate how the proper construction and care of jigs can increase standardization, reduce hand fitting, and increase the rate of material flow. Or, a team may demonstrate how reducing set-up times in the cutting or machining department reduces scheduling difficulties in the finishing department and, ultimately, delivery times.

Developing action plans.

As individuals in the various enterprises become more familiar with the new principles of production and organization they will be better equipped to construct performance criteria which contrast their factories with the benchmark, or world class plants. The refinement of action plans will also serve to more precisely identify what resources are needed to make the transition. At this point the common services that are most critical to success will be clearer. This, in turn, will enable the industrial policy making agency to refine its instruments based upon real needs. Success will depend upon the state making the transition to flexible specialization as much as the business enterprises. The establishment of action plans cannot be achieved by turning to organizational blueprints. The flexible specialization vision is about, in part, seeking market niches and developing unique competences to satisfy them. For example, a number of Jamaican companies seek to combine carver skills with the new principles of production in ways that will allow them to offer products that cannot be reproduced by machines alone.

One tool that facilitates the development of action plans within companies is the 14 key self-evaluation programme. The concept was developed by Iwao Kobayashi and published as *20 Keys to Workplace Improvement*. We have custom fit it for wood processing and altered a number of the features substantially. The idea, however, is the same: companies can conduct a self-evaluation that enables them to compare themselves along a number of production fundamentals with world class companies. The clarity of the criteria for distinguishing amongst four levels simultaneously suggests the changes that have to be made to transform production consistently with the new principles of production and organization. We have used the 14 key programme in both the furniture and the packaging industries in Jamaica with considerable success.

Furniture/Enterprise Examples

What follows are five examples of companies that are in the process of restructuring according to the principles of flexible specialization. While they are outstanding examples, they are not the only ones. Two or three others have made similar progress and several others could well become the leaders in future years. Well over 10 companies have made substantial progress in the restructuring programme including, besides the four listed below, Magnificent Crafted Masterpieces, Cameron Industries, Ledon Furniture, Leodor, Ultramod, Kitchens R' Us, Original Bamboo Factory, and Discovery Bay Designs.

1. McIntosh Furniture Company: Workshop and Progress

While many companies have participated in a series of workshops on upgrading production capabilities, a few stand out in applying the new principles. McIntosh Furniture Company is one such case. MFC used the Pareto product quantity analysis to identify core products and the process flow analysis to identify families of piece-parts and groups of similar machining sequences. Application of these tools enabled MFC to reduce the product range from 168 to three broad ranges.[10]

The key range, cribs, is distributed piggyback with the Sealy Bedding distribution network throughout the Caribbean that is managed by McIntosh Bedding Company. With hindsight, cribs are a natural for MFC; the problem in the past is that cribs were caught up in the three month production lead time caused by the proliferation of product lines and the view, mistaken, that cribs were much less important than numerous other product lines. Consequently, customers were not able to get short or even dependable delivery times on cribs and MFC did not develop the product line. To deliver in the quantity, quality, and with dependable delivery times the production methods were transformed from mass batch to flow. Flow production methods in furniture involve similar techniques as JIT or cellular methods found in world class manufacturing plants established in high volume industries in industrialized countries, but with allowances for adaptability and flexibility required in fashion industries like furniture and unstable markets as found in less developed countries. MFC is now working on developing production cells for the other core product ranges.

In October 1992, over 30 industry and training people attended a workshop held at MFC and Donald McIntosh's management team demonstrated how a two week production lead time could be established. Most of the leading furniture firms had representatives and all were impressed. It was a most successful workshop because the principles were demonstrated with actual advances made by MFC. In this, MFC is a demonstration laboratory for application of modern, JIT production methods in the context of a less developed country. This is no small accomplishment, as such a vision is rarely established effectively in the furniture industry in America but more so in Europe.

Demonstrating the factory to individuals from other furniture companies is the best way to convince them of the benefits. Even demonstrating their success to potential competitors makes commercial sense to MFC. The long run success of MFC depends upon building networks with other companies that can also meet the demanding lead time, quality, and cost requirements that are being established at MFC. Only with such a group of companies can the lucrative hospitality (tourist industry) market be tackled. This US$120 million annual market is now supplied almost entirely by imports. Instead of MFC producing chairs, tables, cabinets, beds, 'what nots', and every other item required to fit out a hotel, MFC will specialized on two or three items and cooperate with others to fill in the range. Then each company can develop flow lines and the requisite specialist machines and quick changeover attachments to be able to generate the productivity required to be competitive.

The results of the production changes at MFC are becoming evident. Production lead time dropped from three months to two weeks, and sales have increased sharply. Crib sales, in particular, are booming. This is an accomplishment with which most American furniture companies would be proud; to transform an enterprise from mass batch to flow methods is no simple task. To do so without a long and difficult transitionary period is also uncommon. MFC was a good candidate for the transition because of their past investment in product engineering: the company has routing sheets for every piece-part, a rarity in the Third World.

Unfortunately, roughly 40 cents on every dollar earned at MFC is going to pay off interest and penalty charges on long term, mainly foreign, debt. No company involved in a tradables sector can survive such high financial charges. This is the private sector counterpart of the public sector debt which has expanded to astronomical levels by devaluations.

2. Taylor Wood Products

A detailed restructuring programme for TWP, a kitchen manufacturer, was established as a second model for furniture companies. TWP sales for the first six months of 1992 were nearly J$4 million; in all of 1991 sales were J$2.5 million. Production lead time for kitchens has been reduced from six to ten weeks to one week. TWP has implemented many of the proposals including management of accounts receivable, redesign of the product for purposes of standardization, abandonment of group contract system, and the development of a time plus goup incentive system. Mr. Taylor is seeking finance to relayout the factory according to the plans in our report. TWP continues to seek means of upgrading worker skills and requested that a workshop be given on documentation for quality control; this was deemed a prerequisite to more effective collaboration with other companies, particularly for export markets.

3. Wood Works Ltd.: Serial Flexible Specialization

Wood Works Ltd., owned by Chris Marley, specializes in custom made chairs. Following the advice of Joel Suris, Wood Works was reorganized according to the logic of the product. Workers were cross trained so that each could operate any machine. Routing sheets spell out each operation.

Several machines were custom designed to facilitate standardization and flow. For example, Suris, with the help of a local machine shop, constructed a horizontal shaper specific to the shaping of chair backs and rails. The machine is virtually useless for making any other type of furniture. This means that a high rate of throughput for an order of chairs can be achieved by developing a special machining line peculiar to the making of chairs. A fourfold increase in output per worker was achieved; the means were demonstrated to the rest of the industry at a February 22, 1992 workshop. Marley explains that one of the most important ideas he got from the workshops was the advantages of multi-skilling. All of his employees can operate the sander, the drill, the band saw, and the joiner. The increased productivity is shared with the workers who are offered a starting pay level of J$1300 per week, 60per cent over the J$800 of most companies.

Wood Works applies the principle of flow and, unlike Henry Ford, the company can run a range of products on the same equipment. Flow comes from establishing a dedicated line. A variety of chair designs can be produced but each product is linked to a specific configuration of the setups, jigs, and attachments peculiar to each chair design. However, unlike true flexible specialization, the machinery is highly dedicated and switching over is a lengthly process. In fact, any sizeable redesign requires the construction of new specialist machines. In this, only one product can be run at any one time. Real flexible specialization requires an additional step as demonstrated in the next case.

4. Island Crafts: Real Flexible Specialization

Again, under the guidance of Joel Suris, Island Crafts produces a range of 38 products with the capability of producing the whole range each day. This is true multi-product flow and demands that setup times be reduced on every machine. Consequently, IC has a two week delivery time. Lot sizes are small. The plant layout is done according to the logic of the product. Every worker is trained in doing setups and in working the entire range of machines including printing machines. Product documentation is impressive. Each product has a file with the following items:

Material per unit (material costs are determined by multiplying the material by cost).

A sample drawing

Rough mill requirements by step

Machining requirements, step by step including jigs, attachments, and machine settings.

Suris has also helped with standardizing the piece parts, which has greatly simplified production. The owner claims that Suris' standardization suggestions reduced production time by one half. His suggestions to specialize on products that require similar machining operations and to build speicalist machines has greatly reduced production lead time as well. Suris was also helpful in training the supervisors.

Island Crafts is a small company producing a basic product which greatly reduces the barriers to transforming the enterprise according to the new principles. But hundreds of successful small companies not only provide a source of jobs but education in the new methods. Together, groups of small firms can generate large orders and rapidly advance the production capabilities of the whole sector.

5. Morgan Industries: Replacing Internal Sub-contracting with Flow.

Morgan's Industries cost structure reveals a problem similar to much of Jamaican industry. As a per centage of sales, raw material costs are 50-60per cent, direct labour is 7.5-10per cent, and overhead is 30-42.5per cent; but finance charges are 20per cent plus. Thus finance charges run two to three times direct labour costs. The reasons are the high rate of interest (50-90per cent), the need to buy lumber in container loads, the three month lead time required to order wood (payment must be within 30 days of the order), a 60 day payment period to customers, the lack of dependable kiln drying in Jamaica which means longer preparation time periods, delays at the ports for both exporting and importing (manufacturing firms must present paid up income tax forms to access raw materials), and high duties on machinery which inflate their costs and borrowing charges.

Morgan has made substantial progress within the 14 Key programme. The company has broken with the internal sub-contracting system. The shop floor has been cleaned up, isles are painted in, material is moved on pallets, an hourly payment system has replaced the group contract system, separate departments have been established, a draftsman has been recruited to make product blueprints and he works directly with a supervisor who understands all of the machining functions, and cabinets have been modularized for size and parts. At present a team is being formed which includes the marketing manager to carryout a marketing analysis with the goal of reducing the present 30 product lines to five or six. The biggest problem the company faces is one of worker skills. A number of HEART, (the national training agency,) graduates have been hired, but they lack skills. At a meeting with 10 teachers at HEART a workshop to to be conducted at Morgan Industries was arranged. The workshop will be taught by a wood production expert and jointly attended by HEART teachers and Morgan workers with the idea of developing a curriculum for both students and continuing education.

The success of these companies suggests a new form of technical assistance at the sector level. It is doubtful that any of these companies would have instituted the flexible specialization vision if not for a series of restructuring workshops carried out over a two year period under the joint auspices of JAMPRO's Design centre and UNIDO. The workshops were attended by a large number of owners, managers, and technicians. A restructuring methodology has been developed by the task force which includes a means of self-evaluation and a set of tools including the ABC analysis, flow charts and process flow analysis. In addition, a new spirit of cooperation exists in the industry. Representatives of many companies have visited Wood Works Ltd and McIntosh Furniture. Not surprisingly, implementation of flexible specialization created a demand for new skills. For example, widescale transition from craft to manufacturing methods will require technical training in product engineering and construction methods; transition from batch to one piece flow will require worker education in operating and setting up for a range of machines. Payments systems have to be overhauled as the skills of the workforce are upgraded.

Packaging and Plastics

The Jamaican packaging sector contributes approximately 8 per cent of total manufacturing value, contains a sizeable number of large industrial enterprises, and is a major industrial employer. But the packaging industry has effects that extend far beyond its direct contribution to gross national product. Packaging is a unique product in that it affects the competitiveness of most consumer goods in two ways. First, it is the interface between a product and the final consumer. While an appealing package cannot sell a poor product, an unappealing and/or costly package is a barrier to the sale of any product. Second, packaging links the production and distribution stages and thereby affects market size. For example, canning increases the distances that a perishable product can be shipped.

The packaging sector is particularly crucial to food processing: they interact symbiotically. Food processing is about extending the product life of food; the processing specifications are determined by packaging imperatives. A recent report on the food processing sector states: 'Packaging appears to be the most serious problem facing the agrofood industry in Jamaica'. The lack of development of the food processing industry is a major barrier to growth in Jamaica because it necessitates an enormous processed food import bill. At present much of the food basket of the poor is imported processed foods: flour, cornmeal, rice, chicken, cooking oil, canned fish, and condensed milk. Consequently, improving the packaging industry can have a magnified impact on economic growth to the extent that it reduces imports and thereby relaxes the major constraint on growth. The size of the food process gap is indicated by the fact that in Jamaica only 10-12 per cent of agricultural production is processed in contrast to 80-85 per cent in developed countries.

Sector Analysis

In plastics and packaging, firm changeovers from one product to another or even from one size of the same product to another often take several hours or in some cases days. The managing director of one company we visited stated that it could take as many as 10 to 15 shifts to get a certain production line running correctly in his factory, all the while producing scrap as the new set ups were 'made right'. If the factory ran six days a week the total number of shifts on the production line would totally approximately 310 assuming a six day a week schedule. The manager indicated that the line changed over roughly ten times a year. Using ten shifts to get the set up right this amounts to approximately 100 shifts a year spent getting jobs to run properly out of 310 total production shifts for the year on this particular machine. Even if these approximations are slightly off this amounts to close to 33 per cent of production time lost, staggering amounts of completed work stockpiled in warehouses and excessive amounts of scrap and rework as the setup is perfected.

A major bottling plant suffers from much the same problem. Its production lines make it extremely difficult, if not impossible, to produce different size bottles if customers want to develop and package new products in glass containers. The color of the glass being manufactured is set by what is being produced at the moment resulting in certain types of jams and jellies being packaged in green glass bottles rather than clear glass which would present the product more attractively. The jelly and jam maker takes what it can get — the result strawberry jam in green glass jars!

The consequences of excessively long setup times can be easily detected. First, all but one packaging firm appears to suffer from low working capital productivity as indicated by inventory turns (annual sales divided by work-in-process plus final good inventories) of one and two. A world class competitor enjoys inventory turns of 25 to 30. Given the high cost of working capital in Jamaica, the effects on cost structures are devastating: in several cases firms were paying as much in finance charges as direct labour costs. Second, the final goods warehouse in many Jamaican packaging companies holds several months of supply. Because the changeover costs from one product to another are now so high, plant managers will produce runs that will satisfy months of sales before switching over to another product. Inevitably, since the product is consumed at a much slower pace, the level of final good inventory is excessively high and the financial charges mount. Third, quality generally is low in the Jamaican packaging industry. High levels of waste, rework, and rejects are commonplace. Quality problems are indicative of batch as distinct from flow production systems. One of the primary benefits of flow production is that defects can be spotted soon after they occur and the causes can be more easily identified because 'the trail is hot'.

Fourth, new product development is nearly non-existent. The food processing industry is particularly critical of the packaging makers' failure to develop new products. The following quote captures this sentiment:

...in packaging, there is no longer any aseptic packaging on the island, while radiation, sterilization, controlled atmospheric packaging, or co-extruded thermally processable tray techniques, are yet to be deployed in the industry. Largely, packaging in Jamaica consists simply of open filling bags, boxes and bottles.

A Success Story.

In folding cartons we can describe a Jamaican success story. Labels and Boxes Ltd. stands out as a Jamaican company that has adopted many of the characteristics of the flexible specialization vision. Annual sales of J$8-10 million are generated with 25-30 employees for a sales to worker ratio of roughly J$300,000. If every Jamaican company could achieve this level, Jamaica's per capita income would take an approximately five-fold leap. (This extremely rough calculation is based on an estimated average sales per worker figure of J$60,000).

Labels and Boxes specializes in labels and folded cartons which are sold to 20 companies, many on an automatic monthly call off or level scheduling basis to well-known companies such as Grace Kennedy, Nestle, Procter and Gamble, Beecham, Jamaica Flour Mill and Scotts. Air Jamaica purchases Baggage Labels, each of which must be individually numbered. The level scheduling allows the Company first, to plan raw material purchases and deliver on a just-in-time basis thus greatly reducing inventory and inventory finance charges and, second to schedule production efficiently.

Labels and Boxes has a plate-making department, an impressive group of Heidelberg presses for offset printing, cutting and creasing, and two glueing machines. The technological centrepiece is a state-of-the-art five colour press.

Labels and Boxes does not design, do artwork, or make the die cuts. Die cutting has considerable economies of scale and is jobbed on a two day turn around basis to a CAD equipped specialist die maker with whom Pascal Lee, the owner, has a close relationship. Mr. Lee also jobs all artwork to a group of artist/designers.

Production throughput time is short as the small factory is organized into product (not function) departments. The box making department is flexibly organized to accomodate boxes with different printing requirements. The label making department also has a printer and a cutter which are organized into a manufacturing cell. The jobs requiring glueing go to a third, specialist department.

Flexibility is further enhanced by the labour education and payment system. All machines are purchased from the same company to simplify parts and maintenance; but the purchase agreements always include a training provision at the machine makers training centre in Germany. The first task for every trained worker is to train another. Everyone is on an hourly pay system and given extensive cross training workers can move from machine to machine. Set-up times are short and bottlenecks are not obvious. A skilled worker receives J$1100 per week, a new trainee J$250. Piece rates are ruled out by Mr. Lee as threatening to quality.

The Company is a candidate for the highest space productivity of any in the sector, if not in manufacturing. Mr. Lee's philosophy is not to expand but to increase efficiency. Efficiency is increased through incessant rationalization or improvement in methods. The Company began in the same space in 1982 and has doubled sales every year up to the present. Labels and Boxes is a candidate for tours by study groups in companies seeking to better understand how flexibility works in practice.

Sector Strategy and Workshops.

A sector strategy document for the packaging industry titled 'Flexible Specialization and the Jamaican Packaging Industry' was written by one of the authers. At a March 1, 1992, meeting attended by 30-40 people from the sector to discuss the report a range of problems facing the industry were addressed. The goal of the meeting was to arrive at an action plan consistent with pursuing the strategy of flexible specialization and the 14 Key programme for factory restructuring. Eventually a consensus was arrived at that the biggest, single, common barrier to increased flow and reduced waste was slow changeovers. It was also agreed that a starting point should be the plastics group within the packaging sector rather than seek to tackle companies working in entirely different materials (including paper, glass, and metal). Plastics was chosen mainly because it comprised the most firms and total employment.

In response to the consensus, JAMPRO and UNIDO organized a one day workshop conducted by Michael Chludzinski, an expert on quick changeovers which was conducted on 20 May, 1992. The enthusiastic response led to the organization of a one week intensive workshop, from 15-20 June, 1992, conducted by Alan Robinson and Michael Chludzinski. The workshop focused on housekeeping and quick changeovers. Twenty seven participants from eight companies and the Toolmakers Institute attended lectures for three hours each morning and then returned to three host plants to carry out assigned projects for six hours each day. The workshop emphasized improvements that did not cost money but which could save substantial amounts of money and learning by doing. The actual progress was measured by conducting a 5S good housekeeping audit before and after on each host company and by comparing changeover times before and after.

A report of those attending the workshop included the following advances in specific companies.

1. S&T Limited.

Fitroy Berry, plant manager, says that the Company is 'lighter and better' since implementing good housekeeping. Now a five minute cleanup period concludes each shift. When machines are cleaned a worker noticed a lose bolt; a valuable tool was found in a pile of waste; when a fault was found in a roll the roll was immediately sent back to the earlier department to find the cause rather than being stacked beside the machine where it could sit for weeks; the tools were organized; the machine layout has been altered and all of the material not being processed has been cleared away making much more space and improving working conditions; and a suggestion box system has been introduced. Mr. Berry said that the one week workshop gave him time to 'get settled in, go into field, get more experience, get involved' had time to set examples. Mr. Berry stated he went away full of ideas that he could implement.

2. Plastic Moulders.

Keith Bailey, maintenance manager, was sold on the idea of good housekeeping at the workshop. He was especially impressed with the video of Japanese plants in which people could work without shoes because the floor was so clean. He was in the process of writing a report to convince top management of importance of the implementing a 5S housekeeping programme. Mr. Bailey greatly enjoyed the opportunity to borrow two books available at the workshop: *Total Productive Maintenance* by Seiichi Nakajima and *The SMED System* by Shigeo Shingo. At present the Company sells at the bottom end of the market because of the difficulty in making high quality moulds (Plastic Moulders makes 90 per cent of their moulds). It hopes to move to shorter run, higher quality products in the future and needs to upgrade its maintenance, quality, and changeover capability to do so.

3. Plastic Containers.

Seven participants came back convinced of the need to reduce inventory. Since the workshop changeover times on one machine have been reduced permanently by 60 per cent and by lesser amounts on many machines. But the effort to concentrate on quick changeovers has changed the consciousness of the whole company; it has also pointed to problems. For example, the lack of spare parts has become obvious as has the lack of good maintenance. Changeover teams become frustrated when they have to replace parts and do maintenance while they are doing a changeover. But for the first time the company has careful labeling of all parts and tools and an understanding of the importance of good housekeeping. The company seeks to upgrade its documentation and standardization of procedures in the future as part of a TQM programme. They have found that data collection is crucial to impressing foreign purchasers. Plastic Containers sent seven people because they, including top management, had become sensitized to the issue by reading the UNIDO sector report and the follow up visit. Mr. Murray, the plant manager and the seven who attended were extremely pleased that seven and not three had attended because it greatly facilitated implementation. Since the workshop the seven had 'bonded' and were fully confident in the new ideas as they talked often with one another. They were thankful that a handout had been given to every participant. Their next task is to convince top management of how much improvements could be made with small investments. The 'guys at the bottom' also need a training programme in the near future.

4. Plas Pak.

The Company has been able to reduce orders for raw materials substantially (Crafton Miller sales manager estimates by 25 per cent) by decentralizing regrinding. Before, regrinds went to a separate regrind department and were then stored until another order was needed for the same colour (it could be months). Now the regrind is put back into the same order as it is being processed; the loop is closed at considerable reduction in inventory. Mr. Miller estimates that total inventory has dropped from two months to five weeks since the workshop; this represents three weeks cash throwoff or increase in cash flow. The reduction in inventory is immediately obvious upon entering the factory. Enormous increases in usuable space have been created. The Company is particularly interested in improving product costing systems.

5. Wisynco.

Five individuals attended from Wisynco. July was declared housekeeping month as a means of implementing much that had been learned. On one machine changeover time has been reduced from 2 1/2-3 hours to 45 minutes by standardizing the size of moulds, developing quick coupling, and adjusting the rails with pulley systems. This has introduced an expansion in throughput of 15,000 pieces since the machine produces 6000 per hour. The company now concludes that the old changeover cost them 21,000 lost pieces because long changeovers were taken for granted. Wisynco has reduced setup times on 15 of 39 machines. In addition, the Company has reduced the scheduling period from 2-3 weeks to 1 week. Finally, Wisynco has reduced work-in-process stock from 90 to 30 days. Raw material inventory has dropped from 93 to 62 days. The workshop was attended by maintenance people who also do the training and the company hopes to develop certificates for workers who successfully pass courses on the new methods.

Several lessons can be drawn from the success of this programme. First, the strategic sector study convinced top management of the importance of world class manufacturing methods and of the relevance of the 14 Key programme for self evaluation and self improvement. Second, the workshop was targeted at two clear goals: good housekeeping (Key 1) and reducing inventory by quick changeovers (Key 5). Third, the workshop combined ideas and learning by doing; the project teams went back to the host companies for assigned projects each day. Fourth, the teams knew that they would have to present results on the final day.

At a meeting with representatives of all of the plastics companies on 25 July1992, several points were agreed. First, the programme was based on significant impact with low cost input. Second, the programme should be extended to non-plastics companies in the packaging sector. Third, a need exists for learning how to do work process documentation to prevent backsliding (supervisors and engineers need to work together on this). Fourth, the idea of a visual factory was compelling. Fifth, the CEO's have to be targeted so that they back the programme. Sixth, while the middle level people in the firms understood the need for the new principles, the people at the bottom have to be targeted as well as the CEO's. Here there is a need to sell the 14 Key programme, particularly Key 6 on Small Group Activity and suggestion box systems. Seventh, a model for cost savings has to be developed. Eighth, a return visit by Robinson and Chludzinski was highly desireable. The Companies agreed to work on documenting cost savings and JAMPRO and UNIDO representatives agreed to work on making the return visit of Robinson and Chludzinski a success and to have it address some of the issues raised.

Metalworking

There is no accurate count of the number of metalworking firms in Jamaica. A detailed survey of firm capabilities and needs is being conducted now through JAMPRO and UNIDO. The sector is dominated by small firms – 25 workers or less – working almost exclusively on a contract basis with larger manufacturers in the sugar, bauxite, clothing, furniture and packaging sectors. A few have developed some proprietary products but these are produced in limited quantities. Many firms are using less than 25 per cent of their capacity weekly. The majority of equipment is old. This is compensated for by the fact that owners and lead workers are highly skilled and have developed ingenious methods to 'get the job done'.

The relative fortunes of this sector and the larger manufacturing sectors are inextricably linked. In developed countries these firms are the touchstone for new product engineering, machine tool modifications, critical repairs and mould making. There are several examples of how these relationships are firmly established in Jamaica.

Caribbean Casting: Mouldmaking Capacities Enhanced:

One key to setup reduction is the utilization of new moulds designed for quick changeovers. It is now possible to produce these moulds in Jamaica using the skills of Kingston-based Caribbean Casting (CC) to design and rough cast the mould and the related skills of a metal working firm to perform the secondary machining operations and assist in designing quick change setup techniques. Such collaborations are not so far fetched. With improvements in design and raw material capabilities at CC and the introduction of improved mould machining skills through a series of workshops for small metal working firms this is becoming a reality.

CC has acquired and brought on line a new furnace that will give it the flexibility to pour castings of sufficient quality and quantity to make moulds for the glass making, plastics packaging, and shoe making sectors. Since mould making is a first step in the development of new products, as well as the repair and production of machine tool spare parts, these plans are a major enhancement for manufacturing opportunities in the country.

The new capacity to pour castings for other industries, creates the opportunity for collaborations between CC, manufacturers who need moulds, and machine shops capable of doing the final machining work on them. For example, a plastics firm that needs a new mould made to produce a bottle for liquid will, under the current circumstances, acquire the mould from abroad at considerable expense. But with the new capacity at CC to pour the material required to make a mould, and the design capabilities being enhanced at Toolmakers Institute the mould may be designed quickly, rough cast, and then machined at nearby precision machine shops. This is an efficient way to get work done and draws on the strengths of firms in a complimentary, not competitive manner: *each firm develops its strengths as opposed to trying to perform every manufacturing function in-house.*

Mullings Tool and Die: Reducing Set-up Times In Practice.

Ryan's Muffler, a manufacturer of replacement mufflers and parts for automobiles, has a series of machines that press out a variety of parts needed to produce mufflers in a variety of sizes to fit several kinds of automobiles. The change over of machines to produce these various sizes was time consuming and resulted in scrap as each machine had to produce several pieces before the set-up was just right. Because the change over was costly, machines were not utilized well. Long runs of various sizes were made, whether there were orders for the mufflers or not. Raw materials were tied up in finished products that were not being sold. Customers looking for a certain size muffler may have been turned away or told to come back when the machines were changed over.

The owner of Mullings Tool and Die (MTD) was contacted and a fixture was designed and built that allowed an operator to change over the machine without removing a heavy fixture, replacing it with another, and getting good parts by making a series of bad ones. Instead, with the loosening of a few screws the entire fixture can be altered to accommodate several sizes of work and the pieces are produced accurately the first time. Each change-over can be done quickly, allowing the factory to make products virtually on-demand without any investment in new machines. The need for an expensive inventory of finished parts is reduced as well.

Industrial Tooling: Problem Solving At Your Service.

For flexible specialization to work, manufacturing firms are integrated into consultative, problem solving, long term relations with suppliers and service agencies in pursuit of continuous improvement in production capabilities. A small Kingston-based firm, Industrial Tooling (IT), is a representative example of such a problem-solving shop. It has experience working in the plastics, furniture and food industries. The shop builds and repairs moulds, machines gears, trouble shoots and repair machines at factory sites. The firm's owner describes himself as a problem solver. He is a Toolmakers Institute graduate and he currently volunteers time instructing metal-working students at the school. The shop's marketing flier states: *'We also design and implement systems that will eradicate bottlenecks in your production line.'* IT guarantees its work by doing follow-up customer visits. The firm has developed mini-production lines in the shop to produce large numbers of gears and other spare and replacement parts for a variety of firms and has built table saws for the furniture sector.

Caribbean Tooling: Developing In-House Skills.

Caribbean Tooling is part of the Thermo-Plastics Ltd. (TPL) group of companies located in the industrial district of Twickenham Park. TPL is organized as though it were several firms with distinct product lines producing a wide range of plastic products including buckets, baskets, bottles, and pipe and tubing. The firm has a tremendous inventory of machine tools for the manufacture of plastics products, in all likelihood the largest in the Caribbean. Several of these machines are state-of-the-art, purchased from top line machine tool builders in Germany and the United States. The tool shop was originally established to service TPL's machines and repair the hundreds of moulds and dies used in the daily operations of these various manufacturing facilities and is well equipped (it has computer controlled equipment), organized, and capable of performing a wide range of machining operations to extremely close tolerances. To fully utilize its machine shop capacity, the firm does contract machining work for several other Jamaican companies.

Bells Engineering Work: Contract Machining in Small Batches.

In Mandeville, in Central Jamaica, Bell's Engineering Works performs contract machining chiefly for the bauxite and pulp and paper industries. Bell's wants to develop worker skills in the facility so that it can offer its services as an all-around engineering company. In other words, it has begun a process to become identified in Jamaica as a problem-solving company, one that any other manufacturer can call in to help reorganize a production facility. They employ College of Arts, Science and Technology graduates and provide extensive in-shop training to technical high school graduates of machining programmes. The firm does a great deal of small batch production with runs of 20 - 30 considered a large job. Bell's has an established network of other machine shops to which they subcontract work. They indicated that they will use the best skills available to complete the projects they are contracted to do. The firm is well organized and has production meetings each day to monitor work in progress. The hours spent on each job are recorded by the machinists and reviewed at the completion of the job. This helps them analyze where bottlenecks are in the shop as well as determine the accuracy of the quotes they make on work they perform.

Precision and General Engineering: A Small Service Firm.

Precision and General Engineering in Kingston provides a number of precision machining services to local industry. The firm has taken apprentice metal-working students from several Kingston-area vocational high schools. The shop has an ongoing arrangement with several of the country's oil companies to repair and service their equipment. This combination of industry work and work for oil firms has provided Precision with a stable work base. The firm has recently built machine attachments and spare parts for the furniture industry.

Paharsingh Engineering Works: Product Development Works.

In Spanish Town, Pahsrsingh Engineering Works manufactures several large pieces of equipment for the sugar industry and has been exporting throughout the Caribbean for 28 years. The owner started the business by first making a utility wagon for his own small sugar plantation. When the sugar plantation saw the wagon it asked that several more be made that it would purchase. The business was launched from there. Products manufactured in Spanish Town include in-field transport systems for sugar cane, tractor mounted grab loaders, sugar cane planters and several types of field preparation equipment. The firm also distributes heavy motorized equipment for a major US manufacturer. The firm has engineering and design capacity and produces equipment appropriate for Jamaican agricultural conditions. A large well equipped training centre has been set up and courses are run for farm workers on the proper use and maintenance of the equipment. Agricultural students from local high schools attend seminars and workshops at the site. All equipment is designed after careful consultation with the customer so that whatever is manufactured meets the needs of the customer. Ongoing service is provided, in the farmer's field when necessary. Area machine shops are used to manufacture parts and pieces for the equipment.

Caribbean Steel: Why A maintenance Programme Makes Sense.

The benefits of a well planned maintenance programme are demonstrated at Caribbean Steel. The steel firm makes various sizes of re-enforced rods for the construction industry. It had its own furnace in place which was closed down a few years ago because of high energy costs. Its ingots are now imported from abroad. While the plant and equipment are old, it is highly efficient because of a well thought out production schedule that builds repair and maintenance into the normal work schedule. The first five hours every Monday are spent doing basic housekeeping in the factory. In addition there is a constant recycling of new parts onto machines as they wear out during the steel-making process. The firm's tool room is always working on the production of a variety of replacement parts which are ready to be installed on machines at a moments notice. Change overs from one size steel rod to another are quickly done because the dies needed are always ready. These efforts are aimed at driving down the cost of production according to the plant manager. Goals are set to increase energy efficiency, cut down on scrap, and reduce raw material wastage. The work-force is involved in establishing these goals and shares directly in the benefits of any improvements that are made through monthly and annual incentive programme payments. Workers can earn close to an additional 40 per cent annually when productivity goals are reached.

V. A New Industrial Policy Paradigm

Strategic Industrial Policy in Poor Countries

The first task of industrial policy making is not to pick winners in sectors or firms, it is to facilitate the transformation of firms from old to new principles of production and organization. In this, governments in low income countries, as well as high, can assist in developing interchangeability, flow, and multiproduct flow. These transitions are not simple. They cannot be done without developing the accompanying organizational principles. For example, piece part interchangeability, which rarely exists in Jamaican industry, demands product engineering and toolmaking capabilities.

All too often, industrial policy initiatives in less developed countries concentrate on marketing in America and Europe. Market theory suggests that low prices are sufficient to sell goods. But such marketing initiatives are based on an implicit assumption that is false, namely that the production principles of interchangeability and flow are established in their business enterprises. Without these principles, the products they are offering are samples, not products in the interchangeability sense. The well-intentioned efforts are successful, oftentimes, at getting orders; they run aground once the delivery dates or the quality standards are not met. At that point the structural problem is personalized and scapegoats are sought. The real problem remains obscured: namely, the lack of production capabilities. The successful trading companies of Japan, Korea and Taiwan did not suffer similar delusions. The organizational principle of system integration meant that marketing was interrelated with production.

A second task of industrial policy is to facilitate the entry of new firms and the product diversification capabilities of existing firms to maintain the entrepreneurial firm in general if not in particular. While this dimension of industrial policy is similar to the free market perspective, the infrastructural institutions that enable the flourishing of the entrepreneurial firm are not.

There are several implications here. First, investment in labour intensive products can be profitable. Second, any targeting of sectors for the development of export potential must be based on an in depth strategic analysis that accounts for the extent to which the new principles of production and organization have been or are likely to be developed by firms in the rest of the world but particularly the target market. Third, any inward flowing private investments must be assessed in terms of their contribution to the development of local production capabilities including the development of local machine and tooling capabilities. Once the latter are in place they can become central elements in an industrial district which feeds into other domestically based sectors. In this way, sustainability can be enhanced. Fourth, and crucial: industrial policy in low income countries should give priority to conquering the domestic market first. Here is where the practice of getting close to the customer can be learned. Equally important, firms can develop the production capabilities required to compete on the basis of short delivery times and customized products. Only after the fundamental principles of production and organization have been developed can firms be confident of beating foreign competitors in their home markets and have the capabilities to consider building markets abroad.

Choice of Sectors: Market vs. Production Perspectives

Industrial policy, like development theory, is not subject to different principles depending upon the degree of industrialization or the level of per capita income. In all cases the task is to develop entrepreneurial firms so that the inhabitants of a region can develop their production capabilities and enjoy an acceptable standard of living. The task in this section is to draw out some implications of the above analysis on production restructuring for strategic industrial policy in countries that are followers in industrializing. It is not to explain why particular regions have more or less obstacles to developing entrepreneurial firms as a consequence of historical and cultural legacies.

Ironically, conventional theory of comparative advantage and the production and organizational principles perspective developed here point to the same sectors for specialization in low income countries, but for entirely different reasons. The market perspective dictates that low wage countries specialize in labour intensive products because they offer a price advantage; the production principles perspective also targets labour intensive products but because they offer the most potential for developing and upgrading production capabilities of the greatest number of people in the shortest time. Labour intensive industries such as footwear, garments, furniture, and food processing produce democratic goods that are widely consumed: together, such labour intensive goods constitute a sizeable portion of the family consumption budget in low income countries.

Capital Accumulation: Two Perspectives

While both the market and the production perspectives hold that labour intensive industries be the first targets of industrial policy in low income countries, the market perspective does so because of a shortage of 'capital', while the production perspective does so because of the need to develop capital. But the meaning of capital is entirely different in the two perspectives in part because of the different conceptions of competition.

From the production perspective, competitiveness and sustainability depend upon competing on the basis of product, including quality and new product development capabilities. Product-led competition dictates that consumer making firms be networked with machine shops that can facilitate the repair, maintenance and tooling needs that are required for continuous improvement. Flexibility in production requires the custom design of jigs, fixtures, attachments, dies, moulds, and assorted tooling repair and maintenance. While a big firm can have a machining shop, often the task of the machining shop is to assist in the specification of a needed part which can only be accomplished by a precision metal working shop which, in turn, may depend upon other shops that specialize in heat treating, foundary work and casting.

Seeing production as a social process suggests a different interpretation of capital and capital accumulation from the conception in development literature of a physical entity and a 'factor of production' that can be purchased in the market. What is missing in low income countries is not capital in the sense of equipment; what is missing are problem solving, consultative networks that can make equipment useful, that can maintain, upgrade, modify, alter, repair, rejig, and retool it. These capabilities are indispensable for the New Competition: product competition demands production capabilities to enable, for example, quick change overs, synchronization, and quality designed into the process. Without these capabilities, much technology cannot be used effectively. Developing such capabilities can be done either internally by teamwork or externally in the form of networks. Such networks are social relations which, like teamwork relations in the firm, take time and cannot be done alone. The implications for what has to be done are substantial: the capital accumulation challenge is as much organizational as technical, physical, or financial.

Most, if not all, of the NICs built up strong, light, labour intensive industries including furniture, footwear, and clothing. But they also built up repair, maintenance and tooling as a leveraged sector that feeds into a whole range of light industry, consumer good sectors. Without a repair, maintenance and tooling sector, product-led competition and flexible specialization production capabilities are not possible. But with the build up of machine repairing and making capabilities a set of vibrant, problem-solving networks come into being making product-led competition possible. Only then can companies and regions move from being sub-contractors to products designed elsewhere to becoming market forces (the New Competition) with independent industrial design capabilities. Put simply, sustainability requires machine altering and making networks.

This is fundamental to explaining the success not only of the NIC's but the small firm industrial districts of Europe, many of which sustain high per capita incomes in 'mature', 'labour intensive' industries including furniture, clothing, and footwear. In all such cases, design is combined with firms built on the production principles of flow, system, integrating thinking and doing, and networking.

Towards a Sector Strategy Methodology

Seven stages in developing a sector strategy can be distinguished. This list is not meant to be exhaustive but to be suggestive of the methodological approach.

1. Conduct a strategic sector analysis. The first step is to visit a large number of firms in a sector and along the production chain with the purpose of analyzing the strengths and weaknesses and challenges and opportunities facing the enterprises. The strategic dimension involves a comparison of the regional group of firms with leading regions in other parts of the world. A sector analysis must be conducted by an individual with knowledge of sources of competitive advantage of the world's leading firms and regions.
2. Conduct wide ranging discussions amongst industry insiders on the results of the sector analysis. The purpose is to shape a common vision, develop a shared language, establish a plan of action, and identify common services.
3. Develop benchmark analyses for individual companies. The purpose here is to contrast the performance indicators of target companies with world class companies and to use the resulting gaps as targets for developing action plans. The 14 key programme is particularly effective as a needs assessment tool for three reasons. First, it provides clear

criteria within each key for progressing toward world class or best practice methods. Second, the evaluation exercise is simultaneously an educational exercise which makes important distinctions clear to everyone involved. Third, it provides a common language within and across firms which highlights what is otherwise not discerned or even seen.

4. Establish implementation plans. This involves the development of pilot projects in individual companies, establishing workshops for attacking common problems and skill upgrading, and sharing the results of implementing the pilot projects with all involved companies.

5. Redefine the mission and upgrade the skills of individuals in the industrial policy bodies. A global, team, proactive approach to offering services to firms which share the common vision is superior to a fire-fighting, reactive approach.

6. Diffuse the practical restructuring ideas widely in the sector. Videos, workshops, reports, contests, and exhibits which illustrate principles with local examples can facilitate the diffusion of effective production practices.

7. Develop performance indicators to track the progress of individual firms. The performance indicators should be production based such as work-in-process turns, measures of waste, set-up times, defect rates, and skill upgrading programmes. These are all indicators of the transition to the fundamental principles of production, namely interchangability, flow, and flexibility.

Progression through each of these steps simultaneously creates a common language within the industrial community and reinforces the social fabric of community that distinguishes an innovative industrial district from atomistic, disconnected competitors. The existence of community provides the social context within which regionally specific interfirm institutions develop and evolve. Examples of such institutions include marketing or retailing consortia, industrial parks, technology transfer guidelines, vocational educational programmes, fashion institutes, quality standards enforcement procedures, and consultantcy agencies. The organizational form of interfirm institutions may be private, public, or quasi-public. Their purpose is to manage and nurture collective services so that the famed free-rider effect does not erode the requisite cooperation of world class productive organizations.

VI. Conclusion

Adam Smith got it wrong: the sole purpose of production is not consumption; rather it is both consumption and learning. Without learning, the production capabilities of a nation can be quickly eroded. The examples of interfirm collaboration discussed here, from the furniture firms in Kingston to the small metalworking firm on Marcus Garvey Drive designing and producing time-saving machine attachments, are instructive in considering a proper role for the public sector in promoting the 'learning environment' required for flexible specialization to flourish. Rather than earmark scarce resources for efforts in specific firms, a better role for an economic development agency is twofold. First, it must provide a vehicle for creating a sector strategy and thereby a vision from which firm level action plans can be conceived, tested and implemented. Without a sector strategy every firm is left to develop action plans against world class competitors about which it knows little. Second, it must assist in the targeting resources towards:

— the development of comprehensive technical assistance, training, marketing, and financial loan programmes that will help two or three key industrial sectors move forward.

— the development of comprehensive, coordinated manager and worker training programmes.

— the proper funding of training institutes so that they can purchase badly needed equipment to effectively train.

— help for firms in learning about cutting edge technology developments.

— the establishment of a comprehensive national research and development programme.

In successful industrial districts cooperation among firms on issues of strategic orientation, education and training strengthens the entire economy over time. Specific industry centres can be established to meet the training needs of key manufacturing sectors. The various levels of training institutions can then figure out what equipment is needed, where it is appropriately housed, and where training on particular subjects should take place. This is an efficient way of leveraging resources, as opposed to each institution working in a strategic vacuum.

Seminars can be offered on developing problem-solving teams in firms and improving quality. Endeavours like this require little technical material. Without such courses, all the technical equipment in the world will not increase firm productivity and efficiency. Sebastiano Brusco writing about the formation of industrial districts in Italy states that this kind of cooperation, particularly in skills development and research led to 'advance by means of tiny successive steps, with strong links between sectors, which in the end manages to achieve success in terms of production process and product.' Brusco goes on to state that a system of small firms cooperating in this way survives better during economic crises than larger firms.

Flexible specialization needs to be understood as *a work in progress.* It is not a plateau that a firm, industry sector or nation 'gets to' and then possesses on a permanent basis. It is dependent upon a strong base of support from training institutions and government agencies capable of helping it get the highly skilled workers it needs, the research support it requires, and access to loans and other financial support necessary to acquire new equipment and the inputs. It is the workers, managers, owners, technical experts and support institutions of the country attempting to make this transformation, who are best able to manage this process. It results from heightened social relationships between very different but interdependent institutions, firms and people.

To compare, the IMF vision is one in which industrial enterprises will spontaneously emerge by the invisible forces described by comparative advantage theory once prices and markets are freed from government interference. Here, industrial policy is about promoting the ideal of perfect markets for only then can prices do the job of illiciting internationally competitive business enterprises. The dependency school suggests that public ownership of the means of production is a prerequisite for economic development in the periphery. Here, industrial policy is about administering price controls and dictating to firms what to produce. The ideal is the perfectly administered plan created by an omniscient, centralized industrial accounting department. What is clear is that neither vision has been successful in Jamaica. This paper poses a third, production-led vision, that grows directly out of an understanding of, and in close consultation with, the firms the policy is being designed to help.

Notes and References

1. We have focused on three sectors; clothing, food processing, and finance are also being developed in the JAMPRO/UNIDO project. The 14 key methodology

for enterprise self-evaluation are available at the Productivity centre at JAMPRO We wish to thank Christian Gillen, who initiated the project from UNIDO's side and Valeria Viera, Director of the Productivity Centre. We would also like to thank the hundreds of people working in Jamaican industrial enterprises who treated us with a warm hospitality that is unique to Jamaica.

2. Both market and stage driven economic development visions, we would suggest, are informed by the same plan or market dichotomy that informs conventional economic theory. The free market version, which guides the IMF, defines the barriers to economic growth in terms of market restraints introduced by the government; the state planning version perceives the barriers to growth in terms of the anarchy of the market and the power of monopoly capital. The first seeks growth via freeing of markets; the second by replacing markets with planning and capitalists with central planners. Each vision is the mirror image of the other; both deny conceptual space to the organization of production. Lacking a theory of production, both have pursued policies that have been antithetical to the development of a national industrial base capable of supplying the domestic needs of the populace.

3. The section is a condensed version of arguments that are made more fully in *The New Competition: Institutions of Industrial Restructuring*, Harvard University Press, 1990.

4. See Alfred Chandler, *The Visible Hand: The Managerial Revolution in American Business*, Harvard University Press, 1977.

5. PIOJ, Five Year Plan, 1990

6. This example was worked out in consultation with three Jamaican furniture companies and Joel Suris,a wood processing product engineer. Saris contributed substantially to the furniture industry company analyses, workshop and to transformation projects for several companies.

7. The relationship among throughput, operating expenses, and inventory is elaborated in Goldratt and Fox, The Goal, North River Press, 1984.

8. Dieter Haas, a leader German furniture consultant for many years makes the point as follows: 'For the majority of business firms, terms such as all-automation or CIM/CAM/CAI etc. will remain marketing slogans of the manufacturers of electronic appliances and computers. However, in the furniture industry there will not be the complete automatic solution in the foreseeable future. The variety in design and constructive possibilities, as well as dynamics of change, set limits' (n.d.).

9. For more examples of real services see Brusco 'The Emiliar Model' *Cambridge Journal of Economics;* a summary can also be found in Best, *The New Competition,C47. Vol. 6, 1982.*

10. For a brief report of Pareto Analysis and Production Flow Analysis see Appendix E of m. Best Final Report, May 20, 1992. For a more extended anaysis see the workshop materials in Part Six of the May 20, Final Report and the principles of flexible specialization reports on the packaging industry (Part Two of the May 20, Final Report or Part One of the July 1, Final Report). All are on file at the Production Centre, JAMPRO.

11. Arnoldo K. Ventura, Outline of an Agro-Food Science and Technology Plan for Jamaica; a report commissioned by the Ministry of Development, Planning and Production, September 1990, p. 36.

12. Ventura, p.12

13. The plate making department first, converts the original artwork into a negative composed from the four basic colours; second, burns the negative onto a series of screens; and third, produces the plates to be attached to the press. At present, the company is developing its CAD capability to speed the process and facilitate the storing of negatives for remaking worn out plates. One of the owner's sons has been studying at Rochester Institute of Technology's printing department– one of the world's best.

14. For a more detailed review of the sector see Forrant, UNDP reports, September 1991, February, 1991.

15. Brusco,'A Policy for Industrial Districts,' 1989.

CHAPTER 4

The Korean Economic Development Experience: Its Relevance to Jamaica

Sung Sang Park

Korean Experience

Poverty Before Economic Development Plan

The Republic of Korea was founded in 1948 after World War II. It was a typical Asian agricultural economy with no natural resources and a dense population, most of which was engaged in farming. After the three-year-long Korean War from 1950 to 1953, which destroyed the country's limited production facilities and commercial buildings as well as dwelling houses, reconstruction of the Korean economy had to begin from scratch.

In 1961 the gross national product was $2.1 billion compared with today's $210 billion and the per capita GNP was $82 compared with $5,000 today. I will give you a good anecdote of poverty-stricken Korea in the fifties and early sixties. Before harvesting spring barley, many farmers went up to the mountains to peel off the skin of pine trees in order to feed their starving families. Total exports amounted to no more than $41 million in 1961 compared with $72 billion today, an increase of more than 1,700 times.

I still vividly remember the USAID report about Korea, published in 1959 by the US State Department. It said, 'Koreans are the laziest people in the world. They never appear on time when they have conference meetings'. Koreans as well as Americans refer to this one hour delay of meetings as 'Korean Time'. It disappeared when our economy started growing very rapidly. Koreans have become punctual. They realized that punctuality was one of the most important elements in doing business in the international market place.

Successful economic development provided us with more jobs and made our people work harder. Business became busier and busier as Korean industrialization progressed. As you see, Koreans cannot afford to be lazy today. Do you know what the US State Department's description of the Korean people is today ? It says, 'Koreans are the hardest workers in the world' in contrast to 'the laziest' 30 years ago.

Industrial Policy of Five Year Plan

Now you can understand the poverty prevailing among the Korean people at the beginning of the first Five-Year Plan in 1961. One month after the military revolution of 16 May 1961, the chairman of the Supreme Military Council of the Revolutionary Government wrote a letter to the governor of the Bank of Korea saying that the Bank should formulate a Five-Year economic development plan within one week. I was ordered to draft the Five-Year Plan because I was in charge of the national Accounting Division which estimated GNP growth. While I was working on the plan, I thought that a macro-economic development plan itself might do nothing for real economic development. There are many countries in the world whose economies are not so successful even though they have set up macro-plans several times. There are many development plans in developing countries which describe only the nature of forecasting in the future, without containing the micro project lists indicating the potential investment seeking to attract domestic and foreign businessmen. If the government's announcement of an economic development plan alone guaranteed economic success, then no country in the world would remain as poor as before.

I would like to tell you why the Korean economy has been so successful in accordance with the Five-Year Plans. It is very simple. I presented a list of micro projects with a macro model development plan.

I was fortunate to receive the order to draft the First Five-Year Economic Development Plan as the head of the team. When I stayed in Washington, D.C. for one year as a USAID participant, I pondered on the question of why Americans were rich compared with Koreans who were so poor. By observing the individual life of Americans, I thought that they were making the necessary consumer durable and nondurable goods by themselves while Koreans were incapable of producing radios, phonographs, telephones, television sets, refrigerators, cars and so forth, which made them richer than us. If Korea could afford to produce these goods, the Korean people could become as rich as Americans. But when we discussed this problem with American economists, they always insisted that Korea should not produce these goods because if Korea produced these goods, their prices would be very expensive. They therefore insisted that Korea should import these consumer durables from the US in order to supply cheap consumer goods to the Korean consumer. I said to them that I understood their theory, but that we had no money to import cheaply produced goods from the US. We had no products which could be exported to the US.

When I visited New York from Washington, D.C. in 1959, skyscrapers made a very strong impression on me and I felt that they were the art of iron, steel and cement. I therefore made a list of the factories and plants that could produce basic raw materials for the production of durable and nondurable consumer goods. I thought that Koreans could be as rich as Americans when we were able to produce those goods as listed in the First Five-Year Plan.

While preparing the first Five-Year Plan, I looked at the opposite side of the street in the evening. The shops across the street were waiting for customers with candle lights. There was a blackout every night from 7 o'clock until midnight for every household because of the shortage of electricity. Total electricity supply was only 190,000 kilo watts per hour for the whole nation, the same quantity of electricity power consumed by Pohang Steel Mill alone today. In order to increase the supply of electricity, I listed power plant projects. Without an abundant supply of electric power no manufacturer can dare to start producing new products.

In order to make an abundant supply of cement for the construction of houses, commercial buildings, bridges and roads, I presented cement plant projects. Fertilizer plants are necessary to increase the productivity of crops per hectare of land. The shortage of fertilizer supply resulted in a situation in which Korean rice products were, per hectare of land, less than two-third of the products in Japan. Korean consumption of chemical fertilizer per hectare of land was 210 kg compared with 384 kg in Japan in 1967. The fertilizer consumption per hectare of land in India and Uganda was 11 kg and 1 kg respectively, in 1967. Petrochemical products are essential to produce all kinds of goods and commodities ranging from textiles, shoes, dishes, electronic home appliances, cars, etc. Without petrochemical products, no country can produce any modern commodities. Iron and steel products are also essential intermediate raw materials which can be used, not only as raw materials to produce all kinds of consumer goods and machinery, but also as frames for all kinds of construction.

These five basic intermediate raw materials, namely, electricity, power, cement, fertiliser, petrochemicals, and iron and steel must be supplied abundantly so that industrial production and construction activities can be increased by utilizing them. Besides these five basic intermediate raw material production plans, telephone receiver assembly factory, transistor radios, television sets, refrigerators, bicycles, and car assembly plants were also included in the production programme of the first Five-Year Plan.

The energetic promotion of these plants and factory construction projects was encouraged by the late president Park Chung Hee. He actively participated in tape-cutting and ground-breaking ceremonies and, also, when these plants and factories were completed, Korean entrepreneurs successfully implemented these production projects. Today's economic prosperity in Korea could not have been achieved without the strenuous effort of both the Korean government and private businessmen.

In my view, government should initiate the basic industrial and financial plans, and the actual construction and management of factories and plants should be carried out by the private sector. The Korean government initiated the basic industrial and financial plans, and private businessmen accomplished the actual construction and management of factories and plants. In this sense the role of the Korean government has been quite significant in carrying out the Five-Year Plan.

These intermediate raw material production factories were built with government assistance. Cement, fertilizer, and petrochemical plants were built and managed by private firms helped by the Korean government, because Koreans did not have big firms to build such huge plants by private capital in the 1960s and early seventies. Electricity plants and iron and steel mills were constructed and managed by government-appointed presidents but the employees, except for the presidents, were not government officials. Telephone receivers, transistor radios, TV sets, VCRs, refrigerators, washing machines, bicycles, all kinds of automobiles and trains were produced by private business, assisted by government industrial and financial policies. This process was not interpreted as 'intervention' but 'assistance' for the private entrepreneurs.

The output growth with these new plants and factories became the engine of economic development. The rapid GNP growth began from this stage. Plants and factories were built consecutively year after year and the output growth continued and never stopped growing.

Cement production, before the launching of the Five-Year Plan, was only 470,000 tons compared with 35,000,000 tons per annum today. In view of the Korean economic development experience, the abundant supply of cement creates its own demand for cement. Say's Law, which was discarded by Keynes, is absolutely correct not only for the Korean economy but also for developing economies, in that without an abundant supply of cement or any other basic intermediate materials, no one can dare to plan to construct or produce anything. The same is true for electric power and steel mill productions in Korea. The 190,000 kwh capacity of electricity power plants has grown to 20,000,000 kwh today: a 100 times increase within 30 years. Again the abundant supply of iron and steel made possible the growth of new industries which use iron and steel; that is, ship building, machinery, the defence industry, and so forth. If we had not had Pohang Steel mill at that time, the Korean economy could not have afforded to launch the above-mentioned heavy industries and to attain the level of economic development evident today.

While promoting basic intermediate material production projects, the Korean government launched petrochemical plant construction projects under the Second Five-Year Plan. The petrochemical products had been imported in order to produce textiles and plastic products. Locally produced petrochemicals became an export industry later.

The process of industrialization of the Korean economy took the path of an import substitution process. The importation of cement was substituted by the construction of cement plants which then later produced for export. Fertilier was import substituted and exported. Steel imports were substituted by the construction of Pohang Steel Mill, and steel is now a big export item today. Television sets, VCRs, passenger cars, and radios were all import substituted by the construction of factories for these products and were exported when their quality and price gained international competitiveness.

I know why industrial policies are not favored by economists of developed countries. They might be right in the case of industrialized countries because it is difficult to identify new goods for production since such countries already produce every good and service. They therefore emphasize the demand-oriented government policy as Keynes rightly suggested.

In contrast to industrialized countries, the problem of growth in developing countries is supply-oriented in nature. Demand is huge but supply is short. Supply holds the key to economic development. Developing countries can identify what commodities or what raw maerials should be produced. Because of this difference, the industrial policy of developing countries is easily formulated and justified as was the case in the Asian Newly Industrializing Countries (NICs) compared with the difficulty of formulating industrial policy in industrialized countries.

Desirable Nature of Industrial Policy

In my view, the difference in success or lack of success in economic development comes from whether or not the government has been pursuing industrialization by industrial policy which contains a specific list of production items and the means to furnish the local and hard currency required for the projects. Industrial policy should be precise so that local businessmen and investors from abroad can know which commodities are produced for the domestic market as well as for export.

In view of population size big businesses, such as car production, ship building and heavy machine production industries, are not appropriate in Singapore and Hong Kong. Jamaica might be in the same position because of population size.

Singapore's industrial policy has not been much different from that of Korea's and Taiwan's. It will be observed that Korea's, Taiwan's, Hong Kong's, and Singapore's export items in the international market are more or less the same. Their products are competing in the same foreign markets. Textiles, toys, etc., were low quality and extremely cheap in export prices because of cheap domestic wage costs in the 1969 and the seventies.

For the Jamaican economy, you can identify the import substitutable items easily by looking at the lists of import items. The items for import substitution selected by the government can form the basis for industrial policy. The items for import substitution produced by private business with or without joint ventures will become exportable goods if Jamaica used 'high-tech' imported machinery to produce those items. There are many countries in the world which failed to achieve economic development even though they adopted an import substitution strategy. The reason for this lack of success derives mainly from the failure to produce exportable goods without using high quality 'high-tech' machinery imported from the best producers in the world.

Singapore's success comes mainly from foreign direct investment which makes internationally competitive goods of high quality. It is also derived from the strategic concentration on manufacturing rather than on service industries. The service industries were left to foreign investors who were given incentives to earn money by being allowed to do business without restriction, as was done in Hong Kong. But manufacturing business was helped by the government's financial policies, especially credit policy which encouraged business investors.

Development Strategy: Hong Kong, Singapore

To my knowledge, the basic industrial policy of Singapore, Hong Kong, Taiwan, and Korea was more or less the same in fostering manufacturing businesses, especially export manufacturing. Moreover, the financial support of their governments to manufacturing was the same.

Hong Kong

In Hong Kong there is no actual development strategy to be assessed. There are many economists in the world who recommend the Hong Kong-type development strategy which is based on completely free trade in exports and imports, free capital inflow and outflow, and no monetary authority to print excess money for political necessity. The conspicuous stability and rapid economic development of the Hong Kong economy were brought about by the favourable business environment created by the British traditions of the Hong Kong government. In my view, the Hong Kong government has been maintaining the profitability of export business by using national macroeconomic policies without change in order to attract the continued inflow of foreign capital.

Firstly, in order to maintain price stability, Hong Kong dollars are strictly tied to the foreign exchange reserve in the Hong Kong Shanghai Bank which issues bank notes in the form of the Hong Kong dollar. There is no room to create excess money supply of more than 15 per cent on average per year. By avoiding inflation, the Hong Kong economy has earned the confidence of and has established a good reputation with foreign as well as local businessmen.

Secondly, the foreign exchange rate of Hong Kong dollars is very well controlled in order to maintain exporters' profitability. This policy also stimulates the confidence of the local businessmen and potential foreign investors.

Thirdly, the interest rate is always kept at the international level. The reason is quite simple: interest rate is kept freely floating without government intervention. This policy worked very well in keeping interest low because the commercial bank's lending rate is determined by the borrowed source. For instance, bank credit is available in the form of Japanese Yen at a 4.5 per cent rate of interest during the period when the US dollar rate is more than 10 per cent. Businessmen in Hong Kong can borrow investment funds from low interest rate currency rather than the Hong Kong dollar. Because of this, commercial bank loans in terms of Hong Kong dollars are not in a monopoly position that would enable them to charge high interest rates to the customers. The low interest rate made profitability sustainable for exporters and local suppliers of commodities and services.

Fourthly, the profitability of manufacturing business stems from the cheap labour supply from mainland China in the form of refugees. The Hong Kong population has grown from 2 million to 5.5 million.

Fifthly, among other favourable conditions in Hong Kong, the government is very efficient in creating infrastructure that is convenient for visitors and businessmen. There is no shortage of basic raw materials such as electricity power and water supply which cannot be imported from abroad. Housing and roads are well designed and constructed without interruption. But, the government policy of maintaining the profitability of the export business might be the key element in the success of the Hong Kong economy. Without profitability, no business in the world contributes to economic development by producing, exporting, and investing because entrepreneurs are profit-oriented by nature.

In this context, if Jamaica wants to copy the Hong Kong model, the profitability of exporters and of producers should be kept as the principal emphasis in formulating macro and micro policy measures.

In the Hong Kong model, government macro policies are regarded as non-interventionist. This is only a superficial observation. The profitability of foreign investors might not be created or maintained without careful adjustment in the macro policies of the Hong Kong government. If the profitability of the exporters in Hong Kong disappears for some reason, disaster cannot be avoided. This simple but important factor of development has often been ignored.

Singapore's Development Strategy

I would like to describe the economic development strategy and policies of Singapore which might be a better reference for Jamaica's economy. Jamaica's population size, climate, and island country environment are quite similar to Singapore's.

The book, *Singapore 1990*, published by the Singapore Government states that economic development has always been a key priority in its strategy. As a small country with no natural resources and little industrial experiences, how could enough jobs be created to meet the basic needs of the people?

The policy option we chose was one that has served us well over 'The 25th Year of Industrialization'. The decision was to insert the nation into the global economic system in two ways:

1. By the promotion of foreign investment in Singapore. Such investment would bring jobs, technology, markets and industrial management expertise;

2. By adopting a free trade policy that would enable free import and export of goods and services. This would ensure that the production of goods and services in Singapore would be internationally competitive. The policy of partnership with multinational companies has provided us with opportunities for economic upgrading.

The government's description in the book is not unique and uncommon. There are many countries in the world which have tried very hard to copy the Hong Kong and Singapore model of economic development, that is, attracting and inducing foreign investment but, unfortunately, they have been unsuccessful.

Korea also tried very hard to attract foreign direct investment, but was unsuccessful because of the northern threat. Taiwan faced the same difficulty. Instead, Korea borrowed heavily the required capital from abroad, that is, from the export-import banks of the developed countries, the World Bank, and the commercial banks of advanced countries. But Singapore did not borrow the required capital from abroad: instead, it invited foreign direct investment by creating a profitable and attractive domestic investment environment.

We should ask the question, again: why have some countries been successful while others are not despite their policies to attract foreign capital, as in the case of Hong Kong and Singapore.

My assessment of this issue is as follows: First, economic stability can only be pursued practically by price stability. Price stability can be achieved by an adequate supply of money. Without economic stability attained by price stability, social stability and political stability cannot be assured. Inflation widens the gap between the incomes of the rich and the poor. The failure seems to be the result of inflation.

Second, once inflation is created by maladjustment in the money supply, the foreign exchange rate adjustment will be delayed for years because of the fear of a cost push. This makes balance of payments deficits caused by imports profitable and exports unprofitable.

Third, once inflation is installed many governments, advised by economists, raise interest rates up to the level of 5 per cent to 50 per cent per month rather than per year in the hope of curtailing inflation. This high interest rate policy produces an adverse effect by fueling galloping inflation because of the cost push effect of the high interest burden on the producers. Investors from abroad might be threatened by the high cost of borrowing local currency for production operations.

For these reasons, foreign investors as well as domestic producers and exporters lose confidence in the policies of many governments. Hong Kong- and Singapore-type strategies then become ineffective. In this connection, inflation is the number one public enemy of economic development.

Singapore's industrialization strategy was to copy the Hong Kong practice but to preserve sovereignty as an independent nation. Unlike Hong Kong, Singapore established a monetary authority to help finance industrialization in accordance with the government's policy direction.

The above-mentioned macro-economic policies are managed by the monetary authority in Singapore.

Role of Government

As I have explained so far, government's role in the process of development in the Asian NICs is a predominant force in bringing about successful growth rates and export growth because an individual businessman, or businessmen as a group, have no power to control national macro and micro policy to create a favourable and attractive investment environment, as we saw in the case of the economic development strategies of Korea, Singapore, Hong Kong, and Taiwan.

Denis Benn rightly expressed his views on the issue of the role of government in his article 'Beyond Adjustment: Toward a New Development Paradigm'. He said that a primary responsibility of government is to provide the broad policy framework to guide economic activity. He pointed out that, in fact, a recent World Bank analysis has suggested that Korea's prosperity is not attributable merely to a private sector-led development effort, but also to the strategic role of the government in stimulating and supporting private sector development.

I would like to explain the importance of government macro and micro economic policies listed below in creating a favorable business investment and production environment or in damaging business activities.

Government macro policies are: *(a)* Money supply policy: curtailing inflationary pressure in order to stabilize prices and restricting-imports by restricting over-consumption beyond national means; *(b)* Foreign exchange rate policy: encouraging exports and discouraging imports. Export-led growth can be expected by sustaining profitability of export business and; *(c)* Interest rate policy: encouraging business investment activity or discouraging business investment. Reduction in the cost of products or increase in the cost of products by increasing capital cost, that is, interest rate.

Government micro policies are: *(a)*Industrial policy; *(b)*Trade policy and; *(c)* Credit policy for effective use of national loanable funds, that is, bank loans.

I would like to explain government's macro and micro policies in detail.

Money Supply Policy

Money supply policy should be strictly pursued in accordance with the Irving Fisher quantity theory: that is, $M.V. = P.T.$ This means that money supply should be limited, for instance, to 10 per cent of GNP growth (T) and 5 per cent increase in consumer prices (P), and 2 per cent of velocity change (V) (when manufacturing growth of more than 10 per cent) equal to approximately 17 per cent at the maximum. (If GNP growth rate is only 5 per cent, then, money supply should be limited to 10 per cent or less). This 17 per cent is still high compared with Singapore and other industrialized countries. In order to avoid inflationary pressures and balance of payments deficits in developing countries, including Jamaica, the money supply must be kept within a limit of less than 17 per cent per annum. This means that national loanable funds from the commercial banks to all kinds of businesses in a country should be limited by 17 per cent at most. If the interest rate is more than 17 per cent, the increased borrowing of 17 per cent will be all paid back into the bank in order to pay interest income to the rich depositors. There will be no incentive for manufacturing ventures. At this high interest rate of 17 per cent, the increased loanable fund of 17 per cent will be ineffectively used, that is, not for productive investment, but simply for interest payments to the previous debt. If the interest rate is approximately 5 per cent, which is competitive with industrialized countries, the products from domestic manufacturing business could become exportable goods. Foreign investors will rush into that country.

The demand for bank loans in some Latin American countries when the interest rate is 50 per cent per annum, is much higher then when it is 17 per cent per annum; and the loan demand from the business at the period of 17 per cent interest rate is much higher than at the period of 5 per cent because of the need to pay high interest rates by borrowing more and facing difficulty in using these high interest bearing loans for productive investment. For this reason, high interest rate policy at the time of inflation resulted in snowball effects of money supply expansion. We never before experienced galloping inflation of 3,000 per cent per annum in human history.

The budgetary deficit will cause one of the fueling effects of inflation because the revenues are collected from past income, but expenditure must be at the current price of 3,000 per cent increase. Jamaica's sale tax of 10 per cent is courageous and is an appropriate measure to reduce government's budget deficit. Inflation is the main cause of budget deficit because of this.

When we observe the performance of Singapore's economic development from 1976 to 1990 the money supply, M2, increased 14.6 per cent per annum for 15 years and the cash currency increased by 10.3 per cent. The consumer prices increased 3.1 per cent per annum and the economic growth rate was 10.2 per cent on average per year. The foreign exchange rate was kept stable, that is, 2.34 Singapore dollars against one US dollar in 1977 and 1.9 Singapore dollars to one US dollar in 1990. This means that Singapore prices are more stable than those of the US.

The 14.6 per cent increase in money supply, M2, means that national loanable funds from commercial banks are limited by 14.6 per cent if there is no government deficit to reduce the national loanable fund. The 14.6 per cent increase in the credit to business made a remarkable economic growth rate of 10.2 per cent per annum without fail. Why do we need to expand money supply up to 100 per cent? In this sense, the credit policy of the Singapore government and monetary authority was so efficient that the limited and precious national loanable funds were fully utilized for economic development.

Basic Economic Indicators				
period	Money supply		Consumer	GNP
(15 year average)	M2	Currency	Price increase	Growth rate
1978 / 1990	14.6%	10.3%	3.1%	10.2%

Exports Growth Rates (Unit: Million Singapore Dollars)						
Year	1984	1985	1986	1987	1988	1989
Export Growth Rate	51,340.0	50,178.8	48,985.5	60,265.7	79,051.3	87,116.5
		-0.2%	-2.4%	23.0%	31.2%	10.2%

In terms of the US dollar, the value of its exports in 1989 was $44,675 million dollars.

Foreign Exchange Rate Policy

As has been explained, an appropriate exchange rate policy is essential to sustain the profitability of export business. There are many developing countries which would not adjust their foreign exchange rate properly at the time of inflation. A 10 per cent revaluation in the rate means that exporters are losing sales of 10 per cent in terms of local currency revenue while exporting the same amount of goods at the same export price. The profit will be reduced to zero or less because of the 10 per cent revenue decline. Thus international competitiveness will be lost because of the revaluation of the foreign exchange rate. The same effect of 10 per cent revaluation explained above is exactly applicable to the inflation of 10 per cent in comparison with hard currency countries.

We have been emphasizing that the export growth of developing countries is an essential factor for economic development. Export growth is attainable only when export business is profitable. The profitability of export business can be assured only by prompt adjustment of the foreign exchange rate. There are many developing countries which do not observe this simple rule in respect of their foreign exchange rate policy.

Interest Rate Policy

High interest rate policy (here I mean the nominal rate but not real interest rate) prohibits economic development. The investment in the manufacturing business requires long-term finance for the construction and gestation periods of productive operations. Without an internationally competitive interest rate for loans, foreign as well as domestic businessmen could not dream of new manufacturing ventures. When the interest rate is 30 per cent per annum, the cost of constructing a factory and supplying equipment will double before the completion of factory and plant.

The high interest rate policy (nominal) will not only make the price of the products higher for the newly produced goods by foreign investors, but will also make the prices of currently produced goods and services higher, because the high nominal interest rate is one of the production costs of goods and services. The average cost of the product comprises 60 per cent of raw material inputs, 20 per cent of wage and 20 per cent of capital cost (the interest of borrowed money plus necessary profit). I therefore want to advise that the interest rate should be reduced to the level in industrialized countries in order to avoid cost-push inflation.

Demand-pull inflation is also created by the government's high interest rate policy because manufacturers need to borrow heavily just to pay high interest, not only against the burden of previous debt, but also against the ever increasing debt. Because of this, foreign investors are afraid of the high interest rates of that country. The cost of the products should be lower in order to compete in the international market. This is done by keeping the cost (interest rate) of capital, wages, and raw material inputs lower. Without the low cost (interest rate) of local currency borrowing, there will be no hope of attracting investors in manufacturing from abroad.

Creating Entrepreneurs by Maintaining Profitability: Importance of Business Savings

We must recall the classical model of economic growth summarized by Benjamin Higgins' book on economic development. Output (O) is

the function (F) of Labour (L), Capital (K), Land (Q) and Technology
(T). This model holds that:

(1) the growth of labour employment (▲L) depends on the rate of
    capital accumulation (▲K);
(2) technology progress (▲T) depends on capital accumulation
    (▲K);
(3) and the rate of capital accumulation (▲K) depends on the level
    and trend of profits (R).

In view of the classical model of economic growth, output growth
and employment growth are entirely dependent on profitability. This
is absolutely true when we observe economic performance in the four
'tiger' countries, namely, Korea, Taiwan, Singapore, and Hong Kong.
The business tycoons in these countries are the typical creation of
capitalism. Without the profitability of manufacturing business, business tycoons in the four 'tiger' countries could not have been created
within a period of 20 to 30 years. In some sense, the government
development policies in these countries created the multinational
business tycoons in order to compete in international markets with
their products. This is also a very important lesson for Jamaica's
economic development strategy.

We should also realize that there are two types of national savings
which could be invested for the growth of output and employment.
The most important national savings at the per capita income level of
less than $1,000 are 'Business Savings' which are created only from
business profits. At the low level of individual wage and salary income,
household savings are not large enough to provide the resources for
national productive investment, because the population is living at the
subsistence level. For them, there will be no room for household
savings.

Economists of developed countries often overlook this fact and
recommend a high interest rate policy in order to increase household
savings as the resources for investment. Unfortunately, this high interest rate causes the cost push effect on the manufacturing business
profits. Thus production and export businesses are discouraged. A
high interest rate will produce the opposite effect by causing galloping
inflation and reducing national business savings in low per capita
income countries.

Micro Policy for Effective Utilization of National Loanable Fund

Credit Policy to Secure Continuous Economic Development: Germany, Japan and Korea

In my view, industrial policy does not work when financial policy does not support it. At the same time financial policy alone cannot promote an optimum level of economic development, especially for developing countries.

We must ask the question why some countries are developed and others are not, despite the fact that the financing through bank credit increases 15-200 per cent per annum without exception in every developing country.

The financial cooperation between banking institutions and industrial enterprises has been the main cause of the success of the German economy. German industrial enterprises are controlled by major German banks who do so by holding stock shares of major enterprises. As the owner of the plants and factories in terms of holding companies, banking institutions provided financial support for the investment projects of the industrial enterprises. Financial help for investment projects was essential for the prosperity of the production business. The prosperity of the production business was to be the main factor in the growth of the German economy. Japanese economic development was also assessed the same way as in the case of the German economy. The financial support for the production business by the banking institutions was essential for the success of economic development of Japan's war torn economy. But the difference between Japan and Germany was that the Japanese government pushed industrial projects under the guidance of MITI and Japanese banking institutions had strongly supported MITI's industrial policy by giving financial support, while the German government did not push explicitly to help finance the government projects in support of the private sector. In fact, unlike Japan, West Germany did not have an industrial policy.

Korean economic development, as I described earlier, has been successful because the government financial policies were designed to finance government industrial projects. In this regard, the difference between success and failure depends mainly on whether the national loanable funds are used effectively by the credit policy of the government or the Central Bank.

Basic Principle for National Credit Policy

The available money for a household or business must be used most efficiently and profitably and not wasted. The same is true for the nationally available loanable fund for a nation. This must be used for economic development purposes in order to create jobs for unemployed people and to increase production, and ultimately to increase national income.

We should not increase bank loans infinitely in order to avoid inflationary pressure. National loanable funds are limited like water in a reservoir for irrigation. The reserved water should be channelled into the most productive rice paddies to maximize the year's harvest. If the water is allowed to flow into weedy or unproductive areas, it is natural that we should not expect a bountiful rice harvest.

Let me introduce an example of the inefficient use of financial resources in relation to economic development efforts — the land-reclamation project headed by the former First Lady of an Asian country. She wanted to extend the coastline of the bay near the capital city and create new high-valued real estate by borrowing money from commercial banks. This new coastal land, with a spectacular seaside view, was sold at a high price so the project had no problems with respect to return on interest and principal. To the commercial banks, the loan was allocated to the most profitable project, following the market principle. It quickly became evident, however, that this project contributed almost nothing to that country's economic development. This land-reclamation project involved mainly the transfer of earth from mountain to sea. Precious national financial resources were therefore wasted.

Efficient Credit Policy of Government and Central Bank

When we want the credit policy to support economic development, we should allocate our limited loanable funds to the industries which could best promote the nation's economic development. The next task is to determine which industry is to play the locomotive role in economic development.

In my view, national industries are mutually related to one another. This interindustrial linkage explains why the manufacturing is the locomotive industry which contributes to the growth of the related service sector. When manufacturing output increases by 20 per cent, the transportation requirement, the demand for communication and insurance, warehouses and advertisement will all increase by 20 per cent in order to take care of increased commodity transactions. Wholesale business will prosper by dealing with 20 per cent more commodities, and the retail business in terms of the nationwide spread of shops and stores will also be busy by dealing with 20 per cent more commodities which are the output of the manufacturing industry. This is the real process of economic growth and development.

This linkage effects of manufacturing output to the related service sectors explain why the manufacturing industry is the locomotive to pull the rest of the service sectors at the same speed. National service businesses could be viewed as freight cars connected to the locomotive by chains just like a train because the locomotive industry of manufacturing pulls every related service business at the same speed. If the manufacturing sector does not increase its output, the linked service industries such as transportation, communications, insurance, warehouses, advertisement, banking, wholesale and retail businesses have no way to increase their businesses at all. The speed of the whole train is determined by the strength of the locomotive. For this reason, I can say that the speed of the national economic growth is highly dependent upon the output growth of manufacturing industry.

Because of my intuitive observation of the interindustrial relationship, I have found the theory of employment multiplier which says that an increase in the employment of manufacturing industry by 1,000 persons would increase the employment of other linked service businesses by 3,200 persons. The 3.2 times increase in employment in relation to manufacturing can be explained by the analogy of the locomotive and freight cars.

It is clear that the limited national loanable funds of the commercial banks should be directed toward manufacturing output growth in order to obtain maximum GNP growth, because the output growth of the manufacturing industries all stimulate income and employment growth of all other linked service businesses. From an economic development point of view, manufacturing is the heart of industry that makes other related businesses prosper.

In terms of world trade, 70 per cent of this trade is composed of manufactured goods. In order to earn foreign exchange through exports, exportable goods should be produced in the manufacturing sector.

Financing for the growth of manufacturing output is not only assessed as the industrial policy but also regarded as the financial credit policy for the growth of the national economy as a whole. In this respect, banking services are just like the fuel tank connected to a locomotive. The locomotive cannot run without an adequate supply of fuel, that is, 'money'.

Credit Policy for Balance of Payment Surplus

During my tenure of office as the Governor of the Bank of Korea, the Korean economy, which was the fourth largest external debtor country in the world, achieved a significant turning point from 1986 onward by producing a balance of payment surplus.

The realization of a balance of payment surplus for the first time in Korea from 1986 onward, was accomplished by embarking on the localization of components and parts which had previously been imported mainly from Japan in order to assemble commodities for exports. By reducing the import requirements through this import substitution programme of components for assembling TV sets, VCRs, cars, etc., the trade deficit with Japan has been declining. The Korean economy has been relying heavily on Japanese components and parts for assembly lines. They can afford to reduce the imports of the parts and components while exports are growing. The balance of payment goes into the black when the import substitution by the localization programme begins to materialize through the credit policy of the Central Bank.

Credit policy has also been adopted to discourage consumer loans in order to discourage the growth of consumption by household. The decline in consumer credit will produce a suppressing effect on national consumption. Thus, imports for domestic consumption have shown relative decline which seems to contribute a trade surplus for the balance of payments. Credit policy for the import substitution of the components and parts for assembly line products on the one hand and financial policy for discouraging household consumption by restricting consumer loans on the other hand, were effective in creating a turning point from a deficit to a surplus on external trade. As a result, national consumption grew only 7 per cent per annum while GNP grew 12 per cent per annum for two years from 1987 to 1988.

This is a very simple credit policy that can be copied by some heavily indebted countries of the world. There are many countries in the world in which a large proportion of the bank loans is directed toward consumer credit which encourages consumption, by households, beyond their means. Thus national consumption has been increasing beyond national means, which results in the trade deficit and accumulating external debt beyond their control.

The national credit policy by the government or the Central Bank is very important in view of its effects. When banks are expanding credit to the enterprise to support speculative land purchase as was done in the Philippines by the first lady, land prices will increase. And recently in Japan, bank loans, which were extended to purchase land, were also blamed for the speculative land price increase.

Because the demands for land are created by speculative bank loans for now, if you increase housing loans for the sake of poor people, the credit facilities are mainly used for purchasing larger apartments than they possess especially when inflationary prices are increasing in real estate. There are numerous examples of misuse of the valuable and scarce national loanable funds increased by the rediscount facilities of the Central Bank.

Strategy for Technology Transfer

The transfer of technology from developed to developing countries is a very important issue. In spite of its importance, the solution to this problem has remained vague to the leaders of the developing world. They are actually neglecting to understand how to transfer technology from developed to developing countries.

There are three different stages of technology transfer for the industrialization process of developing economies.

The technology transfer for the first stage of industrialization, that is, from the primitive stage, is very simple. In order to produce import substituting commodities, the developing countries should import the machinery which can produce such commodities. The imported machinery already embodies the advanced technology which was developed by technically advanced countries. This means that the task of technology transfer could be accomplished by simply purchasing advanced technology attached to productive machinery. Factories and plants can be built only by importing them from technologically advanced industrialized countries. The imported factories and plants will produce the specific products which are required not only for domestic use but also for exports.

Even if we do not have technology to produce machinery and to construct factories and plants, we can produce the required commodities by operating the imported factories and plants, because the machinery exporters are always ready to teach the technology of the machinery and the plant operation for the sake of more exports for the future. This is the most important strategy of technology transfer from highly industrialized countries to developing countries.

It is unfortunate that the leaders of the less developed economies of the developing world do not understand this simple, practical and important strategy of technology transfer for their economic development. The failure of socialist production systems was caused not only by state owned operational shortcomings but was also due to the failure to import advanced technology attached to machinery. Because of this shortcoming the precious foreign exchange, earned from the exports of naturally endowed resources, is wasted. If leaders of the developing world practiced this simple strategy of technology transfer, the poverty of the developing world could have been relieved in the same way as was done in the Asian NICs.

They should realise that most of their daily necessities which are imported from advanced countries can be produced locally by importing machinery which manufactures such products. They have no reason to be criticised in terms of free trade principles because developing countries are importing the same amount of machinery instead of consumer goods within their available foreign exchange reserve. Developing economies do not have enough foreign exchange to import both consumer goods and machinery.

The second stage of the technology transfer for further industrialization might be a little more difficult because it requires more sophisticated technology than the first stage in order to widen and deepen the industrialization process. The technology transfer at this stage, the second stage, must be based not only on importing high-tech attached to advanced machinery but also on importing technology in the form of Licensing and Royalty payments. The hiring and importing of foreign technicians are also one of the methods of achieving the required technology transfer. Joint ventures with 'high-tech' production companies from the developed countries provide one of the solution to this problem.

We should emphasise that the technology transfer for the process of further industrialization at the second stage, might be overcome through the strenuous efforts of businessmen and government.

The third stage of technology transfer could be described as the phase in which the newly industrializing countries are struggling to achieve the stage of production technology up to the level of advanced countries. The third stage might face the most difficult task of high technology transfer. Newly industrializing countries like Korea, Taiwan, Hong Kong and Singapore, have pursued the technology transfer of the first stage and second stage successfully and smoothly by adopting the above mentioned relatively easier measures.

Despite shortcomings in technology, industrial development of the NICs reached the stage where they were able to make high quality goods which are competing against the products of advanced countries. They now face severe competition with the highly advanced industrialized countries in the production of exportable goods for domestic use.

Conclusion

The above-mentioned analysis deals with a number of central issues relevant to the role of industrial and financial policies in the economic development of Korea and also in other NICs, such as Singapore and Hong Kong. It is hoped that the analysis will prove useful in identifying some options available to Jamaica in accelerating the pace of development as it prepares to enter the twenty-first century.

PART II

The Jamaican Production Environment

CHAPTER 5

The Industrial Relations Culture:
Perspectives and Change

Trevor Munroe

I mean by the industrial relations culture the complex of beliefs, values, attitudes and behaviour associated with the labour process, and inter- actions at the workplace. I also mean to refer to these dimensions of consciousness and of action primarily of those involved directly at work-sites but also, secondarily, but no less important, the attitudes and behaviour towards the workers of citizens in other capacities: in the capacity of judge or policeman, journalist or planner, arbitrator or conciliator or indeed the attitudes of the so-called man in the street.

If we understand industrial relations culture in this way then three observations immediately suggest themselves. Industrial relations cul- ture is, by definition, one of the most vital elements affecting any serious effort at raising the quantity and quality of national production and of improving levels of productivity. Second, it is an area about which many talk, even pontificate, about which perhaps nobody is without opinion but very few ground their analysis in scientific re- search or serious study. Third, the industrial relations dimension is one of the more vital zones in that fundamental precondition of appropri- ate preparation for the twenty-first century, namely the management of cultural change.

In this context, the basic argument of my presentation is this: Jamaica's industrial relations culture is in a state of transition from an old, colonial, plantation mould to a more enlightened, humanist culture. This transition is by no means smooth or certain in the short and medium term as elements of the old and the new coexist and contend; as national and global factors serve to reinforce one or the other; as there exists both real dangers of relapse as well as definite potential for positive transformation. At this moment, in this conjuncture, more than is normally the case in societal affairs, conscious will, consistent action, and determined intervention by human agency can make the decisive difference between whether we return to the negatives of the past or facilitate the transition to a more positive future. As I speak I have a strong sense that the situation is very much in the balance. We are talking about a fifty-fifty chance of going forwards or of going backways, with all the implications of one or another course for national development.

What then are the main elements of what I have called the old colonial industrial relations culture? To my mind there are four.

The first is its exploitative character. The factors involved in production, the human beings and the natural environment, are regarded as elements from which as much is to be squeezed for as long as possible for as little in return, with almost no regard for sustenance, nurture, or replenishment of the social or natural environment. It is as if there is a belief that the factors of production exist in unlimited, inexhaustible abundance and the elements in the labour process, those who direct it, as well as, though to a lesser extent, those who are directed exist for the sole reason of one trying to 'get round the other.'

The second is its authoritarian nature. Here, those who labour are seen as 'hewers of wood and drawers of water', with neither the training, intelligence, nor the interest to contribute anything but 'hard work' to the productive process. The experience and expertise of the workman is disregarded. Decisions are made, directives given and orders implemented without prior consultation or communication. Authoritarianism is disguised by the misnomer 'discipline' and rationalized by a range of racist, classist, and sexist prejudices against blacks, lower level employees, and women. These subordinate elements in turn repay the compliment by treating workplace authority as the boss to be resisted or as 'bucki-massa' to be cultivated. Such attitudes are rooted in dictatorial relations of long-standing whereby the top is vested with sole authority to hire and fire, to dismiss and suspend, to expand or to lock down.

Authoritarianism leads to our third characteristic: that those involved in the productive process regard one another as opponents, as antagonists who are expected to struggle with one another, sometimes openly, more often covertly, but all the time in a never-ending tug-of-war to determine who is to get the upper hand.

The fourth is voluntarism. This means that the old industrial relations culture leaves the different elements at the workplace to work things out on their own with little or no interference from the law or from state regulation. Naturally, this voluntarism within the broader framework of colonial property law and legislation which provided for the maintenance of an unequal law and an order prejudiced in favour of its maintenance and in favour of the advantaged, meant that it favoured the powers that be: capital more than labour, management more than worker, the strong over the weak. In the voluntarist culture the nonrecognition of labour unions was, until recently, not only quite legal but even today the employer who manages to 'keep out the union' is, by virtue of this, highly regarded, indeed, looked up to with admiration by his or her colleagues.

When we take these four main features of the old colonial, plantation industrial relations culture together it is apparent that it is both unproductive and dehumanizing.It also underlays negative perception of the workplace amongst employees.

Table 1: Whether employers give workers a fair deal			
Question: Do you believe that workers in Jamaica get a fair deal from employers? If not, why not?			
Answers:	Yes	No	Not sure
unionized workers	5%	95%	0%
non-unionized workers	7%	92%	1%

Main Reasons for NO answers
Low wages.......................................62%
No respect for workers................... 11%
No justice for workers............ ....7%
Job insecurity....................................6%
Workers have no say in decisions.......5%
Denial of union rights........................5%
Sexual harassment.............................3%

Table 2: Rating of employer in treatment of workers

Question: At the place where you work, how would you rate your employer in the following areas of treatment of workers

Areas of treatment	Answers	Good	Notbad	Poor
Respect for workers	Unionized	15%	51%	34%
	non-unionized	33%	36%	31%
Respect for workers rights	Unionised	21%	40%	39%
	non-unionized	31%	29%	40%
Appreciating workers contributions	Unionized	31%	28%	32%
	non-unionized	40%	28%	32%
Paying workers what they deserved	Unionized	7%	26%	67%
	non-unionized	16%	19%	65%
Co-operating with unions	Unionized	29%	38%	33%

Source: Dept. of Goverment / Carl Stone Survey - *Jamaica Workers Views*, etc. Nov. 1987

Table 3: Non- Involvement in the Decision Making Process

Question:Based on your observations, how are decisions usually made in your organization? (See Key to choices)

Key to Choices:
1. System 1 - Exploitative, Authoritative (Management decides unilaterally without prior information to workers
2. System 2 - Benevolent, Authoritative (Management decides, but workers are informed before decision is put into effect)
3. System 3 - Consultative (Consultations take place, but management goes ahead if no agreement is reached)
4. System 4 - Participatory (Decision-making done throughout the organization, although well integrated, through linking processes provided by overlapping group)

Systems	General	Utilities	Tourism	Banking / finanace
Exploitative, Authoritative	48.8%	5.2%	46.1%	59.3%
Benevolent, Authoritative	21.7%	18.8%	22.7%	23.0%
Consultative	18.6%	67.6%	24.3%	11.3
Participatory	10.7%	8.1%	6.6%	5.7%

Source:Kenneth L. Carter
The Structure Of Worker Dissatisfaction In Jamaica — p. 67 (unpublished manuscript circa 1989)

Table 4: Opportunities To Communicate Feelings, Etc.		
Question: How well do you feel about the opportunities for you to communicate your feelings, suggestions, grievances, etc. to management?	Supervisors	Workers
Very satisfied	2.0	1.0
Satisfied	2.3	2.3
Dissatisfied	89.2	92.9
Don't Know	2.0	2.8
Not stated	4.5	1.0
An overwhelming section of the workforce (92%), both supervisors and workers, feel that the organization's structure and practices do not make it possible for them to communicate their grievances, feelings or suggestions to management. This forcefully explains our findings that workers and management do not get along very well because they are perfect strangers. The findings below superfluously lends additional support to this substantially structured conclusion.		
Source: Carter *op. cit* p.85		

Table: 5 Consultation re changes in your job		
Question: When changes which affect your job are made, how often are you consulted?	Supervisors	Workers
Very often	12,2%	1.3%
Often	21.8%	17.8%
Seldom	42.0%	23.5%
Very seldom	23.6% 66.8%	29.7% 70.9%
Never	1.2%	27.7%
Source: Kenneth L. Carter *op. cit* p.85		

Table 6: Attitude Responses

Question:If you had the power to change just one thing about your job, what one thing would you change?

	General Profile	Tourism	Utilities	Nurses
Improve Personnel and Industrial Relations Dept.	17.8%	9.4%	17.1%	1.6%
More Pay	14.0%	38.7%	18.2%	9.9%
More recognition and appreciation	38.4%	20.8%	49.6%	52.9%
Acceptance as equal human beings	13.4%	16.8%	0.0%	5.1%
Better physical accommodation	16.2%	14.2%	5.0%	25.4%

Source: Kenneth L. Carter *op. cit* p.124

In general, during the colonial and for much of the postcolonial period, this industrial relations culture held sway without significant or successful challenge from alternative values and attitudes. The overall reason for this state of affairs was that, by and large, this culture did allow room for the fulfilment of some vital interests of the contending parties. Moreover, the environment, both national and global, was either congruent, facilitative or, at any rate, did not render it disastrous from the point of view of the 'national interest'.

We might mention one or two of the more important environmental factors. In the first place the world economy was experiencing, in the two and a half decades following World War II, unprecedented rates of growth, what some have with reason called the 'Golden Age' of capitalist development, as such societies and economies like Jamaica's linked to relatively powerful engines of growth, experienced relatively significant expansion, fuelled by comparatively favourable trade relations and investment inflows.Colonial and postcolonial production was primarily in this context for domestic and international markets that were protected and, therefore, low productivity was shielded against the consequences of uncompetitive costs, poor quality, etc.

A second factor was that the colonial and postcolonial states, in keeping with the orthodoxies of the time, intervened in the market place to provide subsidies and incentives, to regulate prices, guarantee quotas, etc. Moreover, until the early seventies we were living in an age of cheap energy and, relatively speaking, fairly balanced external accounts.

In this context, where the national cake was growing and rates of inflation were comparatively low, exploitative, adversarial relations, alongside competitive party politics, could further develop its own institutions, achieve increased profits and real incomes for the main combatants, facilitate social services and social mobility for the disadvantaged and contribute to the attainment of political independence as well as postindependence clientelism.

Management and labour made their name on the basis of the ability to fight each other to a standstill. Unions rivalled each other in relation to wage and fringe-benefit bargaining at the workplace and in the delivery of working class votes to associated parties in national elections. During the 1970s however, many of the conditions which rendered this industrial relations culture unchallenged began to change. In the first place cheap energy disappeared. The global economy reflected much reduced rates of expansion and, in relation to the Caribbean, more adverse terms of trade, reduced capital inflows and higher rates of imported inflation. At the same time, secondly, and perhaps not unrelated to the more adverse situation, enlightened values more hostile to authoritarianism, supportive of greater democracy, enhanced social justice and practical concern for the environment began to gather momentum on a global basis.By the end of the seventies 'statism' in economic policy which, in its western social democratic or eastern communist variants had enjoyed hegemony, was now challenged and by the mid eighties, displaced, not least of all by the conditionalities attached to IMF programmes and World Bank Structural Adjustment Loans.

Less and less could producers for either the domestic or the export market rely on protection from foreign competition and other forms of state subsidy. The risk of rising local production costs and uncompetitive markets now added a significant constraint to the viability of the adversarial industrial relations culture. With the removal or reduction of protection each of the contending parties as well as the nation as a whole developed a renewed interest in lowering production costs.

Wage guidelines, introduced between 1977 and 1991, and sharply reduced social expenditures, constituted a formal constraint on both the economic and social wage of the employed labour force and resulted in a significant transfer of resources from labour to capital. A new blow was struck at the efficacy of the old industrial relations culture. Wage and fringe-benefit bargaining would henceforth have to be more professional and creative as well as complemented by attention to national economic policy parameters.

As the same time, infusions into the labour force of young workers and managers formed and socialized in postcolonial circumstances introduced segments of the labour market with higher skill, greater information levels, more self-esteem and self-confidence, with less tolerance of authorian relations which, characterized not just work-place but internal union relations as well.

This leads us to examine what I have earlier described as the coexistence and contention between the old and the new in the prevailing 'mixed' industrial relations culture. To sketch the contours of the 'new' requires some extrapolation from relatively recent incipi-ent tendencies, from as yet underdeveloped attitudes and imperatives only now being fully recognized. From these, however, it is necessary and possible to identify and to encourage the main elements of a new culture as follows: the first is more equity in the labour process. There is clearly a new intolerance amongst more enlightened managers, employees, arbitrators, planners, and other elements within the indus-trial relations culture of widening gaps between the top and the bottom.

The second is a new concern for participation, for employee involvement in meaningful consultation and decision making at the workplace. Amongst all sections of the industrial relations culture, there appears to be a new and growing appreciation that high motiva-tion of the work force is a vital precondition for productive labour. More important, and perhaps as fundamental to this motivation as pay are relative intangibles such as 'respect', 'recognition', 'appreciation', most of all what workers call 'treatment as a decent human being' (Table 6 and 8). To facilitate this, human resource development practitioners in the new mould and managers and supervisors at all levels are increasingly appreciative of what employees have for long been saying — substantial improvement in meaningful communica-tion is the single most important element to attain in the new culture. Directives from the boardroom, edicts from on high, orders from air-conditioned offices without prior consultation are perhaps the most damaging relics of the old culture which, in this regard, is regrettably still too alive and well.

The third is a partnership, team-work, problem-solving approaches to the labour process and to raising levels of productivity. Adversarial-ism, in all its manifestations, is still very much evident amongst man-agers, workers and, of course, trade unions and employer associations. One does, nevertheless, detect the elements of a new approach. Cer-tainly, contrary to popular perception, there has within recent years been a very definite impulse amongst workers to use the strike weapon less and as a last resort.

The fourth is a new quality of professionalism in the approach to industrial relations matters. There is now less reliance on generalist, amateurish, and instinctive impulses and an increasing appreciation of the need for relevant expertise to prevent, conciliate, and settle disputes.

Table 7: Work Stoppages In Jamaica

YEARS	TOTAL	ANNUAL AVERAGE
1960 - 1963	250	63
1964 - 1967	257	64
1968 - 1971	316	79
1972 - 1975	568	142
1976 - 1979	702	176
1980 - 1983	450*	112
1984 - 1987	216	54
1988 - 1991	252	63
* Incomplete		Source: Economic & Social Surveys, Jamaica

Table 8: Industrial Disputes Reported By Cause

Year	All Causes	Wages/conds of emp.	dismissals / suspensions	Bargaining rights	Misc
1987	370	65	138	66	101
1988	372	51	155	82	88
1989	308	74	112	81	41
1990	275	71	81	66	57
1991	269	54	79	68	68
Total	1594	315	565	363	355

Source: Economic & Social Survey, Jamaica 1991, Planning Institute of Jamaica

It is necessary to emphasize the following: colonial-type exploitation, authoritarianism, adversarialism as well as unconstructive voluntarism and legalism remain strong in our industrial relations culture, perhaps in most instances even stronger than new attitudes to equity, employee involvement, partnership, and relevant professionalism. The significant factor, however, at least in my perspective on change, is that for the first time the old is being seriously challenged by the new and, in terms of the environment, there are now important ingredients militating against elements of the old and facilitating the birth of this more humanist, democratic, productive industrial relations culture.

In conclusion I will mention some of these factors. Economic liberalization and market-driven economies on a global basis require not only, as was previously thought in economies like Jamaica, cheap labour but as much highly motivated, productive, and skilled labour. This can hardly be attained in the old colonial industrial relations culture.

There is now increasingly apparent a very definite limit to the extent to which labour market segmentation can be allowed to fuel the levels of poverty, immiseration, and inequality permitted by the old industrial relations culture. When these limits are passed no class, colour, nor creed can insulate themselves from the accompanying social decay. Neither productive activity nor peaceful, satisfying lives are possible in the face of abuse of the social and natural environment reflected in, for example, rising crime and violence, the spread of the drug culture, the probability of epidemics, and the deterioration in the educational, housing, and health status of the working population.

The growth of the informal sector as well as of free trade zones, for the foreseeable future — a concomitant of export oriented industrialization — is going to render an increasing proportion of the labour force nonunionized and perhaps, nonunionizable with traditional methods.

Equally, constraints on the level of high wage employment, in say, state enterprises, and on the level of real wage increases will encourage if not compel labour unions to break with the traditional culture and adopt a more positive attitude on questions like worker ownership. Otherwise increasing marginalization is the unavoidable consequence.

My perspective, therefore, on change in the industrial relations culture is one of realism and cautious optimism. It is founded on the fact that the old shall always seek to hold on but, invariably, enlightened self-interest will come to demonstrate the necessity of the new. In facilitating this birth and growth clear vision, consistent effort, and

mature management of cultural change are indispensable midwives of
the historical process

CHAPTER 6

The Jamaican Party System and Political Culture

Carl Stone

Introduction

Jamaica has had a relatively stable two party system since independence in 1962. The country benefitted from an important prior period of preparation for parliamentary democracy between the first adult suffrage election in 1944 and full autonomy in 1962.

As the country approaches the twenty-first century, it is important to assess the weaknesses and strengths of Jamaica's party democracy and to suggest where the party system, the governing institutions and the political culture need to be changed to accelerate the country's political development.

My analysis begins by looking at how the party system has changed and developed over the 48 years between 1944 and 1992. This analysis of qualitative changes over this early period sets the stage for a discussion of the contemporary party system and political culture.

The Final section examines an agenda for political change and reform to strengthen the parties and party system to improve their capability to take on the public management tasks of the twenty-first century.

Changes in Party System (1944-1992)

Major changes have occurred in Jamaica's party system over the 1944 to 1992 period. Many of these changes have gone unrecognized in contemporary discussions or have been forgotten.

Participation

To begin with, participation rates for voting have impressively increased from 50 per cent of the adult population in 1944 to 80 per cent of the adult population by 1980 as shown below. This has been due to the effective mobilization of voters over the years by JLP and PNP party machinery.

Table One: Voting as % of Adult Population	
Parliamentary Elections	% of Adult Population Voting
1944	50
1949	60
1955	61
1959	62
962	72
1967	56*
1972	57*
1976	72
1980	80
1989	72
*Voter registration declined due to changes in the registration system in these two elections.	

From the early period Jamaica's political parties have always drawn stronger organizational and voter support from the lower income urban and rural citizens than from the middle class, the professionals and the business class. This is like India and in contrast to democracies like the USA and Canada where the party system attracts stronger support from the middle class. The poorest, lowest income and most marginalized in Jamaica provide the hard core emotional support for the political parties and the party system. As a result, third parties, new parties and new leadership have not been able to penetrate these marginalized communities or to turn their loyalties away from the JLP and the PNP. This factor is a major source of party stability in Jamaica and it has not diminished or changed over the 48-year period since 1944, but it is also a source of intense and violent party tribalism.

Information Levels

Information levels within the Jamaican mass public have grown very substantially since 1944. The average Jamaican citizen is much more aware of world affairs and of national politics and policy and has a much better grasp of public management issues, politics and matters relating to the economy and its management in the 1980s and 1990s than in the 1940s and 1950s. Indeed, Jamaicans are more politicised and politically aware than citizens in most industrialized democracies. A major contributing factor to this high public awareness has been increased exposure to public affairs by the mass media, especially radio and television. Seventy five per cent listen to radio and in urban areas 65 per cent have access to television. Another contributor is that high levels of politicization have induced considerable citizen interest in global, regional and local public affairs and political developments.

Campaign Issues

In the early period, party campaigning centred mainly around open-air mass meetings where platform speeches concentrated primarily on personality issues, personal gossip and personal abuse, directed at candidates and party leaders, with little focus on policy issues. All of this is now changed. The content of current party political campaigns centres on policy issues and how well or badly parties have performed policy making. Personal gossip and personal attacks are no longer major areas of emphasis in election campaigning. The trend is growing similar to the industrialized democracies where political communication is channeled mainly through the electronics media. Election campaigns in Jamaica now concentrate more on media advertising than on open-air mass meetings. Huge sums are spent on media advertising (newspaper, radio and T.V.) combined with motorcades, marches, roads signs and graffiti and high profile playing of popular reggae music.

Minor Parties and Independent Candidates

The two major political parties had to compete with many smaller parties and independent candidates in the early years as the following voting statistics confirm. In 1944 independent candidates and minor parties earned 36 per cent of the vote compared to 41 per cent for the JLP and 23 per cent for the PNP. In 1949 the independent candidates and minor parties experienced a dramatic decline in voter support. In 1955 the two major parties the PNP and JLP had consolidated their voter support into a virtual monopoly of the vote. Since that early period, 99 per cent of the votes goes to the JLP and the PNP.

Table Two: Vote shares for parties (%)				
	1944	1949	1962	1989
JLP	41	43	50	43
PNP	23	43	49	56
Other parties and Candidates	36	14	1	1
TOTAL	100	100	100	100

In the earlier elections voters had more choices. In 1944 there were 130 candidates competing for 32 parliamentary seats or four candidates per constituency. In 1989, 124 candidates competed for 60 parliamentary seats or about two candidates per constituency.

From the early years party candidacy in Jamaica has been dominated by the middle class. This has not changed. The two main class interests from which candidates are recruited are professionals (teachers, lawyers, doctors etc. and small and medium scale business–farmers, shopkeepers, contractors, owners of retail outlets, merchants, etc.). Middle sector dominance of party candidacy remains unchallenged.

Table Three: Main Occupation of Party Candidates (%)		
	1944	1989
Professionals	33	40
Small & MediumLevel Business (farm & non-farm)	54	43
White Collar Employment	6	7
Working Class	2	0
Full Time Politicians	5	10

Contrary to popular belief, full time politicians make up only a small percentage of party candidates, although their numbers have been growing between 1944 and 1989. Over the years the ranks of the professionals have grown and now match the large number of party candidates from the small and medium scale business class. Working class representation has disappeared after a very small beginning. A small number of candidates have always been drawn from the ranks of white collar employment.

Political Violence

Party violence has always existed in early Jamaican party politics. In the early years political violence was confined to stone throwing, disturbing party meetings, stick and stone clashes between groups of activists going to meetings and the occasional political mob killing. All of this changed in 1967 when armed political gangs entered the picture in the inner city area of the capital as guns replaced the sticks and stones.

Political gun violence subsided in 1972 but returned on a massive scale in 1976. It escalated and achieved the highest point of turmoil, killings and property destruction in 1980 when it is estimated that 20,000 persons abandoned homes that were burnt down and some 500 Jamaicans were killed in political warfare between JLP and PNP gangs, mainly in the capital Kingston, St. Andrew and Spanish Town.

In 1980 the police were almost helpless in being able to contain this high level of violence in which the political gangs were armed with high power assault rifles, semiautomatic pistols and submachine guns. The army had to be brought in to assist the police.

Between 1980 and 1989, political violence was reduced but residues of the problem remain in constituencies where local politicians still have connection to political gangs. Many citizens fear a reescalation of high levels of political violence in the next elections.

Centralization

In the early period, both parties were relatively decentralized with local political personalities being able to make decisions in their local areas and national party leaders being forced to respect their autonomy. What existed then was 'stratarchic' rather than a rigidly hierarchic structure of centralized control as local leaders enjoyed great autonomy.

As the party leaders took over the management of public policy and came into control of huge public sector expenditures, as government expenditure grew from 13 per cent of GDP in 1950 to 40 per cent by 1980, a patronage or clientelistic system developed whereby party leaders catered to the needs of hard core party supporters through state patronage (jobs, contracts, benefits, favours, houses, etc.).

The effect was to consolidate party centralism in both JLP and PNP by Independence, giving the top party leaders and top officials purse string controls to force local leaders into compliance. Activists increasingly looked to the political centre in Kingston for benefits. Respect for local leadership diminished rapidly.

This trend towards political centralization and power concentration in both parties increased as the trade unions, which were an integral part of the early party machinery and a source of internal party democracy ensuring grass roots influence on the parties, distanced themselves from the parties. This was due to unionized workers wishing to see politically independent trade unions unhinged from party politics. This working class perspective emerged in the 1950s and was consolidated by the 1960s, weakening the union-party link.

Organizational autonomy between affiliated trade unions and the two parties evolved between the 1950s and 1960s. Unions became more specialized in collective bargaining withdrawing from vote seeking and party politicking by the 1960s and 1970s. The parties, in turn, developed strong and centralized political machinery that took over their earlier voter mobilization functions.

Centralized power in both parties increased as a consequence and this process was consolidated by Independence in 1962. The two parties gradually evolved into powerful centralized oligarchies with power concentrated in the hands of top party leaders. As these oligarchic tendencies consolidated party democracy diminished.

This tendency was even further reinforced by the leader-centred character of the parties and their domination by high profile popular leaders (Bustamante, Michael Manley, etc.) whose personalized authority held sway over the party machinery. This discouraged independent thinking in the parties, dissent, leadership challenges, serious policy debates and democratic mechanism for decision making in these two dominant political parties. This style of leadership has been a plus for mobilizing political loyalties but at the expense of encouraging and motivating internal party democracy.

Thuggery, violence and what I have defined as 'garrison politics' have crept into internal party power struggles in both parties. This was very evident in the PNP in the 1970s. It is now rampant in the JLP in the 1990s. For example, in St. Catherine North West, the use of thugs and goons to determine the JLP selection of a candidate denied the selection to the most popular of two competing candidates and follows the trend that was set at the party conference at the Arena where intimidation was used against party dissidents.

The Contemporary Party Systems and Political Culture

In spite of seemingly polarized positions between the JLP and the PNP on ideology in the 1970s (JLP capitalism versus PNP socialism), there has always been a fair amount of policy continuity between successive JLP and PNP Governments even in that turbulent period. Party policy continuity was the trend in the 1950s and 1960s when there were no significant ideological differences between the PNP and the JLP. It continued at a diminished level between the 1970s and 1980s.

Table four summarizes some of the main PNP policies in the seventies and the JLP reactions and responses in the 1980s.

Table Four: Policies continuities	
PNP Policies (1972 - 80)	JLP Reactions (1980 - 89)
Cooperatives in sugar industry	abandoned by the JLP
State owned food farms	abandoned by the JLP
Imposed bauxite levy	continued by the JLP
State trading Corporation	continued by the JLP
Foreign exchange controls	continued by the JLP
Wage guidelines	continued by the JLP but later abandoned
Controlled basic food price	continued by the JLP but later abandoned
Promoted worker participation	abandoned by the JLP
Close ties with Cuba	abandoned by the JLP
Housing Trust	abandoned by the JLP
JLP Policies (1980-89)	PNP Responses (1989-92)
Deregulation of economy	intensified by PNP
Privatization of state owned enterprises	intensified by PNP
Dismantled import quotas	no change by PNP

Auction system	changed to full currency liberalization
Civil service retrenchment	continued by PNP
Tight monetary policies	continued by PNP
Tight fiscal policies	continued by PNP
Set up export promotion agency	continued by PNP

Four of the ten PNP policies were thrown out by the JLP after coming to power but six of them were continued although another two were eventually abandoned. Seven of the eight policy measures carried out by the JLP in the 1980s and listed in that table were continued by the PNP in the 1990s, indicating that policy continuity has increased and has returned to the very high levels of the 1950s and 1960s.

The high degree of centrist-rightist policy directions which inform the current JLP-PNP policy consensus, leaves no obvious opening for minor parties to emerge to the left of this new policy compact.

Leadership Credibility

There is a crisis of credibility in the party system as cynicism towards political leaders has increased over the 1990-91 period. What has happened in Jamaica is similar to the declining popular support and confidence in politicians which has surfaced worldwide in North America, Europe and the Third World. This trend has been aggravated by the inability of government spending to satisfy the needs of citizens (roads, health services, education, water supplies etc.). Negative ratings of most members of parliament in Jamaica among the electorate has increased from 40 per cent to 70 per cent between 1989 and 1991.

A major factor influencing this new negative voter attitude towards political leaders has been public exposure of corruption by politicians and huge increases in the salaries and emoluments of ministers of government and parliamentarians that have been way above the rates of pay increases being earned by most sections of the Jamaican labour force.

The increased cynicism towards political leaders in 1991 has been accompanied by reluctance to register to vote. Voter registration has been problematic as voters seem reluctant to participate in the system. We have, however, tended to exaggerate the implications of this trend, some even believing that the two party system was about to collapse.

Support for the parties is cyclical. Interest in parties peaks at election time only to decline in the interim periods. It is quite normal for 35 per cent to 40 per cent of voters to completely lose interest in parties and party leaders during these 'dead season' periods.

In 1990, after voting out a governing JLP party and discovering that the newly elected PNP was carrying out the same policies of the JLP, voter apathy increased rapidly. But we have had similar periods between the 1976 and 1978 elections when 40 per cent of voters turned against the political parties, only to return to the fold by 1980.

In 1992 voter registration has considerably increased and the current trend suggests that high voter turnout (80 per cent of registered voters and 70 per cent of adult population) is likely to be the norm in rural parishes in the next elections due to an increased desire to vote out the existing PNP government. Interest in voting in these rural parishes has grown by 10 per cent between 1991 and 1992.

Urban Corporate Area voting is likely to remain very low (50 per cent — 55 per cent) although it is likely to be disguised by bogus voting in inner city area. Outside of the Corporate Area the deep alienation towards party politics has been rapidly declining as a resurgence of antigovernment militancy is motivating some rural voters to register and vote.

Concern is being expressed over garrison constituencies (both JLP and PNP) where one-party hegemonies take elections rather than win them genuinely. In these areas one party dominates but uses strong arm tactics to consolidate its majority by bogus voting. Those big vote majorities in this minority of inner city constituencies are not entirely fabricated as we have done polls in these areas which allow us to compare real support for the leading party with the controlled balloting that occurs on election day. Table five sets out these data for the 1989 elections.

Table Five: Voting and estimated party strength in garrison constituencies (%)				
	Actual 1989 ballots		Stone Polls estimate	
	JLP	PNP	JLP	PNP
West Kingston	82	18	67	33
Kingston Central	43	57	41	59
Kingston East	19	81	38	62
St. Andrew South	27	73	40	60
St. Andrew South West	2	98	35	65

In these five garrison constituencies, only in Kingston Central did the actual vote match the Stone Polls estimated. In Kingston

East,St. Andrew South, Kingston West and St. Andrew South West the 1989 vote inflates the dominant party's strength by 15 per cent to 33 per cent.

Political Dissent

The 'Gang of Five' in the JLP in which five party leaders were accused of being disloyal to the party's leader, represents a continuing conflict between independent minded party leaders and the JLP party's top hierarchy. The party has clearly become paranoid about leadership threats and this has created deep distrust between its leader Edward Seaga and these prominent JLP persons. The evidence is not convincing that Errol Anderson, Pearnel Charles, Karl Samuda, Douglas Vaz, Ed Bartlett, Joan Webley, Cliff Stone and Denis Wright pose challenges to Seaga's leadership. Only Bartlett has survived. A longer list of early defections from that party (Frank Phipps, Winston Spaulding, Ian Ramsey, Tony Abrahams and Ronnie Irvine) reinforce reasonable doubts on the prob-lems of independent persons being able to survive in the JLP under Seaga's highly personalized and centralized leadership.

The 'laid back' consultative and low profile leadership style of the new PNP leader P.J. Patterson is a sharp contrast to the current 'take charge' and 'take control' leadership style of the JLP leader. Laissez-faire and looser political management in the PNP will avoid any such similar problems emerging in spite of the Portia Simpson challenge. In the past purging of party dissidents has been the norm due to ideological divisions in the PNP between leftist and rightist tendencies and factionalism, power struggles and competing cliques in the JLP. Authoritarian tendencies exist in both parties but they have always been stronger in the JLP. In the late 1950s the JLP party leader Alexan-der Bustamante canceled a party election unilaterally because he did not favour the persons elected to office.

The Party Union Link

The continued formal party-union link between the Bustamante Industrial Trade Union and the JLP and the National Workers Union and the PNP has been a major factor weakening trade union leadership. Outstanding labour leaders tend to run for office in both parties and invariably become ministers of government. The effect is that their leadership becomes lost to the trade unions. The trade unions have lost most of their outstanding leaders in recent years to party politics.

These include Carlyle Dunkley, Pearnel charles, Errol Anderson, Michael Manley and Clifton Stone. The process is continuing as trade unions leaders are still running for political office and are likely to end up being lost to the labour movement (Dereck Rochester, Ruddy Spencer, and Dwight Nelson).

Economic Management

Since the 1970s the PNP has acquired the image of being the party that is most concerned for the poorer classes and this image was reinforced in the socialist period of the 1970s. On the other hand, the PNP has failed to attract a reputation for sound economic management. The JLP by contrast does not have a strong populist image in the current period but enjoys a strong image as being the party better able to manage the country's affairs and the economy.

Over the years, and especially since the 1980 elections, in addition to the dominant issue of economic hardships on the poor (cost of living, unemployment, declining buying power and high inflation), the issue of economic management has surfaced as a major factor influencing voters' choices.

The general view among the Jamaican electorate is that the current parties and leaders are not doing a great job of managing the economy to benefit the majority. The overall perception is that the politicians have a diminished capacity to solve Jamaica's economic problems and this is why there appears to be a huge gap between campaign promises and delivery. These perceptions have been reinforced by objective economic realities including massive inflation levels, high youth unemployment, drastic declines in living standards, failure to achieve significant and substantial economic growth since the early 1970s (compared to rapid growth of the 1950s and early 1960s), the economy's chronic indebtedness, real declines in public spending, drastic deterioration in government funded social and economic services and an economic climate characterized by constant crises and crisis management.

JLP leader, Eddie Seaga, is currently the only Jamaican politician who is perceived by many voters as an effective economic manager and as having the skills needed to run the country's affairs efficiently. His strong managerial image is likely to be a major political asset when the parties contest the next elections. His rating as an economic manager is twice the level of that enjoyed by PNP leader P.J. Patterson.

Many voters however are gradually scaling down their expectations of the flow of benefits from government and this is likely to ease some of the negative political opinion pressures towards government and politicians.

Uniform Voting

In the early period (1940s and 1950s), candidate appeal was a major factor influencing voting with 30 per cent to 40 per cent of votes being attracted by candidate appeal. This has ceased to be an important factor influencing voter choice. As candidate appeal has declined in importance, weak candidates get elected due to party voting and some strong candidates lose elections due to swings in party voting. As a result the number of safe seats has declined. That decline is also due to a drop in loyal party voting. Loyal party voting was approximately 90 per cent in the 1950s and 1960s, 80 per cent in the 1970s but has since declined to 48 per cent of likely voters, as 'issues voting' has increased from 10 per cent to 52 per cent over the past 48 years.

In the earlier period (1950s and 1960s), 65 per cent of the constituencies voted only for one party while the remaining 35 per cent shifted from party to party reflecting the national swing. Today, 80 per cent of the constituencies swing from party to party depending on the national swing. That national swing factor has also increased from five to six per cent in the earlier period to 14 per cent and 16 per cent swings in the current period. These big swings are usually large enough to eliminate majorities in traditionally safe seats.

As a result of all of these factors, safe seats have declined, the dominant party tends to win in most parishes and constituencies, and the country now tends to vote like a single constituency, except for a few inner city urban constituencies where party majorities have remained stable.

The Challenge of the Twenty-first Century

And what of the future and the challenge of the twenty first century?

Party Democracy

There is need to promote greater internal party democracy in both parties. This can be achieved by increasing the recruitment of party members from the middle strata and the more educated; by making internal party activities more visible, transparent and open to media scrutiny; by establishing more orderly and accurately documented membership lists in the political parties to reduce thuggery and bogus voting in party elections; by encouraging rather than attacking independent thinking in the parties and by purging from the parties' leadership ranks persons associated with violence.

Proportional Representation

The uniform trend in voting across the constituencies which has eliminated most safe seats means that winning parties get a disproportionately large 75 per cent to 85 per cent share of the seats from 56 per cent to 59 per cent vote majorities. The country needs to seriously examine the adoption of proportional representation for elections to parliament. Such a move would encourage the return of small third parties and open up the political system to a more diverse range of parties.

Table Six: Votes and seats by winning parties (%)						
	1962		1980		1989	
	votes	seats	votes	seats	votes	seats
JLP	50	58	59	85		
PNP					57	75

A Presidential System

Most members of parliament end up having ministerial or junior ministerial responsibility in top heavy administrations and there is virtually no back bench in the parliament. In the current parliament 37 PNP MP's have either cabinet rank, junior ministerial portfolios or are parliamentary secretaries. In addition to the 15 opposition JLP members of parliament, there are only eight PNP MP's without ministerial responsibilities.

As table seven demonstrates, most of the working time of MP's with ministerial jobs and responsibilities is concentrated on ministerial tasks and very little is available for constituency representation. This is in sharp contrast to the MP's without ministerial jobs and responsibilities who devote more than twice the time of ministers, junior ministers and parliamentary secretaries to constituency work and representation.

Constituency representation needs to become a full time occupation and this can only be achieved by changing Jamaica's Westminster style parliamentary system to a presidential system and have voters vote separately for an executive president and parliamentarians. This change would stabilise voting for MP's and create longer periods of incumbency that would increase the experience and competence of parliamentarians. The mix of proportional representation electoral systems and presidential systems of government is very prevalent in South American democracies (Chile, Venezuela, for example)

Table Seven: Breakdown of working time of MP's		
	MP's with Ministry jobs	MP's without Ministry jobs
Constituency work	19%	45%
Attendance in parliament	10%	7%
Ministerial jobs	66%	0%
Personal business unrelated to public office	5%	48%
	100%	100%

High levels of poverty and youth unemployment and a tradition of patronage politics mean that political handouts to 'party faithfuls' can never be eliminated in Jamaica. What is needed to counter-balance it are community empowerment strategies such as regular town hall meetings where MP's give account of their stewardship, answer questions and engage in dialogue with voters, and the creation of constituency management bodies on which ordinary citizens and community leaders sit and can have a say in local constituency decision making.

Decentralized Management

For this to be meaningful, the whole structure of centralized government management has to be dismantled and a more decentralized regional system of government created around the following four administrative units or areas listed in table seven. Over-centralized administration is a major negative factor influencing low levels of efficiency from health service and educational management to police administration and road maintenance.

Table Eight: Suggested administrative units for a more decentralised government administration
1. Corporate Area and urban St. Catherine
2. East (Portland, St. Mary & St. Thomas)
3. Central (St. Ann, Clarendon, Manchester and rural St. Catherine)
4. West (St. Elizabeth, Westmoreland, Hanover, St. James and Trelawny)

There is need for concern about the quality of leadership being recruited into public office in both parties. Most are unfamiliar with government and management and terribly ignorant of economic policy issues. This problem is aggravated by the existing high turnover of MP's as incumbents lose elections after short periods of representation. We need adequate training programmes in management, economics, public law and civics to better equip these persons to assume leadership roles in public management.

Our politicians are also intellectually lazy, reflecting tendencies from their middle class life styles. Only a few of them (Hugh Small, P.J. Patterson, Maxine Henry, Peter Phillips, Michael Manley, Eddie Seaga, Bruce Golding, Karl Samuda, Audley Shaw, Anthony Johnson, Arnold Bertram, Trevor Munroe and D.K. Duncan) do not fall in this category of intellectually indolent politicians. They do not read and keep up to date on what is happening in the world of global politics, international finance and even in the area of local politics. For example, most MP's still believe that elections are won by candidate appeal although extensive research and publications by me in books, articles and newspaper columns have established that Jamaican voters vote for parties and party leaders. No more than two to five per cent of Jamaican vote preferences can be attributed to candidate appeal.

Easily read books written on party politics and voting such as my *Politics Versus Economics* published in 1989, shortly after the 1989 elections, are not being read by our politicians who remain in a state of ignorance on these matters, continuing to hold unto folk wisdom.

Party Financing

The funding of political parties by big business is a continuing problem as it has become a source of influencing the parties. There is no simple solution but what we need is a mix of state financing and public listing and disclosure of all party contributions.

Administrative Corruption

Extensive corruption remains a major weakness of public management in Jamaica. Juries are corrupted. Customs officials and policemen collect bribes and politicians take money to administer favours. Big business frequently uses its money to influence decisions in its favour.

We need special laws with heavy punitive sanctions against corruption in government and indefinite banning of persons found guilty of corrupt acts from public office.

But most importantly public opinion is too soft on corrupt practices and needs to be more militant in punishing politicians for dishonesty. The press has a major role here in exposing corruption as radio commentators Wilmot Perkins did on the recent furniture scandal. But except for a few journalists (like Perkins, Beth Aub and Dawn Rich) the media tends to be easily intimidated by politicians, big business and thugs.

CHAPTER 7

Crime and Violence: Its Implications for Economic Expansion

Gladstone Bonnick

Introduction

I have been giving thought to the social environment for the growth of the Jamaican economy over the long term. In trying to provide me with some data on which to gauge the impact of crime on the economy, the PIOJ sent me an excellent article by Carl Stone entitled 'Crime and Violence: Social-Political Implications'. In this paper I am presenting I will do little more than repeat what Stone has said, but I will recommend for your consideration a slightly different viewpoint on the relationship between crime and the economy and will attempt to sketch a slightly different strategy for the future.

Citing a recent study by an American Criminologist, Dr. Klaus de Albuquerque, Stone reminds us that:

1. Jamaica is now among countries with the highest rate of violent crime including murder, rape, robbery, and aggravated assaults. It has much higher rates compared with low crime rates found in Eastern Caribbean countries such as Dominica, Barbados, Guyana, and Trinidad/Tobago;
2. Official crime statistics understate the actual incidence of crime, especially thefts, minor robberies, and praedial larceny;

3. Between January and November 1978 about one-third of persons he surveyed in the Corporate area had been victims of theft, robbery, burglary, and praedial larceny. In addition, about one-fifth of persons surveyed in the rural parts had been victims during the same period.

Regarding the trend in crime, research by Stone and other sociologists has shown that after being stable for most of the post World War II period leading up to independence, the crime rate has increased rapidly since independence. Initially, there was a steady increase in crime rates during the 1960s but these have accelerated since the early 1970s.

Crime and Violence: Its Causes and Effects on the Economy

Stone makes some well reasoned arguments to support the following.
1. Poverty does not explain the varying levels of violence among either Third World or industrialized countries. There are vast differences between the level of crime and violence among countries with similar levels of economic development. The homicide rate for Japan and Western European countries is very low — fewer than four per 100,000 each year — while in the US the figure is about 10. The data on robbery is similar for the comparison between Japan/Western Europe and the USA. In Jamaica violent crime equals or exceeds US levels.
2. The image of the criminal has changed from being that of a despised person to become a 'rude boy' or 'Robin Hood character' defying and challenging an inequitable socio/economic system. Criminals and purveyors of violence now project a new 'macho' image that has made them into role models in the ghetto community.
3. Japan and Europe have modernized in ways that minimized the growth of criminal violence. They manage to preserve in the process traditional social values and order which have had the effect of moderating aggressive social behaviour. In Jamaica, money has replaced traditional values as the mark of success, and its acquisition by whatever means has become the driving force of the society. Japan and Western Europe have retained social security systems that have eased the trauma of the disparity frequency brought about by modernization.
4. Both Europe and Japan managed to retain in the process of modernization strong traditional authority systems.

5. The slowdown in economic expansion which frustrated expectations for a better life exacerbated the situation of rising criminality in Jamaica that was set in train by the disruption of the traditional Jamaican social order by post-war economic changes.

Stone also discusses the impact of crime and violence on the business environment in Jamaica. His analysis divides crime into two levels: the large number of petty crimes involving stealing, burglary, and praedial larceny; and the more serious level of violent crime associated with drugs and street gangs. The former he associated with unemployment and lack of economic opportunity; the latter with the accumulation of alternative power.

He correctly concludes that: a high crime rate can potentially be a deterrent to investment by imposing heavy costs on those investments and by increasing the risk of loss of life or injury to all who own, manage, or work in enterprises that have a high casualty rate for armed robbery. The threat to personal freedom and the sense of insecurity occasioned by fear of personal and property crime might also motivate those with skills and capital to emigrate, thereby aggravating economic problems such as the brain drain and the flight of capital.

He notes that 'on the other hand, the drug trade can have both positive and negative effects on an economy': the positive coming from income, employment, and foreign exchange provided by the drug business, and the negative from the disruptive effects on legitimate business associated with the increased supplies of guns and the corruption of public officials.

The study notes that while violent crime has been partially neutralized by aggressive law enforcement, praedial larceny has increased considerably since the 1970s. He estimates that between 10 per cent and 25 per cent of the revenue to farmers has been lost to praedial thieves, thereby rendering agricultural investment both more prone to risks and uncertainty, and more subject to uncontrollable losses. The overall impact has been a decline in agricultural investment. I may mention that, in addition to the direct loss to thieves, the rate of return to agriculture has been reduced because of higher investment costs required for fencing and other protection (e.g. the need to put barbed wire in fish-ponds to prevent thieves from harvesting the fish with nets).

Stone has not failed to mention the distortions in resource allocation caused by the high and rising level of crime and violence in Jamaica. He points out that one consequence of the increased level of crime has been the great demand for security services, and estimated that the security guard industry now employs 20,000 workers in some 200 firms. The effect is that the cost of this security incurred by business is passed on to consumers in the form of higher prices. Another distortion arises from the reduced handling of cash in business enterprises, and the rise in the demand for banking services associated with alternative media of exchange.

While Stone has not mentioned this, attention should be drawn to the vast investment in burglar bars, grilled doors, and concrete block walls and security fencing that is part of almost every dwelling unit, office, and factory building in Jamaica. I would guess that the society has tied up in these protective measures resources which could have added significantly to the stock of housing in the society, and its current use probably has had a negative impact on the supply of housing to the less advantaged groups of the society.

The statistics on murders clearly show the rapid rise over time. While Stone, in trying to isolate the causes, finds it necessary to observe that about 40 per cent are due to domestic conflicts, I would focus on the 60 per cent that are associated with criminal activity. What the statistics do not show but which we all know is the extent to which small- and medium-scale entrepreneurs have fallen prey to the gunmen over the years. Gas station owners, transport operators, retailers, club operators, small contractors, and small scale manufacturers have borne the brunt of the assault over the years. Big capitalists, being able to afford security and to use alternative ways of handling cash have, by and large, been spared.

As a sociologist, Stone is interested in understanding the causes of rising crime and violence in Jamaica with a view to suggesting solutions to the problem. He reasons that, to the extent that the economic situation has been a cause, then improvement in the economic situation could be part of the solution. Looked at from the point of view of the economists, one must ask the question whether higher and sustained economic expansion is likely given the negative impact on investment and the distortions in resource use deriving from the high and rising level of crime and violence in the society; or whether the society might not be in a 'catch 22" situation. The answer to this conundrum depends in part on the economic strategy the society chooses to follow.

The Economy Strategy

The economic strategy which Jamaica has chosen to follow for the foreseeable future is one based on free enterprise in which economic decisions are taken by private individuals who are the sponsors of investment and the organizers of production activities. Some sectors are relatively robust in the face of rising crime; for example, bauxite/alumina, sugar, and, to a lesser extent, tourism based on large hotels, enclave-type of development. But others, such as agriculture, services, small scale manufacturing and construction are more vulnerable. It appears to me that the less vulnerable sectors are unlikely to grow rapidly enough to provide the economic expansion the society needs to meet the aspirations for rising employment and growing per capita income for an increasing population. It therefore seems essential that the society not leave the vulnerable sectors to the depredations of the criminal.

The strategy is also characterized by openness of the Jamaican economy and the expectation of rising participation of Jamaican products and services in the world of international trade based on the ability to compete with other suppliers in the arena. What this implies is that Jamaica cannot be competitive, either in its own market or abroad, if Jamaican production has to bear the direct impact of higher crime rates on the amount and cost of marketable output.

Openness of the economy is expected to result in increasing inflows of investible resources from abroad since Jamaican savings are inadequate to support the level of investment and growth in output to which the nation aspires. Adequate inflow of foreign investment and investors may not materialize if the perception abroad is that Jamaica is a more dangerous place to locate business than other countries. But it also implies the possibility that Jamaican capital may seek investment possibilities abroad if participation in the Jamaican environment carries inordinately higher risk to the entrepreneur, not only of loss of capital, but of life and limb.

Stone's view is that the community has to some extent, adjusted to the high crime rate, and that although the rising crime rate has generated fears throughout the society, its impact on the economy has been contained, and that no major, lasting, negative effects have been evident in the urban corporate economy, especially since 1980. This is not a useful point of view to project, and I beg to disagree. I would submit that a large part of the hoped-for future growth will have to come from other parts of the economy than the urban corporate economy. I also submit that while the urban corporate economy has been able to hire armed guards, passing on the costs to the Jamaican consumer due to the protection against imports that was available, this offset will become less available as the economy becomes more open. It will also become less relevant as the economy attempts to become more export oriented.

Some statistics on the recent situation leave me uneasy regarding the conclusion that the community has accommodated itself to the level of crime. One concerns the rise in the number of murders in the first three quarters of 1990 (over 28 per cent) compared with the corresponding period of 1989, and the data on shootings (over 16 per cent) during these periods. The other concerns the declining percentage of crime related murders that have been solved; the percentage fell from 24 per cent to 12 per cent between 1987 and 1989. Stone attributed this fall to the intimidation of witnesses and the low level of confidence by the public in the police.

From an economist's point of view the continued rapid rate of increase in crime, and especially violent crime, cannot be consistent with an economic strategy which has to be built on a high degree of confidence on the part of the entrepreneur that he will reap the fruit of his labours. Nor can it be based on the assumption of improving Jamaica's competitiveness as a place to locate productive investment and to undertake production for export. It is clear that the society must either change its economic growth approach to one that may be less sensitive to the dysfunctionalities in the social environment, or design into the strategy provisions for mitigating the threat to the economy inherent in the present social situation. In other words, Jamaica must either change from a private enterprise/open economy strategy, or, the economic strategy must include a potent anticrime component.

The Anticrime Strategy

Stone has set out in his paper his views on a short term solution and in general I would agree with them, except that I believe the situation has become so serious that nothing short of shock treatment will be adequate. Once the level of criminality is rolled back to more reasonable levels and the upward trend has been reversed, then less drastic measures may be in order.

The economic principles which should guide the formation of an anticrime strategy are the traditional principles guiding resource allocation and incentives, and those which determine the appropriate role of government in the society. These principles are reflected in the following statements:

a) the resources allocated to fighting crime must be adequate in light of the magnitude of the problem (the costs imposed on the society) and consistency with other objectives (e.g. investment expansion and economic growth);

b) the manner in which the allocated resources are utilized should be as efficient as possible;

c) the system of incentives applied to those involved in anticrime work should be made to reflect the importance of their work to society and should reward initiative and compensate for the higher risk to life and limb which the work involves;

d) the system of disincentives to criminal behaviour should increase the expected cost to the individual of engaging in violent crime to the point of being unbearable. At a minimum the criminal should expect to repay to the society, not only the direct cost of compensating victims, but the indirect costs which his criminal behaviour imposes on the society as a whole, in addition to any punitive damages the society may assess;

e) the importance of social benefits are such as to support the view that the financing of anticrime efforts ought to be collective (through taxation) rather than individual (through direct payment by persons according to use). It is also important to recognise that, like the control of a contagious disease, the society cannot adequately protect itself by inoculating only those who can afford to buy the vaccine. Similarly, the society's security cannot be based on a system of private guards for those who can afford such services;

f) I would submit that on efficiency grounds the society's security cannot be left to private sector initiative to provide the necessary service.

g) under the present arrangements the brunt of the cost of crime is borne by the victims. This is inequitable for it imposes a tax on individuals without regard to their ability to bear it or to previous levels of benefits enjoyed from the society. If criminals are made to pay compensation adequate to offset damage to victims, then the society should have some system of transferring this compensation back to victims. This need not be a complicated or comprehensive system. For example, praedial thieves could be required to work on victims' farms or on agricultural infrastructure — roads, drainage ditches, etc.

The principles suggested above could be useful in guiding the rethinking that should be done as Jamaica gears itself for the future.

Writing from afar without access to detailed data it is impossible to make judgements on all the issues. However, I will allow myself the luxury of some guesses, some observations, and some tentative suggestions.

On the adequacy of resources allocated to fight crime, one can see how the percentage of government expenditure at all levels combined compares with other countries, as well as the comparison of per capita expenditures. One can look at the crude ratio of police to population. On casual observation, the police in most cities of the US are more visible than in Kingston, partly because they are more mobile. I have no doubt that they are better equipped technologically, not just with fire-power, but with computers and laboratories, and have the benefit of sophisticated systems of personal identification which help them keep track of the citizenry. In this regard, Stone's judgement that the superior marginal benefit from community support rather than additional resources would be applicable to Jamaica, must not be accepted without further examination. In Jamaica, where the resources available to the police must be well below US levels per policeman, additional equipment and training might well be the preferred immediate emphasis — although this and the mobilization of community support need not be mutually exclusive approaches. My judgement is that the time has come for a comprehensive review of the resources at the disposal of anticrime forces with a view to making them superior to the opponent.

On the utilization of resources, Jamaica must rethink two issues: the role of the Jamaica Defense Forces (JDF), and how much dependence there should be on the growing army of private security guards. (i) Jamaica needs to rethink the issue of whether it needs a force for defense against external threats or whether the force should be oriented to deal with internal threats essentially as a back-up to the regular police. From my observation the JDF has been used for the latter. As such, thought should be given to whether this arrangement provides for the most effective management of the resources for combatting violent crime and use of equipment and manpower. Does the country really need two forces with separate equipment and under separate command structures? Some countries have a single force. Maybe Jamaica should examine their experience and see if that model may not be more appropriate to its needs;
(ii) Under present arrangements Jamaica underprovides for internal security through budgetary provisions financed out of taxation, leaving private individuals to make further provisions to meet their needs.

The result is the proliferation of weaponry in the hands of a large and inadequately trained force, under a variety of command structures of variable competence but guided by profit considerations. The result is also an inequitable distribution of a basic and necessary service that should be available equally to all. While the present situation is an understandable reaction to the crisis, it is not the way to go. More adequate provision for an adequate force financed through taxation is more appropriate.

The incentive system in the society must be reoriented to offer better pay to those who provide essential services. The police, teachers, and nurses have long been treated disadvantageously compared with those fortunate to be in the glamour statutory agencies responsible for tourism advertising, investment and export promotion, development banking, etc. In the long term these agencies should be considered for privatization and their operations left to the private sector interest they serve; but, in the meantime, the whole question of pay policy in the public sector should be made more transparent and the justification for continuing to treat essential services as low-pay islands reexamined. Police pay should be made sufficient to attract more and higher quality recruits, and offer the expectation of a reasonable standard of life consistent with the average the society can afford. The opportunity for upward mobility should be provided through training to fit officers for the wider variety of jobs that a technologically modern force would provide. In hard economic times when budgetary resources are scarce the likely reaction to the above is that the society cannot afford it. I say that what can and cannot be afforded depends on your system of priorities. The essence of my point here is that higher priority needs to be given to the police.

The disincentive system should be adjusted to make the expected cost to the perpetrators of violent crime unbearable. Stone makes the point by saying that the society should increase the risk to the criminal by improving the rate of solving crimes. This will require more police, better equipped and trained, and highly motivated through an appropriate incentive system. Once caught and convicted, the persons involved in violent crime should be made to bear higher costs than they now do; that is, penalties should be increased. Thus, a criminal who shoots and injures his victim in the process of committing a crime, should face a penalty almost as severe as if he had killed his victim.

While an economist has no basis for getting into an argument regarding whether or not punishment dissuades crime, it is clear that if the society establishes certain sanctions for criminal behaviour and fails to apply them without undue delay then any possible deterrent effect of punishment will be considerably eroded. Those convicted of murder committed in the process of criminal activity should be executed without undue delay. The use of a motor vehicle in the commission of a crime should carry as an additional punishment the permanent revocation of the drivers licence. The photographs of convicted criminals should be on display at public buildings throughout the island so that the criminal cannot hide behind anonymity. These are just examples of how the cost of being a criminal may be systematically raised through a wide variety of measures revoking the rights normally enjoyed by law-abiding citizens. The more general point is that after conviction punishment should be certain, swift, and unpleasant.

I agree that part of the solution must involve the community, and endorse fully Stone's recommendations. I would add that the propaganda apparatus should be brought to bear in stigmatizing criminal behaviour and in reversing in the mind of the community what has become a far too positive image of the criminal. Indeed, it seems no accident that the Jamaican crime situation is close to that of the US. Our acculturation process has been subverted by the US propaganda apparatus operating through the cinema and television which spews forth a continuous diet of violence which has been accepted almost unquestioningly as suitable for Jamaica as it pursues modernization.

While the above thoughts suggest the rethinking that we need to do, and the possible components of a strategy for the short term approach to the problem, one must be mindful of the need to reverse a trend before the underlying patterns of behaviour become so ingrained that the society will no longer even contemplate change. Below I set out some thoughts on changing the trend.

Reversing the Trend: Drastic Solutions

If the experience in other societies can provide some guidance to Jamaica, both that of societies that have modernized without a drastic rise in violent crime and those that have moved from a less to a more disciplined society, the following seem to be some of the main lessons to guide policy approaches to reversing the trend towards violent crime: (a) there must be a return to a strong authority system; (b) the notions of rights and personal freedoms must be consistent with the greater good of the society; (c) there should be no compromise with crime even when there could be some economic benefits accruing from it.

In my view the return to a strong authority system will require a special and sustained effort during an initial period of years. This will be a period in which the society should be put under special arrangements akin to martial law. Among the arrangements should be the institution of a national identity card system, under which each person above the age of 12 years would be issued a card bearing photograph and fingerprint and showing address, and with a magnetic strip allowing easy verification by a scanner attached to a computer system through which additional information about the individual can be accessed. Individuals would be required to carry this card at all times and to present it to law enforcement officers when requested to do so.

The society should be prepared to give up certain freedoms it has enjoyed in the past but which have been abused by criminals and may have to be suspended to reverse the trend to crime. The freedom of movement at all hours of the night and day from one area to another may have to be reconsidered. Curfews may have to be used as they have been in the past, except that they may have to be imposed for long enough to foster an adjustment in movement patterns toward ones consistent with better monitoring by police.

The right to own and carry firearms is a matter to be reviewed in this connection. As things stand firearms are in the hands of the official security forces, the private guard forces, selected (licenced) householders, unlicensed holders, and criminals. Except for official security forces and criminals, the firearms are in untrained and unpracticed hands. Since most violent crime involves the use of firearms, the problem has been seen as one of getting the guns out of the hands of criminals. This approach has failed for a number of reasons. In at least one country, Switzerland, every able bodied male is a member of the army reserves, is trained in the use of firearms, and is required to keep his rifle at home. It strikes me that at present the criminal in Jamaica has the advantage in that the majority of his victims are unarmed or untrained in the use of weapons. This advantage would be nullified if in every household there was a firearm and a capable user. Let me be clear to point out that I am not suggesting that the Swiss approach be transplanted to Jamaica; rather I am suggesting a certain courage in exploring the solutions. Frankly, I would prefer the death penalty for the use of a firearm in the commission of a crime irrespective of whether anyone was killed in the process. But the main point is that the society cannot continue to confer *de facto* rights on criminals which it restricts to the rest of the citizens.

Similarly, I would like to point out that there are other approaches to dealing with drug related crime than that which requires the society to seek a compromise with those who break its rules. Malaysia executes drug dealers. It applies this punishment without regard to whether the drug dealer is Australian or British, or to threats of withdrawal of foreign aid. China executes dealers as well as users of prohibited drugs. Some European countries erode the profitability of drug dealing by making drugs available to registered addicts. The best approach in our situation may not be immediately obvious, but in a situation where the society is close to being overwhelmed by crime strong measures are indicated. If and when the society returns to lower levels of crime then treatment of crime as illness may be an adequate approach. For the time being, the Jamaican society should be honest with itself: Either accept that the economic benefits of drug dealing are important enough to justify decriminalizing the activity and leave the people involved in the trade free to pursue their economic activity, or decide that this criminal behaviour is intolerable to the majority of the society and treat it as such. Compromise is not an option. No special consideration should be given to those in the trade to get them to redirect their energies toward legal activities.

I recommend Stone's article because it addresses an important issue on the resolution of which the future of Jamaican society and economy will depend. But I think that while the paper can serve as a basis for starting our thinking on solutions, it should not be regarded as offering the solution.

The objective of my intervention is to express a doubt as to whether the economic expansion which could reduce the need for criminal behaviour can occur in the present climate of extreme and rising violent crime aimed against key economic actors. I have suggested that we need to reconsider whether current institutional arrangements are likely to facilitate efficient use. I am fully convinced that shock therapy is needed to reverse what is becoming an established trend.

What I have said does not add up to a comprehensive approach to all crime. It is limited to the violent crime which discouraged investment and economic activity. Petty theft and corruption do increase the cost of doing business and to the extent that they are more significant in Jamaica than elsewhere would tend to make our economy less competitive, and should be addressed. The priority is clearly violent crime and praedial larceny — the perpetuators of which do not content themselves with cutting one stem of bananas but in reaping the whole field.

Finally, I recommend that more resources be devoted to fighting violent crime and that the anticrime forces be given better incentives for doing one of the most important yet dangerous jobs in the economy.

CHAPTER 8

Community Involvement:
Responses to the Challenges of the Future

Maxine Henry-Wilson

Introduction

Perhaps in some ways community development can be most appropriately compared to a hardy perennial tree. It survives despite the
absence of consistent nurturing and tending. Its roots run deep and it
can fend for itself. Yet, at some point, the lack of care leads to the
shedding of its foliage and its begins to decline. If it is not given some
new lease on life it will ultimately die.

Such has been the history and experience of community development as movement and activity in Jamaica. It has had a life-cycle in
which it has been practised at various times as paternalism as welfare,
as development, and as service delivery.

Its earliest origins were in the immediate postemancipation years
during which religious sects attempted to resocialize the former slaves
to the norms of freedom. Building free villages (communities), providing basic social services and generally contributing to the creation
of new social organizations and relationships, were some of the activities in which the churches engaged. Their methods and outcomes
represented hybrid community development techniques combining
welfarism, paternalism, and circumscribed impetus for self-reliant social action.

In the late nineteenth to early twentieth centuries, organizations such as the Jamaica Agricultural Society (JAS) were pivotal in providing leadership for the peasantry. The techniques used by the JAS bore the hallmarks of the community development approach. The Society's point of intervention in communities was very specific. Through representing farming interest, the JAS initiated programmes to upgrade agricultural production and trade. It used its various community fora to promote adult education, through which farmers and farm families were sensitized to organisational methods for promoting better farming practices in their communities.

The formation of the Jamaica Welfare Limited in 1937 signalled a spate of community development activity. The Jamaica Welfare Limited was what could be described as a special purpose vehicle established to administer the fund created through the payment of a levy of US one cent by two foreign banana shipping companies on each counted bunch of banana shipped from Jamaica.

The broad mandate of the Jamaica Welfare Limited was to:

1. To promote, manage, and control schemes for, and to do any act or thing which directly or indirectly serves the general interest and social and economic betterment and aids the agricultural and working peasantry, small settlers, farmers, labourers and working people of and in Jamaica.

2. To engage in any work or activity directly or indirectly relating to the health, culture, education, recreation, agriculture, industries, finances, trade, justice and morals of and for the agricultural and working peasantry, small settlers, farmers and labourers of and in Jamaica (*Statutes of Jamaica Welfare Limited,* 1937).

The Jamaica Welfare Limited was a multiservice agency engaged in diverse social development activities. Its guiding philosophy was that of 'teaching (people) to do for themselves' (Eddie Burke, 1938). To a significant extent, the genre of community work carried out by this network represented a consistent, integrated, and holistic approach and aimed at preparing the people for nationhood. This, in a nutshell, had some consistency with the development genre.

The history of the Jamaica Welfare Limited has not only been that of multiple and symbolic name changes, but also of erratic shifts in mission and policy direction. Consequently, in one decade it has been the state's agency for building and operating community centres; in another it has been the vehicle for nonformal skill training. More often than not its mandate has been unclear, overlapping with and duplicating the efforts of some of its offspring agencies such as Literacy and Cultural Development Commissions. The resources allocated to these bodies have been inadequate and political (as distinct from partisan) support a vicarious.

The Social Development Commission (SDC), the contemporary successor organisation to the Jamaica Welfare Limited, has become the state agency for community development, loosely defined. The Commission has provided some rootedness and popular legitimization of this process. However, there have been some changes in the landscape with a proliferation of nongovernmental organisations of diverse vintage including church groups, corporate entities, and overseas assistance agencies.

What this means is that there are several actual and potential carriers of the community development message and activity. The real issue is the extent to which their activities are consistent with sustainable community development and, therefore, have the potential for energizing community residents to take effective responsibility for improving their own lives.

Concepts and Constructs of Community Development

Community development connotes people-centred iniciative using the methodology of collective action. It is not prescriptive in the sense of offering a blue print for social action. Rather, it defines an approach which can be implemented through experimentation. This approach departs from the assumption that any one community is the replica of another.

This is not to deny that there are points of similarity and comparability. What that means however is that while we can benefit through social learning from the experiences in one community we cannot expect to transpose these uncritically to another. Furthermore, community development cannot be based on what is essentially a false assumption that a specific community of interest exists among the residents of a designated geographical area. These residents have also been players in wider historic social situations which have had an impact on their relationships and interactions, creating social fragmentation and conflicts. These occurrences have a deleterious effect on the cohesiveness of communities. Hence, one of the incipient intervention strategies which must be employed is that of community building.

While community development cannot be categorized as uncritically prescriptive, there are certain strategic objectives which give it its defining characteristics. A random selection of definitions of community development reproduced below will highlight some of its peculiar and substantive features.

1. Community development is a movement designed to promote better living for the whole community with the active participation and, if possible, at the initiative of the community but, if this is not forthcoming, spontaneously, this must be done by the use of techniques for stimulating it in order to ensure its active and enthusiastic response to the movement (Stewart McPherson, 1982, p.164).
2. (Community Development) . . .involves popular participation, not so much in the productive sense, but in the economic and social processes.
3. (Community Development) is a process of social action in which the people of the community organize themselves for common action. They define their common goals, determine action plans, and execute these plans with maximum reliance on community resources.

The points of commonality and convergence in these definitions relate to the process nature of community development — the *sine qua non* of popular mobilization for social action and social change — and the access to resources.

One of the naive assumptions which frequently plagues community development activity is that communities are self-mobilizing and self-organizing and that all their indigenous norms and practices are positive forces for effective community development. Our own experiences negates these and demonstrate that there will not always be a spontaneous popular embrace of the methodology and there is need to stimulate and sustain such initiatives. As emphasised in McPherson's definition, in many instances, it will be necessary for there to be appropriate catalytic strategies.

The methodology of community development must be consistent with proactive behaviour rather than reacting to strategies which have failed in other spheres and turning to this approach as a short-term palliative. Contrary to some impression, community development is neither a panacea nor a quick fix solution. Its process-oriented nature means that it is iterative, frequently requiring participants and practitioners to start again 'from scratch' and go over ground which they thought they had previously conquered. Further, it requires and assumes behaviour change, with participants being resocialized to take responsibility for their own environment, to be involved in effective decision making which can enhance their well-being in a holistic way.

Essentially, what is being searched for is a new social architecture which is responsive and facilitates multidimensional development. This architecture must have two dimensions. Firstly, it must have facilitatory linkages with the complementary organizations in the wider environment. In other words, its energy and legitimacy, its capacity to fulfil its objectives are only possible if it is a two-way channel for information and decisions. What this means, in effect, is that nontraditional organizational forms and activities cannot survive in an environment in which there is too much dependence on traditional bureaucratic structures which are inflexible and which emphasize control as distinct from accountability, innovation, and responsiveness. Transformation in existing communities must take place to ensure they have structures and effective linkages with the local level. What this assumes is the fundamental reorientation of the inherited bureaucracy; how it is organized and how it operates. It has to be deliberately prepared and sensitized to the specific characteristics of the community as a client group and be taught to accept the legitimacy of the community groups as decision makers.

Secondly, the ultimate objective of the efforts must be that of *social development*. This is the essential distinction between community development and mere community organization building. The latter can be a tool for achieving the former but, in many instances both are perceived as synonymous.

This architecture has three main features. Firstly, it must proceed from strategic planning and be based on strategic management. It must emanate from the establishment of long-term goals for the society, and consequent resources allocation. Internal and external opportunities in the community must be harmonized with those of the wider society. They cannot be appendages which result in further marginalization of communities.

Secondly, the use of strategic management interventions should result within the communities themselves so that the people have the ability to identify their own opportunities, optimize the use of available resources, and manage their own efforts. To effectively do this they may learn new skills, acquire and gain access to new technologies, and build a knowledge base about such activities as marketing and the use of working capital management. Communities have to be taught to analyse and manage risks. The organisational support to achieve this is critical, given the low thresholds for risk-taking in poor communities.

In all of this what is the starting point for our efforts? A return to the analysis of some aspects of the Jamaican experience might provide a useful signpost. In this presentation the empirical data which is used to inform the observations about the future directions of community development has been based on a sample of community councils registered with the Social Development Commission (SDC) in the 1970s. The study was conducted at two levels: the first step was an appraisal of the positive and negative deviances which influenced community organisation and building.

After this appraisal six communities were selected for intense field study. The criteria for their selection included a range of variables, including, the time of their formation, a socio-economic profile, and their geographical location.

The following conclusions have been drawn in terms of the extent to which our community development efforts have achieved the ideas identified above and present some guide as to likely points for any renewed initiatives in this sphere.

a) The major bursts of community development activity have coincided with those historical junctures at which there have been a supportive political environment. Community development, like any other development process, requires political support. This does not mean state sponsorship but rather policy options which facilitate local efforts in all its dimensions.

b) The point of entry into the community must be programmes which can meet some felt community need. Continued institutional and functional legitimacy must be based on a perception by the community that the activities have social utility.

c) The enthusiasm for the initiatives will decline if there is a perception that the process is geared towards system maintenance rather than systems change or adaptability. In other words, the promise of empowerment cannot be realized if there is no transfer of decision making and/or material resources. In the absence of this the community will see their efforts as being only of symbolic value.

d) Community development efforts are sustainable if they pursue a dominant goal rather than multiple goals simultaneously. In the pursuit of this dominant goal, however, there must be a strategic approach to integrating the provision of the inputs which are required to achieve this goal. For example, it is no use pursuing the dominant goal of skills training without consideration of subsequent employment opportunities or availability of credit to facilitate own account businesses. The most successful efforts have been those which pursue what could be described as sequential diversification of their goal.

On balance, among the populace, there is some rootedness of the community development approach and its potential for empowerment. This is despite the fact that we tend to have a dominance of welfare and patronage approaches rather than approaches consistent with options development. This identification with community development, however, may be a dying phenomenon, as many of those who have been schooled in the principle of and who benefitted from the programmes of community development are now aging. The ethos of collective resolution of problems runs the risk of disappearing with them and being replaced by a crass individualism. Most of all methods, techniques, and promised outcomes, currently identified as community development, engender cynicism in our young who see them as anachronisms. The challenge is to update the technologies and remove the marginalism which is identified with community development efforts.

The wheel has now come full circle and there is a renewed exhortation for the use of community-based solutions. Currently, that prominent recommendation that we embrace this approach is contained in the report of the *Committee of Advisors on Government Structure* (popularly referred to as the Nettleford Report).

In this report, the community is targeted as a partner (in a tripartite arrangement) in the redefined structure of government. The specific role identified for the community is that of an 'effective partner in the participating structure . . . committed to self-reliance in the building, shaping, and maintenance of social institutions necessary for stable peaceful and sound community life with or without direct government intervention (central or local) or the private sector' (*Report by Committee of Advisors on Government Structure*).

The committee correctly notes that 'effective community organizations cannot be effectively built. They have to be generated from within' (p.37) Experience has shown that there are certain preconditions for the internal generation of community activity. This assumes a participatory mode. However, community residents beset by multiple, apparently intractable problems do not view participation as a value in and of itself. It must lead to some specific problem solving.

Secondly, the sustainability of these organizations can only be achieved if they can be successfully led through a life-cycle which includes several peaks and troughs of participation by members, goal achievement, leadership crises, etc. To achieve this, human and material resources for leadership development, consensus building and lobbying, for example, have to be made available. Policy options that stimulate collective efforts must be embraced.

In real terms,the rhetoric of a third partner needs to be supported by appropriate institution-building activity. State sponsored community organizations merely breed dependence and tribalism. However, there are specific policy actions which are a *sine qua non* of an effective community partner.

1. The state needs to facilitate the evolution of a clear policy around the role of community organizations in decision making. For example, the private sector has been established as a *de facto* partner in national development. As partners they are consulted on nearly all matters. A similar approach needs to be adopted to the third partner, namely, the community.
2. Consistent with its role of strengthening civil society in the transitional period, government must support its agencies responsible for community mobilization and education. The consultative process with the third partner becomes cumbersome if the latter does not have coherent institutional form. This is not a spontaneous process. It needs facilitation, massaging, and general activities consistent with institutional building.

The existing government agencies, such as the SDC, are treated with low priority both in terms of human resource and budgetary allocations. Consequently, they have no capacity to deliver service. Core government agencies which have responsibility for human and maternal resources must change their own attitudes to these institution if the rhetoric of community partnership is not to be merely that community organisations must be the vehicles for achieving this partnership.

To effectively achieve these objectives, the organizations must be organically involved in enhancing the quality of life and in controlling community resources. What is the methodology for achieving this?:

(1) each community must be assisted in developing a plan with targets;
(2) resource requirement for attaining these targets must be itemized and possible sources identified;

(3) details of implementation must be formulated.Out of this process must be gleaned the specific areas of collaboration between the public sector and the community, on the one hand, and the private sector and the community, on the other. Out of this collaborative action we must then design real areas of activity.

For example, we must begin to dispel the myth of rural communities as closed, isolated, self-contained and homogenous geographical and social entities. One of the challenges to which we must direct our efforts is the methodology for placing these communities on a sound economic footing, capable of competitiveness, producing quality products based on the demands of the marketplace. As such then, the plans for rural communities must address issues of land reform, agricultural improvement, provision of development capital, and identification of markets. The realization of social development is consistent with identifying the boundaries of activities, the areas of overlap, and the relative weight of each sector.

In both urban and rural communities, preventive education and service delivery at the 'grassroots' can be designed for community initiative. Communities must be involved in introducing and enforcing certain basic rules of social hygiene.It is important for us to recognize that the mobilization of communities in rural areas cannot be to the exclusion of those in urban areas. Community building is not a zero sum game. Both geographical areas have to be given equal priority.

Economic development and empowerment is an indispensable component of social development. Historically, there must have been some discrediting of self-reliance as an approach to economic development. This is definitely an area for further experimentation and redefinition. Clearly, autonomous development is *not* a possibility in the contemporary world. What must become the object of social learning is the methodology of marrying community human and material resources with appropriate technology and dynamic markets to achieve viable enterprises.

While we recognize that no social experiment can be fully replicated, we must explore models and *systematically* document them.

In all of this, the state has a role in fostering a policy environment which is consistent with shifting certain power relations and guaranteeing more equitable relationships.

Critical to this must be the political decision to move the item of community development from being last on every agenda to assuming a more prominent position. The real value of community development is the building of human infrastructure. This is the only method of making the development process irreversible.

CHAPTER 9

Gender Considerations in Policy Design

Beverly Anderson-Manley

No developing country can afford to waste the productive energy of its female population. The challenge facing Ministries and Bureaux for Women's Affairs is to ensure than an awareness of gender implications permeates the highest levels of policy making. (The Commonwealth Secretariat - 1987).

Gender Considerations in Policy Design: the Jamaican Bureaucratic State

Sexism, the domination and subordination of women, is a universal phenomenon with tragic consequences for women and men, and for national development potential.

Increasingly, development literature reveals the link between gender bias and global poverty. A recent report of the International Labour Organisation (ILO) (*Washington Post*, 13 September 1992) — research undertaken by Worldwatch, a Washington based independent, nonprofit research group that studies a variety of global problems — notes, *inter alia*, that:

- women, not men are the family breadwinners in most of the world;
- sex discrimination against women is a major cause of poverty;
- women worldwide still earn less than men for similar occupations;

- gender bias is an enormous stumbling block on the road to a sustainable economy;
- in countries with 3 billion of the world's estimated 5.5 billion people, women are the primary earners for their families and are therefore playing a key economic role but because they are discriminated against in wages, land ownership, and lending, they are inhibited from contributing to their nation's economies;
- bias against women is the single most important cause of rapid population growth; 'where women have little access to productive resources and little control over family income, they depend on children for social status and economy security';
- even though overpopulation is a major problem for third world countries, governments need to focus more on increasing the productivity of women, rather than on simply reducing fertility; *National statistics often overlook women's work. Government needs to recognise women's work as a valuable economic asset and invest in women accordingly*;
- sex bias exists in every country often compounded by discrimination based on class, caste, or race, but it is most pervasive in the poorest areas of Africa, Asia, and Latin America and ranges from exclusion of women from development programmes to 'systemic violence against females'.

From the global to the national: What is the situation here in Jamaica?

Ten per cent of Jamaican women can be considered as successful: this includes teachers and nurses. Of this 10 per cent, therefore, approximately five per cent include women in the top echelons of the public and private sectors. This figure obscures the plight of the remaining 90 per cent of Jamaican women, who together with the five per cent of women who are nurses and teachers are employed in traditional female-oriented jobs (i.e. stereotypical female roles).

Another factor that obscures the reality of the majority of Jamaican women is that while female labour force participation is reported to be one of the highest in the world, the majority of these women are relegated to low paying, services oriented jobs. In addition, there is relatively little movement taking place in the sexual division of labour.

Yet another factor that obscures the reality is that approximately one half of households nationwide are headed by women, and within the 'urban' area of St. Catherine, it is estimated that they head 50 per cent of households. It can be argued then that Jamaica is a matriarchal society. The conclusion is often drawn that this translates to power for Jamaica women. More often than not, these women are heading situations of utter poverty within the household which, in turn, derives from their marginal position in the labour force and translates into their further powerlessness in the wider society.

And now we come to the wider society; let us examine the following: there are four elected female members of Parliament in a House of 60 members; four appointed Senators in a Senate of 21 members; at the local level there are 20 women out of a total of 189 councillors; no political party has ever been able to appoint more than one female member to its Cabinet and, even when there is a female member in the Cabinet, typically, she is appointed to the social service sector; both political parties are headed by men although it is well known that it is the women who do the majority of the party's work, including operating constituencies for male MP's. One of the four vice-presidents of the ruling People's National Party (PNP) is a woman and one of the four deputy leaders in the Opposition Jamaica Labour Party (JLP) is a woman.

Let me hasten to say that I am by no means idealizing women. Research has shown that having a token woman in a position of power does not necessarily take us further on the road to gender equity. But, surely, it is necessary for us to ask ourselves at what cost do we continue to exclude the voices of women from national decision making?

So, perhaps a major challenge to policy makers in their strategic planning for the twenty-first century is how to develop an understanding of gender discrimination; its negative impact on women and men and on our development potential. This is work for both women and men who are concerned about the future of our county. This cannot be women's work only: the discussion is not about women's issues. We are talking about development priorities. At the policy level we can no longer afford the luxury of seeing women as welfare recipients. Instead, both genders must be regarded as valuable resources and agents of social and economic change.

But let us not fool ourselves that this will be an easy accomplishment. For example, in the case of Jamaica, a national Policy Statement on Women was adopted by Cabinet in 1987. The Policy Statement makes it clear that it is the permanent Secretaries who have the mandate to implement the policy. As noted in one of the Bureau of Women's Affairs documents, it has become one of the key challenges of the Bureau to get the Permanent Secretaries to take on this critical role. Following on the creation of the National Policy Statement on Women, a Plan of Action was developed on a ministry-specific basis.

Attempts to get the policy implemented have resulted in a better understanding of the complexity of gender issues; the embedded nature of resistance to change (attitudinal; structure and systemic); the nature of the bureaucrats (both women and men) who 'man' the state; the nature of the state itself; and the role that an active and vibrant women's organisation (outside the state) must play — acting as a pressure/lobby group on the state bureaucrats to get policy implemented.

All of this is not to deny three critical points made by Maxine Henry-Wilson: (1) the vagueness of the language in the policy document, and its failure to identify specifics; (2) the absence of promotional and lobbying machinery to ensure that inputs on behalf of women assume a programmatic format; (3) the document displays a poor understanding of the realities of the policy process and the methods by which access is gained and a public policy demand is moved from the policy agenda stage to actually become a programme.

In addition, since the Policy document was adopted by Cabinet in 1987, there have been significant changes in the context in which policy commitments to equality are to be realized.

So, the policy document has existed since 1987 and has in fact been adopted by successive governments. But how many policy makers or planners know of its existence? How many have attempted to use it as a tool in policy planning or implementation? How many even think that gender is a relevant issue in development policy?

One of the lessons we have learned in the Bureau is the scope of the task, the slow pace of change, the wide variation in baseline perspectives and data and, hence, the important contribution that review of the five years of experience (since the adoption of the Policy Statement in 1987) can make to policy implementation. This review has led us to the creation of an instrument which can assist development planners in all ministries to analyse the impact of gender in development planning.

The Bureau sees the provision of relevant tools for gathering gender specific data as a critical part of its responsibility. This baseline is an objective starting point for planning and monitoring policy implementation through to the year 2000 and beyond. The gender monitoring checklist (GMC) is proposed as an example of such an instrument. This instrument is being proposed within the perspective of other initiatives whose implementation has been characterized by: refusal within the government service to take the policy statement seriously or to even acknowledge that it exists, and difficulty in translating it into meaningful measures. In summary, five years of experience has demonstrated that the present policy statement has been ignored and is difficult for planners and decisions makers to use.

Increasingly, in attempting to play its part from its marginalized position within the bureaucracy (marginalized in terms of staff classification, funding, location), the Bureau is aware that in order to get policy makers, not only to listen but to act, it is necessary, apart from anything else, to have some political compulsion behind women's demands. In keeping with this , staff at the Burean should have classification at the highest levels possiable.

The struggle of the Bureau of Women's Affairs to be accepted as a legitimate and valid agency of the Jamaican government, is not unique to Jamaica but reflects the experience of national machineries worldwide. These national machineries have not only had to cope with external resistance to change in the status of women, but they have had to confront internal confusion and lack of clarity regarding conceptual approaches and appropriate methodologies for improving their status.

As stated before, this is an issue for humanity and its complexity, given the impact at the individual/interpersonal, group level, and institutional and societal levels, demands nothing less but that both genders accept shared responsibility for the process of resolution.

An immediately applicable lesson is that the complexity of gender issues requires an objectivety that has not to date been possible. Gender relations are saturated with personal opinions and emotions; a legacy of traditional socialized attitudes and stereotypes. These constitute potential resources and obstacles. The GMC is proposed as the instrument through which objective determinations of the current situation can be made across all relevant bodies in the public sector.

Over the course of the year 1992/1993,it is hoped that use of the GMC will establish the foundation on which specific action and work plans can be translated into real measures for change. Within a generally consultative approach, the GMC will be adapted and revised in light of experience and use. The result will be a monitoring instrument that bridges the general policy statement with operational strategies and plans. In each ministry, the Bureau of Women's Affairs will be targeting senior policy makers who can constitute a functioning implementation core to ensure the construction of bridges between policy and work-place practice.

The proposal for introducing, supporting, and coordinating the GMC through the initial year of establishing a baseline on policy implementation, is being developed for consideration by this group and by the Inter-Ministry Committee (as representatives of permanent secretaries), and for the Policy Review Unit (PRU) in the Office of the Prime Minister — the former as the group mandated by the Cabinet to implement the policy statement, and the latter as the unit with responsibility for monitoring implementation of all government policy.

The Bureau hopes to work with this senior reference group on policy implementation to (a) coordinate the establishment of meaningful baseline through use of the GMC and (b) stimulate government to use these data to decide priorities regarding policy commitments to gender equity.

Coordinated test use of this type of instrument across the government must be supported at senior levels (at level of the Cabinet and the permanent secretaries) and seen by all shareholders to be a legitimate part of policy planning and implementation; not the isolated action of a marginalised function associated narrowly with 'women'. This can only be done from a function with multisectoral responsibilities, which is why the proposal for a year's test use of the GMC is being made to the PRU. With a better understanding of how gender is influencing specific situations across all ministries and government agencies, meaningful and feasible plans can be coordinated into long-term strategies and short-term work plans. Without those baseline data and the insights they can yield, the Bureau's assessment is that the National Policy Statement on Women will remain marginal and largely ignored to the detriment of development policies and the country as a whole.

Finally, it is important to note that the question of integrating gender considerations into governmental policies and programmes is a complex one throughout the world. In order to integrate women's concerns in development planning, policy makers and planners need to consider the actual and potential role of women in all sectors and the impact of all policies, plans, and programmes on them. 'Mainstreaming' requires the rationalization of resources allocation in all policies and programmes so as to benefit women equitably. In that effort, women's concerns should not be marginalized as the responsibility of only one government agency and only one gender.

However, given the traditionally perpetrated discrimination against women, it may be necessary to supplement such mainstreaming with the adoption of affirmative policies and special programmes for alleviating certain circumstances facing women as supplementary actions.

And what of a new vision for the future?

As Eva Rathgeber notes, this vision: must be based on the more coherent articulation of what we already know: Our task during the 1990s as women and men must be to bring our experience, knowledge and values into the mainstream of global decision making. We must be both researchers and activities and we must point in the direction of a more equitable sharing of the world's dwindling resources. It is a daunting challenge for the twenty-first century. But it is one that must be faced.

Bureau Of Women's Affairs Gender Monitoring Checklist

Checklist Categories

1. BASELINE DATA
2. POLICY LINKS
3. CONSULTATION
4. EQUITY ACTIONS
5. CONTEXT

Checklist Questions

1. BASELINE DATA
   Is sex-disaggregated baseline data systematically collected and used in decision making?
2. POLICY LINKS
   Are links made between existing policy and the work done?
3. CONSULTATION
   Are men and women in the workplace identifying and addressing gender issues that are important to them?
4. EQUITY ACTIONS
   Are actions taken to address gender issues, systemic discrimination and constraints to achieving gender equity?

5. CONTEXT
Are the unique circumstances and relationships specific to the workplace factored into measures for gender equity?

Checklist Benchmarks

1. BASELINE DATA
Is sex disaggregated baseline data systematically collected and used in decision making?
0 sex-disaggregated data is not collected
1 Some sex-disaggregated data is collected but not used in decision making
2 Sex-disaggregated data is collected in an ongoing, organised way, and used in decision making

2. POLICY LINKS
Are links made between existing policy — The National Policy Statement on Women and the international policy commitments made by the Government of Jamaica Convention on the Elimination of All Forms of Discrimination Against Women, and Forward Looking Strategies for the Advancement of women to the year 2000?
0 No links are made between work and policy commitments
1 Some connections are made between work and policy, but the policy does not guide and inform the work
2 Existing policy influences and informs decision and work

3. CONSULTATION
Are men and women in the workplace identifying and addressing gender issues that are important to them?
0 No mechanism or opportunities for consultation on gender issues exist
1 Consultation on gender issues occurs but is not integrated into ongoing functions and the input is not incorporated into decision making
2 Consultation on gender issues is integrated into processes and input is incorporated into decision making

4. EQUITY ACTION
Is action taken to address gender issues, systemic discrimination and constraints to achieving gender equity?
0 No action is taken and no plans exist to take action on gender equity
1   Some action has been taken but this is not part of a co-co-ordinated plan and accountability for follow-through is weak

    2 Action to eliminate discrimination and achieve gender equity are underway as part of a coordinated and phased strategy

5. CONTEXT

Are unique circumstances and relationships specific to the workplace factored into measures for gender equity?

    0 No workplace factors influencing gender equity have been identified or considered in decision making

    1 Some consideration is given to workplace factors but these are not yet integrated into a strategy for change

    2 Workplace factors influencing gender equity are incorporated into a workplace-specific strategy

Checklist Format

	Benchmark Ranking at (date:)	Follow-up at (date:)	Comments
1. Baseline data			
2. Policy Links			
3. Consultation			
4. Equity Actions			
Context			

The Issues

1. BASELINE DATA. Adequate baseline data on men's and women's situations, experiences and needs is either not collected, or if it is collected, it is not used in decision making. Decisions that have a different impact on women than on men continue to be made on a combined basis of socialisation and traditional stereotypes and personal opinion, rather than on actual data.

2. POLICY LINKS. Existing policy commitments are not well know and are not being followed. When decision makers and workers are familiar with government policy, they have found it to be in a form that is difficult to implement or operationalize.

3. CONSULTATION. Employees are seldom, if ever involved in determining whether or what specific discriminatory and equity issues exist in a workplace, or in meaningful and serious dialogue about change.

4. EQUITY ACTIONS.   When sex or gender inequities exist they are often not questioned or challenged, and are accepted by both men and women as 'the way things are.'

5. CONTEXT.   Initiatives to implement policy, for example through the Inter-Ministry Committee in Implementation of the National Policy Statement on Women, have only marginally been able to accommodate the unique and specific circumstances of gender relations in each workplace.

Bibliography

1. Maroney and Luxton- Feminism and Political Economy
2. Jamaica in Independence- Essays on the Early Years (Article on The Status of the Jamaican Woman- Maxine Henry-Wilson)
3. Guidlines for Integrating Women's Concerns into Development Planning in Asia and the Pacific (United Nations Document)
4. Rathgeber- Integrating Gender Into Development: Research and Action Agendas for the 1990's.
5. Documents- Bureau of Women's Affairs:
   a) National Policy Statement on Women (1987)
   b) Gender Monitoring Check-list (1991)

PART III

The Role of Education and Technology in Development

CHAPTER 10

Technology:
Creating Competitive Advantages in Production

Arnold Ventura

The Technological Revolution

The modern global economy is driven by the creative application of technology. Indeed, the contribution of scientific understanding to technological progress has evolved to such a level that technology has replaced nature as the limiting factor in production. The combination of science with technology has been able, during recent decades, to reduce labour costs by 98 per cent, capital costs by 80 per cent and energy costs by some 50 per cent.

Knowledge and ideas are clearly now more valuable than capital, land, or labour. Vision, logic, inventiveness, and innovativeness are the rivets of present civilization, allowing systems of production, service, comfort, relaxation, power, and gainful occupation, to be built on an unprecedented scale. Man now has more freedom and control over his destiny than ever before.

Scientific technologies have had, not only enormous impact in reducing the burden of physical work and improving social welfare, but they have begun to transform life itself and direct the pace and result of evolution. Some of these technologies have improved the generation, storage, processing, retrieval, and dissemination of information to such an extent that most institutions in all societies are being affected. Economic, political, cultural, trade, and diplomatic relation-ships are being profoundly altered and our very perception of our-selves and our place in the universe is being revised and extended by the application of modern techniques. During the last half of this century, our material options have been expanded beyond the imagi-nation of earlier generations because of technological progress in agriculture, industry, and health care.

Limits of Technology

With all of the dazzling progress of technology, it must be remem-bered that both the practice of science and its influence on the creation of technologies are social processes and, as such, are subject to the values and prevailing attitudes of society. As a matter of fact, technological changes will not automatically have desired effects with-out complementary social contributions. For technology to take root and grow, there must be a conducive social, political, educational, cultural, and management environment, as has occurred in the newly industrialized societies. The march of science and technology can exert either a positive or negative effect on economies. The ultimate influence will depend on the level of literacy and the nature and extent of technical absorptive capacity in a society. Development limitations in many countries, therefore, are not often due to lack of technologies, but rather to failures in social organization and fixity of purpose to make use of existing solutions. Science cannot be fully beneficial without a good measure of consensus on goals and wide social support for these goals. The wider the consensus and deeper the support, the easier it is for science and technology to make positive national contri-butions.

Absolute poverty, protectionism in the developed countries, trans-fer of capital from the poor to the rich countries, squandering of local savings on speculative financing, deterioration of the terms of trade, continuous decline in real prices for primary exports, increase in the cost of energy and repatriation of foreign investment, will not be reversed merely by producing more with modern technology. What is required is the will to make serious structural and moral changes which will end widening disparities at the local and international levels. Technology is only an instrument which has the flexibility to take on a host of jobs. Although it can influence the job selected, it cannot dictate the ethics, morality, or values of society which will ultimately determine the application of technology. And, lastly, many of today's environmental problems are due to conventional technologies which were designed without due consideration being given to their impact on the environment.

This paper will examine the major ways in which technology can make a competitive difference in Jamaica and will, of necessity, review the modifications required for Jamaica to join the technological revolution. It introduces new approaches to production and industrialization which have been successful elsewhere in opening up novel options for harnessing technology for competitive advantages.

New Ways to Industrialize

Flexible Specialization

The old mass production methods based on the large scale, rigid, uniform manufacturing, such as the Fordist method of producing cars, are rapidly proving to be less competitive than integrated systems and collective efficiency networks, as is the case with the Japanese system of automobile manufacturing (Ohno, 1988). These networks are characterized by small, dynamic, flexible production units within a continuous operation scheme, linked to consumer demands and markets, which enable them to respond with a variety of high quality goods at relatively low costs. The flexibility of this new manufacturing process is based on multipurpose machinery which allows the production of small batches with the use of reprogrammable equipment.

The new techno-economic paradigm is characterized by manufacturing flexibility and a strong tendency toward knowledge. It is less material and energy intensive. It also depends on economies of scope rather than those of scale and on organisational efficiency based on systematization rather than automation. Management therefore requires objective information rather than intuition or subjective certainty (Perez, 1983, pp. 357-75).

In these circumstances, radical innovations, leading to leaps in technological sophistication, are not necessarily the key to competitiveness. Instead, incremental innovations combined with new organisational forms, enlightened human resource management, and strategic planning at the plant and corporate levels, have proved to be more rewarding. In other words, modern sophisticated technological advancements do not replace, but rather depend on a qualified, well trained and motivated labour force led by informed and confident managers.

It is not cheap labour, but rather small, continuous, technological advances based on imagination, motivation, and technical and organisational creativity, that represent competitive advantage in this new form of production (UNESCO, 1992). So improvements in basic skills on the shop floor, assertive national scientific research, and dedicated experimental development and engineering capability become paramount.

For improved technologies to have their maximum effect, primary emphasis has to be placed on the following: (1) systematic integration of the whole manufacturing process; (2) improvement of the material and component supply systems; (3) the reduction of inventories by just-in-time organization; (4) changes in work processes to facilitate new design in manufacturing; (5) better quality control procedures; (6) economies of scope and not only of scale; (7) reduction of energy and raw material consumption; (8) improvement of the training of the labour force and the treatment of labour as a resource rather than a cost item.

Relevance to Jamaica

These technological approaches and modes of organization of production provide new opportunities for small, underdevelopedcountries. Past constraints to development, such as access to wide markets and heavy investment in capital goods, can now be overcome by servicing niche markets (eg. ethnic and health conscious markets), where the introduction of scientific technologies require less capital investments. Small and medium sized industries can, through sectoral aggregation by way of co-operatives or consortia, acquire the necessary equipment, components, and services necessary to become proficient at flexible specialisation production, as exemplified by the "Third Italy" described by Best (Best, 1990). The basic idea is to achieve collective efficiency in order to respond to changes in the market. Here, shop floor incremental innovations, sharpened by local research and experimental development efforts, can significantly increase economic performance.

Obviously, this kind of restructuring of industry cannot be left to individual initiatives or market forces alone. Government has to play a vital initiating, coordinating, and facilitating role (Porter, 1990, pp.

73-93). For small Caribbean countries, regional integration and close international co-operation between developing countries will, with time, also prove to be necessary.

How Technology Creates Competitive Advantages

The mere availability of technology is not a sufficient condition for improving economic performance and expanding development opportunities because, as indicated before, obstacles to development are more of a socio-political rather than of a strictly technical nature. This, however, should not minimize the key importance of technology in making significant improvements in productivity at all levels of the society. Technical change and innovation cannot have beneficial effects if culturally and politically a society is not prepared to absorb and incorporate them into their productive processes. Jamaica's proximity to the US means that it is continually exposed to the largest and one of the most technologically sophisticated markets in the world, yet its level of technological awareness and application remain disproportionately low.

Although science and technology are undeniably central driving forces of socio-economic change, low production and other social problems, more than likely, will reflect ideological and contextual interests, historical and cultural conditions, and the positions and outlook of individuals concerned. These conditions and interests will not be inspired by technological sensitivity without a reasonable understanding of technological issues. Consequently, an appreciation of technology's importance to production and of the changes in society and at the firm level which are required to make technology maximally effective, becomes crucial. In Jamaica, social innovations are therefore as important, and in some ways more important, than technical innovations for improved productive efficiency (Ventura, 1992).

Here, the media has a central role to play by selecting, in conjunction with the science and technology establishment, important themes for dissemination. The impact of these efforts must be monitored to ensure that the messages are effective.

Endogenous science and technological capabilities will, without a doubt, increase the recognition and exploitation of production choices and opportunities. But this will not happen just by accident. Science and technology must be fully recognized, by all our leaders in the public and private sectors, as a strategic duo of immense importance. Logically then, science and technology will have to be carefully crafted, exploited, and managed before the full effects of these factors can be felt (as happened in the Newly Industrializing Countries of Southeast Asia (NICs), where there were concerted science and technology efforts undertaken by the public and private sectors working in unison). If this is effectively done, Jamaica will be launched unto a new economic growth trajectory. A sense of common purpose, crafted by close working relationships between the public and private sectors, will assure agreed priorities for technical interventions. This will require a serious mobilization of government effort to reach big and small entrepreneurs, as well as consumers, who, by their shopping habits, can influence the search for technological excellence.

Jamaica's national competitiveness will be vastly improved by a dynamic science and technology infrastructure to help entrepreneurs identify and respond to needs in the market place, especially in areas of national priority, such as agriculture, agro-industries, and services. Although common sense can still play a useful role in increasing productivity and fashioning new products and processes, the science content of production is now so high that the range of contributions from the scientifically uninitiated is being significantly reduced.

Jamaica's science and technology management has been improved by the specific introduction of policy and plans, high level cabinet monitoring, the introduction of a broad-based transectoral commission and smoother ministerial working relationships, with the installation of an interagency committee on science and technology. Nevertheless, far more local resources have to be injected into research and experimental development for these changes to have meaningful and sustained effects.

In this connection, it must be remembered that Jamaica is still short of highly skilled, science-minded technicians who are the foundation of production. At the present stage of its development, emphasis should therefore be placed on training a battery of these technical experts in areas such as capital goods production, transportation, fermentation, repair, maintenance and quality control.

With Jamaica's economic hopes riding high on agriculture and agro-industrial endeavours, research and experimental development in these areas must be substantially improved to stem the decline in agricultural productivity (as exemplified by bananas and yams), and enhance competitiveness (as is the case with citrus and pimento). Earnings from primary commodity agricultural exports have been eroded by a reduction in market share and fall in prices. More value must therefore be added to these exports as we assertively diversify our agricultural sales. It is abundantly clear, then, that Jamaica must make better use of it's biomass potential to produce food, fodder, feed, and fuels.

International competitiveness will not be measured by price alone. Increasingly, products which are derived from environmentally friendly techniques will be prized in sophisticated markets: so agricultural productivity, which rests on the application of inorganic fertilizers and a range of toxic herbicides and pesticides, is rapidly losing favour. In the meantime, biotechnology has opened up ways to adapt plants to varied environments and reduce the need for environmentally damaging chemicals. Jamaica is well advised to employ such production and explore the related niches for export.

National technological capabilities are most effectively advanced by strategic technological management; and this will depend on a partnership of action between government and the private sector. This partnership will do much to gain a consensus for action, as it improves the technological awareness of both sides. The more technologically alert the entire society becomes, the better we will be at gaining competitive advantages and the more attractive our productive machinery will be to investors.

Furthermore, one of the chief considerations in today's technological world for attracting foreign investment is the availability of a trainable, or well trained and flexible, technical work force.

Jamaica's foreign service must become an integral part of the machinery to attract investments, especially technological investments, and to supply a stream of relevant foreign technical knowledge. These initiatives will be far more effective if our missions abroad have personnel with more than just superficial scientific and technological leanings.

Although some productivity gains can be made by a more effective utilization of resources deploying old methods, without fundamental improvements in equipment and techniques in many productive areas, there will be few significant competitive advancements. Investments in scientific and technological infrastructural development, including education and training, will help reduce excessive liquidity in Jamaica's financial corps and will provide profitable ways to use national savings. By so doing, technological development will act as a channel for creative investments, and will simultaneously have a direct beneficial bearing on productivity and profitability.

Government has a vital role to play to ensure that savings and other forms of capital have a more pronounced impact on production and productivity. This can conveniently be achieved if incentives packages are prepared to induce investments to innovative applications and targeted technical training. This will also improve the level of local invention and innovation which must occur if our limited resources are to make a significant impact on Jamaica's welfare. Furthermore, more self-employment and improvement in the contributions of the science and technology community to satisfy the demands of the private sector can be anticipated.

The pace of technological innovation is spawning new businesses, transforming old ones, and forcing competition based on novelty and quality. Since this trend is becoming progressively globalized, small countries like Jamaica have no option but to strike alliances between government and the private sector in order to formulate new national technological investment strategies to promote innovation (Ventura, 1992), especially in areas of identified emphasis, such as agro-processing, information technologies, energy, and tourism. Essentially, the private sector has to become more assertive in commercialising existing research results and adopting good ideas to meet specific business needs. Collaborative research between government and companies, and among the companies themselves, will do much to increase innovation and local competitive advantage.

For too long has economic policy been divorced from technological policy. To bridge this gap, Jamaica must promulgate an industrial policy which takes due cognizance of the fact that competitiveness will depend on technological knowledge and its resourceful application. In this way, the nation can set a creative plan for research to achieve clear development goals.

Jamaica's openness makes it imperative that all our social and industrial institutions be provided strong technical underpinnings. This will require the upgrading and better management of technical and research institutions which must be assessed on their ability to enhance local service and production.

Competitive advantage will increasingly reside in the ability to identify and use global information. Successful enterprises, and countries for that matter, will not necessarily be those which can create new technologies. Rather, success will be founded on the ability to absorb new knowledge to improve the management, production, packaging, and marketing of products and services. This will require organizational capacity to spot promising new technologies wherever they may exist, and quickly incorporate them into new products and processes. Individual firms will find it difficult to mount, on their own, complete technological information/intelligence systems, so government has to assist through its various institutions abroad. Government's move to establish functional contacts with expatriate Jamaican professionals to help ease our technical manpower shortages is of great relevance in this regard.

Needless to say, for enterprises to benefit from this type of network, they will have to possess technological investment strategies, based on knowledge of their needs, and a full grasp of their areas of business and the capabilities of their competitors.

Remaining abreast of technological options and marketing demands is a vital factor in being competitive. The present wave of new information and telecommunications technologies allows productive entities to keep up with the knowledge industry. Competitive information outreach and electronic point of scale marketing are now possible because of a worldwide telecommunications network.

Apart from this, countries with up-to-date telecommunication infrastructure and trained personnel are poised to enter the rapidly expanding information processing and software development business. Needless to say, our tourist trade will ultimately depend on the ability of prospective clients abroad to scan timely information on the various properties and their attractions.

Demand articulation and organization response are as important as the specific features of advanced technologies. Government will have to help firms to develop this organizational capability to make use of worldwide technological information. In the age of scientific technologies, this means at least a minimum level of local research and experimental development expertise in areas of forefront and appropriate conventional technologies.

Forms of global competition are being played out by technological fusion, which is the ingenious combination of existing technologies or engineering and science disciplines, to form new hybrid technologies which allow greater efficiency, the production of new products and the provision of new services (eg. opto-electronics, a cross between electronics and optics; and mechatronics, combinations of electronics and mechanical technologies). This new strategy of technological fusion is displacing established technologies in industry. Jamaica should therefore be aware of these developments in order to protect existing production, and to use these methods where possible for new businesses.

Technological fusion brings research and experimental development to a new dimension, where manufacturing enterprises shift from being merely places of production to places for deep reflection and innovation. This is quite prudent, considering that the survival of enterprises will increasingly depend on meeting evolving market demands. A system for facilitating change must therefore be installed, and this system will depend on research and experimental development to stimulate new internally derived developments, as it makes use of innovations from the outside.

Conclusion

It is obvious that technology is a powerful tool for increased production and productivity, but it has limitations in that it requires fertile and receptive ground in order for it to blossom. Technology, if left strictly to market forces, will concentrate wealth and frustrate, rather than aid, true development. If the majority is left in increasing poverty; if workers are faced with a continuous decline in real wages and incomes occasioning dwindling access to affordable food and social services, the conditions for the widespread embrace and skillful application of technological knowledge will not develop. Without an astute, dynamic work-force committed to innovation and efficiency, Jamaica will not become an influential player in the new paradigm of world competition.

Jamaica's comparative advantages rest on the great diversity of its bio-resources and the natural quality of its fruits, fiber, herbs, spices, and flavours. These are relatively untapped and may still be marketed as "organic"; that is, free of contamination with agricultural chemicals. Products created with these raw materials will fetch high prices, not only in ethnic markets abroad, but in the growing health food niches as well. Jamaica clearly cannot compete on the basis of quantities of export. More likely this can be done by high quality products for the high end of markets.

References

Best, M., *The New Competition Institution of Restructuring, Boston: Harvard University Press, 1990.*

Hoffman, K. and Girvan, N., *Managing International Technology Transfer: A Strategic Approach for Developing Countries,* Ottawa: IDRC, 1990.

Ohno, T., *Toyota Production System: Beyond Large-scale Production*, Cambridge Massachusetts: Productivity Press, 1988.

Perez, C., "Structural Change and the Assimilation of New Technologies in the Economic and Social System". *Future*, 15 (4), pp. 357-75, 1983.

Porter, M.E., The Competitive Advantage of Nations. *Harvard Business Review*, March-April 1990, 2, pp.73-93.

Rosenberg, N., *Perspectives on Technology*, Cambridge: Cambridge University Press, 1976.

UNESCO, *Science and Technology in Developing Countries: Strategies for the 1990s*, Paris, 1992.

Ventura, A.K., *The Role of Innovations and Inventions in Building Endogenous Technology Capacity*, New York: ECOSOC/UNDP, 1992.

Ventura, A.K., *Elements of Innovation and Technological Development in Jamaica*, Kingston, Jamaica: UNESCO, 1992.

CHAPTER 11

A Strategic Approach to Technology

Norman Girvan

The main arguments of this paper are threefold. First, Jamaica faces the strategic necessity of shifting from an economy which is driven by the export of natural resource-based goods and services to one that is increasingly human-resource and technology-driven. Second, an active technology strategy is one of the elements in this shift. And third, that such a strategy requires an appropriate partnership between the state and producing enterprises.

The Role of the State in Fostering Innovation

Technical change is estimated to have been responsible for anywhere between 50 and 70 per cent of the economic growth of different OECD countries over the 70-year period ending in 1960 (Solow 1957, Dennison 1974). In Japan 1953-1971, technical change was the source of over 20 per cent of national income growth (Peck and Otto 1981). Similarly, innovative activity has been shown to be a major factor underlying export performance. Studies carried out by the Science Policy Research Unit (SPRU) of the University of Sussex found that investments in R&D, and patenting behaviour were strongly correlated with international market share across 40 industrial sectors for the main OECD countries (Pavitt 1979, 1980).

The relationship at the national level in many respects mirrors firm-level activity and performance. For example, innovating firms played a crucial role in the dynamic evolution of the chemicals and synthetic materials industry in Germany, Switzerland and the United States. An instructive case is I.G.Farben, the German chemical firm, whose strong and sustained R&D effort undergirded German pre-World War II industrial leadership in the synthetic chemicals industry, and was one of the bases of German industrial resurgence post-World War II (Freeman, 1974).

Other research has pointed to the important contribution of incremental technical change, or so-called 'minor' innovations, to increased factor productivity at the firm level (Hoffman 1990, 12). Whereas the initial focus of this stream was on the effects of moving up the 'learning curve' as a function of repetition over time, more recent research has shown that incremental technical change is enhanced where management consciously organizes the firm to maximize learning and utilize its results, engaging technical staff and production workers in a cooperative enterprise to that end.

In Europe and the US, firm-level innovations have always counted on a variety of supports from the state. While the specific kinds and degrees of state support have varied in place and time, two common factors stand out. One is the dominant role of the state in educating and training the labour force. This guaranteed a steadily-growing supply of continually skill-upgraded manpower to the firms and industries with high rates of innovative activity. Secondly, a wide range of direct and indirect subsidies were provided to innovating firms. The most important of these were subsidies to R&D, and guaranteed markets through military procurement for new-technology products.

In the 'late industrializers'—Japan and the Southeast Asian Newly Industrializing Countries (NICs)—the role of the state in fostering technological capabilities became more conscious and systematic. During the American occupation immediately following World War II, US advisers recommended that Japan pursue a policy of labour-intensive industrialization in accordance with its presumed international comparative advantage as a densely populated country with a scarcity of industrial raw materials and indigenous energy resources. (This was very similar to the policy recommended for the West Indies by Arthur Lewis.) Japanese technocrats eventually rejected this, and opted for a policy of heavy industrialization patterned on the industrial profile of those countries which had defeated them. Foreign investment was restricted, and the domestic market protected, in order to nurture the growth of large national conglomerate firms in basic industries like petrochemicals. The focus, at least for the first two decades of industrial expansion, was on the successful implantation of foreign technology. To this end, the terms and conditions of technology agreements were regulated by the state in order to allow/induce national firms to assimilate and adapt foreign technology, and to engage in R&D. The role of the powerful Ministry of Trade and Industry—MITI—and its relationship with Japanese industry, became the symbol of the close state-private sector partnership that underlay Japan's impressive postwar economic performance.

Japan became a model for the industrialization policy of the Southeast Asian NICs. The model was not followed in every detail; it was, if anything, adapted to the circumstances of different countries—as every successful use of a model requires. Korea, with its large domestic market and national conglomerates, came closest to emulating the precise features of the Japanese model. Taiwan, Hong Kong and Singapore were much more export-oriented from the outset. Singapore has relied heavily on direct foreign investment. What has been common to the policies of most of these countries, especially since the early 1970s, is a strategy of *targeted industrial development* whose formulation is led by the state and whose implementation is the joint responsibility of the state and the private sector. Supporting the development of technological capabilities in key industries and activities has been an important element of this strategy. According to Boirus and Simon:

As Japanese producers apply their increasing mastery of high technoogy to the production of ever more sophisticated goods and services, the NICs adjust to their loss to less developed Asian economies of relative labour cost advantage by moving into the production of goods with increasing technological content....All of the major Asian economies are following a model of technologically driven development perfected by Japan, which places aggressive industrial policy at the service of business technological development ...(Boirus and Simon 1989 p.II).

These authors identify four main components of the NIC technology strategy:
1. risk-reducing, capital allocating financial and tax policies designed to encourage firms to adopt new ideas and innovations;
2. policies aimed at facilitating the process of importing technology and permitting its efficient utilization;

3. policy instruments and economic incentives for the rapid diffusion of existing technology throughout the domestic economy;
4. major investments in education and training, especially in engineering and science education.

The case of Singapore, whose population most closely approximates that of Jamaica, is instructive. In the late 1970s the Government identified 11 key industries for technology and skill upgrading and higher wages. These included precision instruments/tools, computers and peripherals, microelectronics, and advanced machine tools. A national R&D policy for the targeted industries (i) allowed firms to deduct R&D expenditures for new product development; (ii) provided state financial assistance for advanced training schemes for their workers; and (iii) provided finance on concessionary terms to firms introducing new skills or technology into the economy. A Science Park designed to attract foreign firms with advanced technology to Singapore was also established.

It is *not* being suggested here that Jamaica can necessarily follow the NIC strategy of shifting into such high-technology industries. The very success of these countries in doing so will make it that much harder for other countries to emulate them. What *is* being argued is the necessity for:

— a conscious *industrial* (or rather, production) *strategy*;
— an *active* rather than a passive *state* in collaboration with producers in the formulation and execution of the strategy; and
— an *active technology strategy* with strong state involvement in support of it.

In this context, some comments on the Jamaican situation follow.

Technology and Jamaica's Export Sectors

The Jamaican economy has experienced considerable structural diversification in the last 40 years. First, the export of primary agricultural commodities gave way in importance to the production and export of primary mineral commodities (bauxite and alumina) in the 1950s-1960s. In the 1970s the mineral-export sector lost ground, and in spite of some recovery in the 1980s it has been displaced by tourism as the principal foreign exchange earner. Nontraditional exports have also been growing. The export (goods and services) profile at the beginning of the 1990s was, therefore, radically different than at the end of the 1940s.

Jamaica: sectoral shares in total exports of goods and services			
	1948	1968	1991
Agriculture	96.4	22.52	7.4
Bauxite & alumina		28.9	27.6
Tourism		18.7	32.0
Other	3.6	29.9	33.0

This diversification is welcome, and must be counted as one of the solid achievements of the post World War II and post-independence periods. Within a long-term strategic perspective, however, it has certain limitations. This becomes clearer if we use a *strategic* classification of the structure of exports of goods and services (XGS) focusing on: (1) the factors underlying the external market position or competitive advantages of the product in external markets, and the degree of vulnerability associated with these factors; and (2) the long-term expansion potential of the product.

With respect to (1), factors may be classified by their degree of vulnerability as follows

Category A: High Vulnerability Factors
    (i) preferential treatment in foreign markets
    (ii) locational advantage
    (iii) low-wage advantage

Category B: Intermediate Vulnerability Factors
    (iv) labour productivity advantage
    (v) overall cost efficiency advantage

Category C: Low Vulnerability Factors
    (vi) product quality*
    (vii) product design
    (viii) product function
    * includes delivery time, efficiency of product support services

In Category A, (i) is self-evident, especially where the product is undifferentiated (most primary commodities) and high-cost relative to other nonpreferentially treated sources; (ii) is placed in Category A because locational advantages can change as other locations are opened up, or as other markets gain in importance (e.g. the Pacific Rim). Low-wage advantages can also be eroded as standards of living and hence wages rise, and/or as a result of competition from other low-wage locations.

External market position is more secure when it is based on Category B factors, which relate to *cost advantages*. It is even more secure when it is based on Category C factors, which relate to *product-type advantages*. A firm can afford a certain level of cost disadvantage if its product is superior in quality or otherwise sufficiently differentiated from that of its competitors that its customers will continue to buy it. Across many firms at the national level, this translates into higher standards of living for the country. Clearly, the most important loci of competition in the global economy is in this area.

The second aspect of strategic classification is the product's potential for long-term expansion. Apart from the country's competitiveness in the product, there are two dimensions to this: that relating to long-term domestic supply capabilities, and that relating to the long-run rate of growth of world demand. The first is constrained most strongly in the case of natural resource based products. The second is more difficult to judge because of uncertainty about the future, but product groups can be ranked according to their *probable* growth rate of demand. As a general rule, growth rates are highest in the world economy today for Category C products.

A crude preliminary classification of the products making up the majority of the value of Jamaica's XGS would result in the following:

Product	Vulnerability	Long-term Potential for Expansion
Sugar	High	Low
Bananas	High	Low
Coffee	Low	Limited
Bauxite	Intermediate	Limited
Alumina	Intermediate	Limited
Tourism I (Conventional)	High	Low
Tourism II (All-inclusives)	Intermediate	Limited
Tourism III (Eco-tourism)	Low	Limited
Garments	High	Low
Non-traditional agriculture	Low	Limited
Other non-traditional	Low	High

In other words, most of our XGS value is derived from natural resource based products with a vulnerable external market position, or with limited long-term expansion potential (or both). Some products, like Blue Mountain coffee and all-inclusive tourism, have secured a niche in foreign markets due to the uniqueness and quality of the product. This is important, and provides clues for future strategy. But the long-term expansion possibilities for these products themselves are limited by resource constraints: the slopes of the Blue Mountains and good beaches. It seems likely that these limits will be reached by the end of the decade.

This analysis points to the general conclusion that long-term strategy should aim at shifting into Category B and Category C products. Accepting that this shift cannot take place overnight, and that a good strategy is one that makes full use of existing production experience and capabilities, the following broad lines of approach are suggested:

1. Although seeking to preserve existing preferential arrangements and existing market positions in traditional products for as long as possible, we should see this as a holding operation that is primarily defensive in nature; while

2. We use traditional products and their natural resource base to develop *more differentiated* products and activities, the production of which is also *cost efficient*; and

3. We see as the long-term strategic imperative the development of *differentiated quality products* which are not natural resource intensive and which have good long-term consumption prospects.

In the next section we explore some of what this means for a technology strategy.

Applying Technology to the Firm

From a technology perspective, the production characteristics of the three categories of products could be identified as follows:

category a products — resource-intensive, undifferentiated, use mature technologies;

category b products — undifferentiated or semidifferentiated, use mature or semimature technologies, labour and/or management intensive, technical efficiency sensitive; and

category c products — differentiated, product quality sensitive, design intensive, use new technologies; and R&D and innovation intensive.

It is notable that as we move from A to B to C there is an increase in the degree of product differentiation and the technological content of production. *The crucial point is that the degree of technological effort required for success increases as we climb up the strategic ladder.* In Category B products, which depend on cost advantages, the principal activities relate to the mastery of process and product know-how and systematic 'learning' efforts at the firm level in order to maximise operating efficiencies and expand the production frontier. In Category C products, where product quality and differentiation are decisive, the key activities relate to design, product quality improvement, and R&D.

As argued in the first section of this paper, the successful conduct of these activities requires purposeful strategies with clearly defined objectives by both firms and the state. For simplicity, we will refer to this as 'active', in contrast to 'passive', technology behaviour.

I would argue that a major problem area to be addressed here springs from the culture of technological passivity within which Jamaican firms have, by and large, operated. The reasons for this may readily be seen by considering the conditions under which the principal types of businesses have operated. Subsidiaries of trans national corporations (TNCs) have access to process and product know-how from their parent companies. Locally-owned enterprises exporting to protected external markets have little incentive to innovate. The same applies to those producing for protected local markets, which have tended to license simple product and process technologies from foreign suppliers. Trading firms, another main area of local entrepreneurship, have little need for all but the simplest technologies. State owned enterprises have been protected by regulation or by government financial supports, and have tended to rely heavily on technical agreements with foreign suppliers (Girvan 1983).

It needs to be pointed out here that a pattern of technological passivity is quite consistent with a process of technological modernization, as shown by successive rounds of investment in up-to-date, imported plant and machinery. Many, if not most, Jamaican firms are continuously 'modernizing'. Secondly, protected markets do not have to result in technologically passive behaviour. Many countries have used selective protection as an instrument of fostering local technological capabilities. In such cases the protection is conditioned on the performance of specific technological effort by the privileged firms, for example the training of workers and professionals to absorb foreign know-how, and the conduct of R&D for the adaptation of process technology and the modification of product design.

Nonetheless, several outstanding examples of innovating Jamaican firms can be found. This writer studied the case of a small welding electrode firm which had made systematic and successful use of worker training, process adaptation and product development as a competitive weapon (Girvan and Marcelle 1990). Red Stripe Beer has an established international market position as a brand-differentiated, quality product. All-inclusive hotels are another example of a highly successful product innovation (Poon 1990). Other examples will spring readily to mind. We need to study the experiences of successful innovating firms in order to better understand why some firms used these strategies as competitive weapons while others did not, focusing on the impact of such factors as the competitive environment, the type of ownership and management, and government policies. This would inform the development of policies aimed at generalizing innovative behaviour across the economy as a whole. Popularization of these cases could also encourage other firms to adopt similar strategies.

Finally, as regards the role of government, several issues arise. One is that explicit science and technology policy has tended to focus on the R&D activities of government agencies, such as the Scientific Research Council (SRC). More recently, stated policies have also been concerned with the problems of the scientific establishment in the public sector. Notably absent has been a recognition of the necessity for a close link between science and technology and the productive sector, and with a long-term production strategy for the economy. I would argue that it is the latter which ought to provide the context, the direction, and the specific content of operational science and technology policies of government.

Hence, such issues as government-funded R&D and the development of the science base would be addressed in function of the needs of the long-term production strategy and the associated producing enterprises. Fiscal, credit, and trade policies would also be crafted to support active technological behaviour by firms following the desired strategic path. Formal science and technology policies would constitute one of several elements in a larger package, ensuring that they are relevant and effective in the totality of government policies and assist producing enterprises where it matters most.

Another issue which arises is the theoretical justification for selective government intervention, which is inherent in the notion of a strategic approach as advocated in this paper. As is well-known, this justification is provided by instances of market failure. The case of the development of technological capacities is well recognized as an outstanding example of this. However, current notions of the need for reliance on market forces to promote competitiveness and the most desirable allocation of resources, do not appear to leave room for selective government intervention. Failures of government intervention are held to be worse than market failure, even when the latter are conceded to exist. This is argued in spite of the well-known pattern of widespread government intervention to promote innovation in the developed countries, and the successful use of selective interventions by Japan and the Southeast Asian NICs.

On the theoretical level, two points can be made here. Markets work best when market power is fairly evenly distributed among producers and consumers. When power is highly uneven, existing patterns of resource allocation tend to reproduce themselves and even become exacerbated over time. A small country like Jamaica which opens itself to the full blast of international competition may, in doing so, sacrifice some strategic opportunities for technical and human resource development. It runs the risk of becoming a reservoir of cheap labour, and a tropical playground for the rich. As we approach the twenty-first century, this is a risk worthy of sober evaluation.

The second point is that the emphasis on the risks and the costs of 'government failure' negates the possibility of the process of social learning. Simply put, this is the process by which a society (and not just government) is able to learn from its own mistakes: drawing on the lessons of previous experience to improve the effectiveness with which it addresses specific problems and pursues its own goals. Like other kinds of learning, social learning will be most successful when it is conscious and systematic. It requires a democratic and mature political culture, a vigorous intellectual establishment, an independent and fearless media. Its key requirements are analysis, reflection, public education, and public discourse. This symposium, looking back on 30 years of constitutional independence and looking forward to the next 30, is a part of that process.

References

Boirus, Michael; and Denis Fred Simon, 'High-Technology in the Pacific Basin: Analysis and Policy Implications", Unpublished MS, 1989.

Dennison, E., *Accounting for U.S. Economic Growth*, Washington: The Brookings Institution, 1974.

Freeman, C., *The Economics of Industrial Innovation*, 1974.

Girvan, Norman, *Technology Policies for Small Developing Economies: A Case Study of the Caribbean*. Mona: Institute of Social and Economic Research, U.W.I, 1983.

————————; and Gillian Marcelle, 'Overcoming Technological Dependence: The Case of Electric Arc (Jamaica) Ltd.: A Small Firm in a Small Developing Country', *World Development*, January 1990.

Hoffman, Kurt; and Norman Girvan, *Managing International Technology Transfer: A Strategic Approach for Developing Countries*. Ottawa: IDRC, 1990.

Ozawa, T., *Japan's technological Challenge to the West, 1950-1974: Motivation and Accomplishment*, Cambridge, MA: MIT, 1974.

————————, 'Government Control Over Technology Acquisition and Firms Entry Into New Sectors: The Experience of Japan's Synthetic Fibre Industry", *Cambridge Journal of Economics*, 4, 1890.

Pavitt, K., 'Technical Innovation and Industrial Development, Part I', *Futures*, 11, (6) December 1979.

————————, 'Technical Innovation and Industrial Development, Part II', Futures, 12, (1) February 1980.

Peck, M. J.; and A. Otto, 'Technology and Economic Growth: The Case of Japan', *Research Policy*, 10, (3), 1981.

Poon, Aulian, 'Flexible Specialization and Small Size: The Case of Caribbean Tourism', *World Development*, January 1990.

Solow, R., 'Technical Change and the Aggregate Production Function', *Review of Economics and Statistics*, August 1957.

CHAPTER 12

Education and Training:
Key Elements
in the Development Process

Alfred Sangster

Education, preparing people for life and living, and training, preparing people for work, are increasingly recognized as critical elements in the development of a nation and its people. They are critical for a number of reasons, not least being their role in developing an understanding and use of the tools of modern technology in the processes of production.

As we approach the twenty-first century, there are some important trends which must be recognized. Here are some of them. First, the development of information technology has made our world increasingly a global village. We were able to watch war from our bedrooms as we saw the CNN report showing the sky over Baghdad 'lit up' by American bombs. Mail and FAX machines have revolutionized the office. I spoke to a man in Australia and the next morning his reply, by FAX, was on my desk.

Environmental decay, both locally and international, is having a profound effect on our nation states. The impact of population pressures on the availability of resources creates a new agenda. The computer is playing an increasing role in our everyday life. We often hear at an office or airline counter, 'the computer is down', and everything stops. Thus the implications of a reliable power supply is also another important consequence.

The global financial crisis and the widening poverty gap are creating dangerous situations at both the macro (international) and micro (national) levels. The introduction of new technologies of all forms, in all areas of human endeavour, also generates major differences between rich and poor. The rapid political and social changes at both the national and international levels are creating uncertainty and a lack of confidence in the development process.

The Education and Training process must take place, not only in the context of increasingly rapid change, but also of significantly reduced resources. The system is constantly being called upon to 'do more with less'. The education/training process does not take place in a vacuum. It deals with people — teachers and learners — equipment and processes, and is essentially a living experience. Most people would agree that education is in crisis and that crisis is in the context of a series of other crises which affect us at the national and regional levels.

I have listed what I call five crisis areas. We perhaps may call them contextual issues in which the educational system must survive.

First, there is the financial crisis. One of today's newspapers has a comment and I will read the first paragraph: 'Ask Caribbean school teachers, what structural adjustment means and most likely they will tell you staff cuts, run down schools and low salaries'. So, the financial context means for us structural adjustment, gaps in income distribution, hyper inflation, high interest rates, the debt trap and low returns from primary products. It is the old tractor argument. Thirty or 40 years ago 10 tons of sugar would have bought the tractor; ten years ago 40 tons of sugar were required to buy that same tractor; today the figure required is even higher. The poor developing countries with their primary products are always the one that take a beating.

There are a number of critical issues which have to be noted when we look at the social and political context. Deteriorating standards of dress, language and life style, and negative attitudes to work, all pose an increasing challenge to our long established value system. Indiscipline rears its ugly head and the weaknesses in the education system threaten the potential for a trained and educated work force. Political violence, tribalism, social stratification all take their toll on the national productive process.

The ecological context is one in which we are looking at our forests being lost, our top soil being eroded resulting in the trend to desertification. Air pollution is becoming more pronounced. Near to Riverton City at a particular time of day when the conditions are right and there is an inversion layer, you can hardly see a hundred metres ahead. Fresh and sea water pollution and environmental degradation are on the increase. Kingston Harbour is now dead.

There is a population and resource crisis. Our GDP has not kept pace with our population growth. The country's resources have to be shared. For example, more people using the transport system creates its own set of pressures on the system and, in addition, engenders indiscipline. Energy and its availability is also related to population pressures. A recent publication by the International Energy Foundation records and I quote: 'Developing countries are emerging as by far the largest energy growth centres.'

Finally, the moral crisis shows up in a number of ways: decay in family life, increased drug use, AIDS, and other sexually transmitted diseases, crime and violence, and a lack of sensitivity to human values. Increasingly, one hears the statement, 'look out for number one.' It doesn't matter how you trample over other people.

These critical issues already have an impact and will continue to affect, in a significant way, the positive development processes of a nation.

How can education and training be positive in the current context? We must delve a little deeper and review some of the problems in the educational system. What are some of these?

Firstly, the quality and relevance of the educational process is questionable. A young entrepreneurial businessman, Robert Bryan, is quoted as saying: 'This is a labour intensive business I run and the quality of labour coming out of our schools does not turn out the skills we need, and when we find experienced people, they can't read'.

Secondly, there has been a significant decline in real terms in the financing of education. The increased reliance on cost recovery issues and methods (mostly fees) is putting increasing strain on the community and the real danger is that education — a major element of social upward mobility of our people — may lose its impact.

Thirdly, the decline in the status and position of the teaching profession has contributed significantly to a lowering of standards. The exodus from the profession of the old and the non-entry of the young are creating a vacuum which will need to be filled.

There are a number of alternatives which have a significant impact on many young people's attitude to the learning process. Among these are the drug culture with prospects of quick money, and the distractions presented by the media which pose a real challenge to the learning process.

The significant decline in the quality of the basic sciences in the educational system is also creating problems in recruiting persons for the disciplines of science and technology.

Given the major problems that face the country and education as a whole, what approach should we take towards the twenty-first century? We need to take some bold and decisive decisions and certainly will have to move in nontraditional directions. Increasingly, we need to develop and maintain a positive posture, and I am suggesting some directions for education and training which are largely directed to the post-secondary or tertiary sector as well as to the work place.

We need to adopt a problem-oriented creative approach to the learning process where relevant economic, social, moral, scientific and technological problems become part of the learning experience. The potential for training in business skills should also be developed. Curricula will have to be reviewed and updated in terms of relevance and appropriateness.

Technology that we use should be relevant and appropriate, with a mix of low and high technology. For example, our post-diploma engineering programme at The College of Arts Science and Technology (CAST), which we developed some years ago, has structured in it a basic problem solving orientation in which the student is sponsored by a company. He/she works on a company-based problem which means he/she is a supervisor at both the College and the company.

We must develop positive work and service attitudes with a serious commitment to discipline and excellence for students, teachers, and at the work place. Earning and learning need to become institutionalized and innovative ways found to finance student education. We are pleased to record some useful experiences we have had with partnership with government in respect of providing financial aid for students through the Student Economic Support Programme. We should be able to work with and help students in need.

We need a critical review of the methods of learning with an increasing use of educational technology. A renewed commitment will need to be made to the teaching profession. Somebody once said that without the teaching profession there can be no other profession. Libraries are increasingly becoming learning centres with media technologies being part of that whole learning experience.

There must be increasing recognition of the appropriateness of 'learning at work' with a greater involvement of business and industry in the total learning process. A greater emphasis will have to be placed on short term modular instruction and job specific programmes with an increasing recognition of the need for job training and retraining as skills change, as professions and technologies change, and as the whole direction of the work force changes. It is interesting to record that some of these trends which give credit for learning involve major cooperation between educational institutions and the workplace. This cooperation between 'town' and 'gown' — called 'cooperate education' in the US and 'sandwich programme' in the UK — is increasingly critical as we relate the experiences of the educational institutions with the work place.

Greater flexibility will be necessary in the educational delivery process with an increased move to Open Learning. Open Learning involves all kinds of models, but we are talking about providing multi-level and multiskills training. We also need to strengthen the partnerships between education/training institutions and supporting individuals, agencies, and professions.

We must develop a list of priority institutions and programmes for funding which must be based on their appropriateness for the development process and the provision of skilled manpower. This has to be particularly relevant in science, technology, and business. There are three major national institutions which need to be recognized and supported in specific ways. These are the Bureau of Standards, the Scientific Research Council and, of course, the College of Arts Science and Technology.

Finally, we need to recognize the role of the computer in the process of catching up with the developed world. There are three terms that are used in computing: we speak of hardware — it is unlikely that as a country we would be able to make any major strides in hardware developments — and we talk about software, which has implications for how we use our computer; but in the middle, between the hardware and the software, comes what people have called the "person-ware" — the people who can make hardware become software. I believe that the use of the computer is critical in all areas in education. We took a conscious decision years ago that all our students at CAST should really have, no matter what they are doing, a 'hands-on' computer experience.

Education needs a national consensus and a strong commitment from all sectors for its future and that commitment has to be made now as time is not on our side. That commitment will be necessary and essential if the education/training process is going to have real meaning and impact on the nation's development.

We need above all to believe in ourselves that our people are our most important resource and our ability to achieve has to be mixed with an underlying sense of vision and faith.

PART IV

Globalization
and
Development

CHAPTER 13

Recent Developments in the Hemisphere: Their Implications for Jamaica

Richard Bernal

Introduction

The global economy and the international economic and political system, which have existed since World War II, are in an advanced stage of metamorphosis. What will replace the now overwhelmed Bretton Woods-GATT institutional framework and its regulatory functions is not clear. The speed and the profundity of the change has been so dramatic that most people have not realized that the world we knew is not changing; it has changed. This transformation ushers in a new era and those countries which are slow to adjust and adapt to the new environment will be progressively marginalized from the mainstream of global economic activity. The global changes are not a change in the weather; they constitute a change in climate. Those who do not adapt quickly enough will be like the dinosaurs; that is, they will not survive. Global changes influencing and interacting with indigenously generated changes within the Western hemisphere will have a profound impact on Jamaica over the next 10-30 years.

Part I   The Context and the Trends

Global context of hemispheric events

This section examines the global context in which developments in the hemisphere emerged. In order to do this, it is necessary to differentiate between economic and political factors operating at the global level. The most important global developments which have had an important impact on events and trends are described below.

Globalization of production and finance

In recent years, international trade and capital flows have grown at a faster rate than world Gross Domestic Product (GDP). This reflects the progressive globalization of production and finance (O'Brien, 1992) which is pressuring governments to minimize, harmonize, or eliminate national barriers (e.g. tariffs, quotas, exchange controls) to the international movement of goods, services, capital, and finance. The driving force impelling globalization is transnational corporate integration through mergers, strategic corporate alliances, and takeovers. Efficiency in resource allocation and profit maximization on a global scale cannot be attained within a world economy fractured into national economies whose policies constrain the degrees of freedom. Transnational corporate integration impels multicountry market integration, initially in a regional context, both as ex-post economic rationalisation and as a defence by the nation-state against the inevitable relinquishing of the vestiges of economic sovereignty.[1]

The transition to a world market is taking place as national economies merge and amalgamate into trade blocs. The deepening of the integration process in the European Economic Community (EEC) and the conclusion of a draft North American Free Trade Agreement (NAFTA) are manifestations of a trend toward the emergence of trade blocs. The compartmentalization of the global economy consists of (a) a European Economic Space (b) a Western Hemisphere Free Trade Area, and (c) some sort of free trade arrangement linking the countries of Southeast Asia and Japan.

Associated with these developments is a trend towards diluting preferential trade arrangements both in the Lome Convention and the Caribbean Basin Initiative (CBI). Already, the benefits of CBI have been extended to the Andean Pact countries and NAFTA will provide benefits to Mexico in terms of conditions of market access, which supersede those provided by the CBI. It is a real possibility that Central American countries could be given access to the banana market of the EEC. Given that their cost of production is much lower than that of other Caribbean producers, the effect could be serious for CARICOM countries.

Tripolar Rivalry

The relative economic decline of the US, the continued growth of Japan, and the consolidation of the EEC have created a situation in which there is fierce economic rivalry between these blocs.[2] The deepening of the integration process in the EEC and renewed interest in various regional trading arrangements has given rise to a trend within the world economy towards the emergence of trade and/or economic blocs. This trend could lead to a compartmentalized global economy consisting of (a) an EEC enlarged to a European Economic Space (EES) encompassing the European Free Trade Area (EFTA) and Eastern Europe (b) a Western Hemisphere Free Trade Area around a core of Canada, the US, and Mexico and, (c) some sort of free trade zone or arrangement[3] linking the countries of Southeast Asia, or a grouping including Japan.[4] The EEC is a large and important market to the US, but after 1992 it will be more difficult for US exporters to penetrate the European market. NAFTA, if it comes to fruition, will include Mexico, Canada, and the US and would, in fact, be a larger market than the EEC. NAFTA would have a market of 363 million people, as opposed to 300 in the EEC, and 380 in the merged EEC/EFTA. The US economy would constitute the core of a Western hemisphere economic bloc of the countries participating in the Enterprise for the Americas Initiative (EAI) which will be characterized by liberalized trade and capital flows. The EAI countries would have a combined GDP of US$6.8 trillion and a market of 719 million (*Enterprise for the Americas Initiative Fact Sheet*, 1991). Japan and the newly industrialized countries of East Asia have a combined GDP of US$3.2 trillion and a population of 199 million (Balls, 1991).

Decline of US Hegemony

The difficulties experienced in completing the negotiations of the Uruguay Round of GATT reflect the relative decline of US hegemony.[5] The Round could end in disarray, or fail to resolve key issues on the agenda. This could be followed by an escalation of protectionism characterized by an acceleration of the coalescing of nascent trade blocs. It could also provoke a proliferation of bilateral trade arrangements and intensify the tendency for the formation of various regional trade arrangements which may, by virtue of a common external tariff, raise protectionist barriers to exports from other groups and nonmember countries.

Slow Growth In The World Economy

The decade of the 1980s was noteworthy for low growth in industrialized countries and uneven growth in the developing countries (*World Bank Annual Report 1992*). During 1990 and 1991 the economies of low income and middle income countries stagnated in terms of GDP per capita.The outlook is not encouraging as GDP growth in the G-7 countries declined from 2.8 per cent in 1990 to 1.9 per cent in 1991.This constrained demand for exports from developing countries and contributed to a 6 per cent decline in non-oil commodity prices, which was the third consecutive year of decline in non-oil primary commodity prices in nominal dollar terms. The volume of merchandise exports from developing countries declined by 2 per cent, however, growth in Latin America and the Caribbean increased marginally. The outlook is not encouraging for primary product exports as technological change is reducing demand by providing synthetic substitutes and reducing raw material input per unit of manufactured goods.

Implosion of Soviet Union / Eastern Europe

The political upheaval and democratization in Eastern Europe has fostered an atmosphere in which the US views the 'Cold War' as over and as thus reducing its security considerations in the Caribbean and Central America. This in turn has induced a complacency about the Caribbean's vulnerability to drug trafficking, poverty, and social unrest. The Soviet Union, driven by expediency, has been dumping commodities on the world market, including bauxite and aluminum, which has had an adverse impact on the price and demand for bauxite. These newly democratic countries' need for assistance will result in the diversion of aid from developing countries.The economic cost of the stabilising role that the US is attempting to undertake has and will reduce aid (both financial and PL-480) available to Latin America and the Caribbean.

Trends in the United States

Economic Recession

The US economy has been in recession, characterized by low and fluctuating growth and persistent fiscal and trade deficits. The trade deficit partly reflects the relative lack of competitiveness of US goods in both the world market and the national market, particularly compared to goods from Japan and the newly industrialized countries (NICs). Protectionism in Europe and Japan has compounded the difficulties involved in increasing exports. In this context there is a need to preserve markets in which the US has a competitive advantage. In recent years, Latin America and the Caribbean have assumed increased importance as export markets. The region accounts for only 14 per cent of US exports,[6] but this is larger than exports to Japan and to the NIC's of Southeast Asia. Latin America has been a market in which there has been a steady increase in demand.[7] Exports from the US have increased by 70 per cent since 1986 — from $31 billion in 1987 to over $54 billion in 1990. The US's share of the region's imports has grown from 46 per cent to almost 55 per cent (*World Development Report, 1990*).

How the US adjusts its fiscal and trade deficits will have a profound influence on economic growth and trade in the hemisphere and, indeed, the world economy. The current strategy involves export-led growth through trade liberalization in the GATT, and simultaneous 'aggressive unilateralism' (Bhagwati, 1992). If, however, the US were to opt for protectionism or an IMF Extended Fund Facility type stabilization/adjustment programme, it would entail devaluation, fiscal compression, and tight monetary policy which would be devastating to growth and trade globally and in the hemisphere.

Domestic Agenda Becomes The Priority

The recession in the US economy and the end of the Cold War have prompted an internal debate about the burden of 'the lonely superpower' (Kauathammer, 1991) and the need for 'selective disengagement'. There is pressure from a growing body of public opinion to have 'America come home', or to put 'America first' (Buchanan, 1991). In June 1992, approximately 88 per cent of Americans felt that the US should give less attention to overseas problems and concentrate on domestic issues (*National Journal*, 1 August 1992; *Washington Post*, 27 October 1991). The demand that certain domestic issues be addressed will find more vocal expression. Its economic difficulties and the implosion of the Soviet Union has resulted in the US retreating from Pax Americana while continuing a reduced but central role in global security (Tondson, 1991; Brzezinski, 1991). Although US expansion and hegemony have been consistent since the late nineteenth century, there have been cycles of isolationism and expansion which affect the modality of its foreign policy. At this time the US is poised on the threshold of a period of inward looking orientation. With all of this in mind, these global forces have impelled the US to consider a Latin American policy which does not rely on financial aid.

Combative Approach to Foreign Economic Policy

The economic recession has led the US to a drive for the expansion of its exports by the opening of overseas markets, and a reduced willingness to provide foreign aid.The emphasis is now on reciprocal, in contrast to concessional trade — such as the Caribbean Basin Initiative — and foreign aid — as was the case with the Alliance for Progress. The EAI, which was launched in June 1990 by President Bush, consists of three components:

(a)Trade Liberalization aimed at creating a hemispheric free trade area, by a series of free trade agreements (FTAs), commencing with the North American Free Trade Agreement (NAFTA) of the US, Canada, and Mexico. Succeeding agreements would depend on the readiness of countries to meet the criteria for membership, which include a suitable macroeconomic environment, market-oriented policies, liberalized trade and investment regimes, the elimination of tariffs and nontariff barriers on goods and services over a specified phase-in schedule, and standards for the treatment of investment and the protection of intellectual property rights. To date the US has signed 16 Framework Agreements on Trade and Investment with 31 countries, which leaves only three small countries outside the Initiative.

(b) Promotion of private investment flows by: (i) the creation of an investment sector loan programme within the Inter-American Development Bank (IDB) to provide resources to support privatization efforts and to create an environment which promotes increased entrepreneurship; (ii) the creation of a Multilateral Investment Fund of US$1.5 billion to be disbursed between 1992 and 1996. This fund would furnish finance and technical assistance to support privatization, private enterprise development, and business infrastructure.

(c)Debt Relief by: (i) Reducing the stock of concessional and PL480 debt. Principal payments will continue to be paid in hard currency, the stock of debt will be reduced and interest on the remaining portion would be payable in local currency. Interest payments will be applied to fund environmental projects and 'child survival'. (ii) Reducing the debt which is owed to the Export-Import (EX-IM) Bank or to the Commodity Credit Corporation through a sale of the debt on the secondary market. The proceeds will be applied to debt-for-nature or debt-for-equity swaps. Although the bilateral debt is a very small portion of total external debt (i.e. 3.7 per cent) for the whole region, it assumes large proportions in countries in Central America and the Caribbean where it is as high as 20 per cent in several countries and 40 per cent in the case of some (Sullivan 1991, Table 3). There is only passing reference to commercial bank debt which, incidentally, is the largest share of the total debt, particularly for Latin American countries. It is suggested that there be a continuation of the Brady Plan measures, and that the IMF and the World Bank try to support debt reduction and rescheduling. This has not been given any specific form but an initiative should not be launched to deal with debt in Latin America which did not even mention commercial bank debt.

The Clinton administration is not likely to persist with the EAI because it is too obviously a programme devised by the Bush administration. The elements of debt relief, investment promotion, development assistance, and reciprocal trade will constitute the components of US policy towards Latin America and the Caribbean. This stance could be described as 'less of the same' since less resources are likely to be made available to support this strategy. A major cause for concern is the more combative approach to foreign trade. Laura Tyson, Chairperson of the Council of Economic Advisors, argues that 'free trade is not necessarily and automatically the best policy'. Her argument rests on the fact that much of global trade is conditioned by imperfect competition, including oligopoly and strategic corporate interaction among firms and governments rather than market forces. Tyson describes her policy disposition as 'cautious activism' which 'in trade policy is not synonymous with protectionism' but 'does sometime involve forceful unilateralism'. She advocates that US 'trade laws be used to deter or compensate for foreign practices that are not adequately regulated by existing multilateral rules' (e.g. GATT) (Tyson, 1992; Tyson et al, 1989).

North American Free Trade Agreement

NAFTA is designated as the first building block of the free trade aspect of the EAI. When it comes into effect NAFTA will make CBI II a depreciating asset in a relative, not absolute, sense because it will provide Mexico with free trade access for exports which currently face tariffs and quotas under the CBI, in particular rum, sugar, garments, textiles and leather goods. These, unfortunately, happen to be products in which Jamaica is and can be competitive. Jamaica is the first Caribbean country and only the second in the hemisphere to have met all the eligibility criteria and is therefore fully qualified for membership in the EAI. Jamaica has already benefitted under the debt relief component of the EAI, when its PL480 debt was reduced by 80 per cent in 1991. The conditions of entry to NAFTA have not yet been set out in detail in the 2,000 page draft agreement, but are likely to be very similar to the eligibility criteria for the EAI. The possibility of Jamaica joining NAFTA through its accession clause is a matter which has to be considered carefully and a decision made at the earliest possible date.

Reduced Foreign Aid

US foreign aid in real terms will continue to decline given the preoccupation with domestic issues and the persistent fiscal deficit. In addition, the Caribbean share of a reduced foreign aid programme could also decline significantly. This is short sighted because some form of aid is necessary to strengthen physical and social infrastructure which would allow developing countries in the hemisphere to support and harness private sector entrepreneurial energy and to take advantage of whatever export opportunities might open up by complementing private investment. Trade liberalization and debt relief are not substitutes for development assistance. They are complementary because an efficient and expanding private sector requires a competent public sector. Extra demands will be placed on the public sector due to resource reallocation which is inherent in a process of adjustment. To effectively support the revamping and improvement in private sector activity, the public sector will have to be transformed and reoriented. This will necessitate additional resources at the very time when liberalization of the trade regime may engender short-term dislocation in revenue raising capacity. This is a particular anxiety in the micro-economies of the Eastern Caribbean where fiscal revenue is based largely on duties on imports. Reduced tariffs and import duties would cause the government's expenditure capacity to be truncated by the erosion of the traditional tax base and this would require an overhaul of tax administration.

Resurgence of Ethnicity and Latin Americanization

The major dilemma in the present conjuncture is that the trend to larger supranational economic units is not consonant with the trend to smaller political units based on ethnic homogeneity. Ethnicity has resisted nationalism, the nation state, and various political ideologies, and will be 'an elemental force' in international relations (Moynihan

1993).[8] The resurgence of ethnicity will affect the hemisphere, particularly the US and Caribbean/Latin American relations. In the US there is a growing disparity between ethnic, racial, and cultural diversity because different groups no longer want to submerge their identities in the 'great American melting pot'. Minorities and migrants want to retain their cultural and linguistic identities. This will become more pronounced as the US moves to the point where, sometime in the early twenty-first century it will be a majority 'nonwhite' country. The most rapidly growing segment of the population, including migrants, are from a Hispanic background. The growing 'disuniting' of America (Schlesinger, 1992), has resulted in responses such as the movement to have English adopted as the official language (by 1990, 17 states had adopted laws designating English as their official language). One possible result is a closer affinity between Latin America and the US, as the southern US becomes Latin Americanized. However, the often mooted closer cooperation and integration between Latin America and the Caribbean may be even more difficult to realize than in the past, despite the compelling economic logic. Canada's continued existence as a unitary state is threatened by ethnic, cultural, and linguistic differences. It is not implausible to predict that before the end of this century Canada could disintegrate into two or more countries. There is also the process of Latin Americanization of areas which were previously English-speaking, the prime example being Belize where migrants from Central America increased so rapidly during the last decade that Mestizos are now the largest ethnic group, accounting for 44 per cent of the population (*Caribbean Week*, 19 October 1992, p.2).

Developments in Latin America

Economic Stagnation and Economic Reform

The extent of the economic stagnation which has prevailed throughout the eighties and into the 1990s in Latin America and the Caribbean, is evident in the fact that GDP in real terms and GDP per capita are actually lower in 1990 than they were in 1977 for the region as a whole (*Preliminary Overview of the Economy of Latin America and the Caribbean*, 18 December 1991, p.3). In addition, the region has suffered a persistent decapitalization through capital flight and heavy debt servicing. Debt servicing required over 40 per cent of export earnings (pp. 53-54) and the debt/exports ratio was an overwhelming 287 per cent in 1991. Latin America and the Caribbean have suffered a negative net transfer of resources since 1980, being as high as US $31 billion in 1983 (p.51). The 1980s was a decade that was lost to Latin American and Caribbean development. The region responded to these developments with new economic policies which focused on economic reform, stabilization, and structural adjustment in an attempt to initiate a private sector-led, market-driven, outward-looking growth strategy. Import substitution and state led development strategies have been renounced and dismantled in favour of outward oriented approaches. Most Latin American and many Central American and Caribbean countries have reduced tariffs, removed quantitative trade restrictions, and vigorously implemented programmes of privatisation.

Democratization

Democratization blossomed simultaneously in several countries throughout the region, but democracy is still fragile in the face of growing poverty and economic deprivation. Democracy is particularly vulnerable during prolonged adjustment and deflationary stabilization, which involve the removal of subsidies on basic foods and public sector services, and directly affect the standard of living of low income groups. Exchange rate adjustment can often cause substantial increases in inflation in the short-term with severe effects on fixed income groups. These situations are often exacerbated by lay-offs in the public sector consequent on cutback in fiscal expenditure. The state's capacity to alleviate poverty and provide services such as health and education is severely curtailed by debt servicing (Bernal, Summer 1992) and support for unprofitable public enterprises. The coup in Haiti and the attempted coups in Trinidad and Tobago, Peru, and Venezuela are graphic reminders of the ever present threat to democracy.

Regional trade liberalization

There has been a resurgence of interest in regional trade liberalization, regional integration, and cooperation (Bernal, 1993). This momentum actually preceded the EAI which did not initiate these developments but rather complemented them and may have added a catalyst to accelerating this process.[9] There has been an escalation of the rhetoric and pronouncements by governments of their intention to pursue regional arrangements for trade liberalization. The Central American Common Market (CACM) has been resurrected; the Mercosur has been created between Brazil, Argentina, Uruguay, and

Paraguay; and the countries of the Andean region have established a free trade area. There has been a proliferation of bilateral trade agreements, such as the Venezuela-CARICOM one way free trade agreement. The number of free trade arrangements and agreements may be self-defeating because, although the intent is to increase trade by lowering and eliminating barriers, the complexity confronting the individual exporter or importer could inhibit trade. There is no guarantee that the announced commitments to regional integration and trade liberalization will come any closer to fruition than they did in the past.

Paucity of Foreign Investment

There is now a paucity of private capital inflows to the Caribbean associated with the reconstruction of East Germany and Kuwait, the reallocation of resources to assist the countries of the former Soviet Union, the attraction of privatization and low wages in Eastern Europe (*Washington Post*, 10 November 1991) and the US's own economic difficulties. There is a capital shortage because savings as a proportion of GNP decreased in both the industrialized and developing countries during the 1980s. Since 1984, 789 companies have invested US $2.2 billion in CBI designated countries employing 142,016 full time jobs and generating US $1.3 Billion annually in foreign exchange earnings (*1990 Caribbean Basin Investment Survey*, p.7). Costa Rica, Guatemala, Panama, El Salvador, and the Dominican Republic attracted two-thirds of the companies and accounted for 92 per cent of foreign exchange earnings, 87 per cent of full time employment and 78 per cent of the assets (p.7). In the case of these countries the main reasons for investing were access to the US market under the CBI, host country investment incentives, and the cost of labour. There is a need for the region to enhance its ability to attract more private capital and to establish the macroeconomic climate to maximize domestic investment and recapture 'flight' capital.

Mexico

Mexico is moving rapidly towards becoming a part of the industrialized world and has even applied to join the OECD. This strategy is clearly manifested in the push to create NAFTA. The prospective conclusion of NAFTA has added to Mexico's political status as 'a middle power' — an important economic role as a new 'growth pole' in the hemisphere — as economic activity concentrates increasingly in the southern US and California. There is a growing worry in Latin America and the Caribbean that, despite an accession clause, joining NAFTA is going to be difficult because the 'Big Three' may lose interest in further expansion or want to wait for a period in order to evaluate its progress.[10] Moreover, expansion may face political obstacles since existing US trade law prevents the extension of FTA benefits to third world countries. It will be necessary to renew 'fast track' authority for each agreement subsequent to the NAFTA (Hufbauer, Schott, 1992). This uncertainty has spawned a 'hub and spoke' development with Mexico as the central node of catenation; and consequently there is now a diplomatic stampede to negotiate, even in principle, a free trade agreement with Mexico to enter NAFTA through the 'back door'. This jockeying could become unsavory and might be detrimental to regional cooperation.

Cuba

Whatever takes place in Cuba politically it is clear that Cuba will increasingly and substantially reenter the world economy. This will have important implications for the Caribbean as Cuba is already well advanced in the reestablishment, refurbishing and expansion of its tourist industry. Cuba will have the advantage of being a new destination for Americans, as well as having a new 'plant' and a disciplined and inexpensive work force. Cuba could quickly become a major destination for cruise ships. Cuba's re-entry to the Caribbean tourist market is taking place at a time when the US economy is in recession and only Jamaica, among the Caribbean destinations, has succeeded in increasing tourist arrivals in the last few years. If the US normalizes relations with Cuba a substantial share of the contracting 'pie' of US aid will be diverted to Cuba, given the political influence of the Cuban community in the US.[11] Cuba will also be a major competitor for private foreign investment and will compete against Caribbean countries[12] in the US market in rum, sugar, citrus, cigars, leather goods, garments, and light manufacturing. If there is a normalization of relations, one of the ironies is that the US will have to purchase Cuban sugar, which it will send to the Soviet Union as food aid.

Drug Trafficking

The poverty which engulfs such a large part of the population of Latin America and the Caribbean makes these countries vulnerable to the corruption and violence associated with international drug trafficking. The small economies and micro-states are particularly vulnerable.

Migration

The migration of people both legally and illegally (French, *New York Times*, 8 December 1992) from economically depressed areas to areas where jobs and higher wages are available is likely to be more pronounced in the next decade or two, as Latin American and Caribbean population growth rates persist at high levels, while these economies produce a limited number of new jobs, most of which are at low wages. This will be a major economic problem and political issue in the US, Mexico, and Canada. The US, in particular, cannot be an oasis of affluence in a sea of poverty, but will face an increasing number of migrants, creating an under-class or a low stratum among the working class, which is racially, culturally, and linguistically different from the rest of US society.

Part II   Implications and Issues

Further Integration With The World Market

There is only one market, the global market, in which the only certainty is change at unprecedented rates. Speed in making decisions based on the latest information will be critical to maintaining competitiveness and market share. Whether Jamaica is able to compete in the global and hemispheric markets to expand exports depends, not only on the policies of governments, but on the private sector's readiness and ability to compete effectively. Even where Jamaican products have a comparative advantage it could, as in the past, be offset by the lack of a competitive advantage by locally owned firms. The expansion of exports will depend on a combination of both comparative and competitive advantages. The state of preparedness varies considerably, reflecting economic and psychological factors.

Erosion of Preferential Trade Arrangements

Developing countries can no longer plan for the continued existence of preferential trading arrangements. Jamaica cannot assume the continuation of existing preferential trade arrangements. It must recognize that the developed countries no longer feel obliged to provide preferential trade arrangements and aid to a region with minute markets, no indispensable raw materials, and of limited strategic importance. The region must be prepared to adapt to the elimination or erosion of preferential trade regimes, such as the proposed extension of benefits of the Lome Convention to Central America and the extension of CBI trade benefits to the Andean countries via the Andean Trade Reference Act which was approved on 26 November 1991. The future of CBI II is in jeopardy as current thinking in the Bush Administration is that it will be superseded by NAFTA and eventually the EAI. Within the long-term vision of a hemispheric free-trade area, CBI benefits will naturally be lost. In the short-term, it is still to be determined how the CBI will operate alongside the EAI. Is it to be upgraded to give similar provisions or is it to remain as is?

The apprehension over immediate and complete reciprocity derives less from the inability to undertake the appropriate policies and institutional changes, but from the social and economic costs of adjustment. This is a valid concern because structural adjustment implies both resource allocation from extinct to emerging or growing sectors and resource creation for new or upgraded productive capacity. There are risks and difficulties involved in improving quality, quantity, and price sufficiently to compete in the vast hemispheric market with multinational corporations, whose assets and sales dwarf the GDP of the combined Caribbean countries. Daunting as this appears, it can be accomplished because there are opportunities and specialized niches in the international division of labour which can be filled by relatively small scale operations.

Adjustment To Reciprocal Trade

A suitable period of adjustment, which can be general, sectional, or product specific, is critical if Jamaica is to compete effectively in a hemispheric free trade area. Product or sector specific adjustment periods, if sufficiently long, will allow these small, 'undiversified' economies to implement orderly economic reorganization. Caribbean fears may be exaggerated since in some areas in the US-Canada free trade agreement the phase-in period is as long as 10 years. In addition, only a limited number of products would require prolonged adjustment periods or exemptions because production is concentrated on a narrow range of goods and services and exports consist in many cases of a few primary products. Sensitive products can be handled by 'snap-back provisions', such as Article 702 of the US-Canada FTA

(*US-Canada Free Trade Agreement*, January 1991) which permits, under specified conditions, the imposition of a temporary duty on fresh fruits and vegetables. There can also be safeguards such as Article 1101 of the US-Canada FTA which allows either country, during the transition period which ends 31 December 1998, to respond to serious injury to domestic producers resulting from the reduction of duties under the FTA by restoring tariffs for a period of no longer than three years.

To Join or Not to Join a Trade Bloc

Countries not included or associated with major trading blocs could face steep protectionist barriers and be marginalized from the growth stimulating dynamic of the industrialized countries.

There has to be a detailed process of evaluation of the costs and benefits of participating or staying outside of the process. Given that the EAI encompasses trade in services, investment, and intellectual property rights, meeting the eligibility criteria imply a particular growth strategy which not all governments in the region are at the moment inclined to pursue. This strategy is an outward-looking, private sector-led, market-driven, growth strategy which involves privatization and liberalization. Governments should only pursue this type of growth strategy out of conviction, not out of expediency.

Should the CARICOM countries proceed individually, or should there be collective participation? If collective participation is available and feasible, given the differences in readiness, what collection of countries should proceed? Should this be CARICOM or some wider version of the Caribbean? Collective participation may prove difficult because it will involve measures which deal with national policy issues; for example, investment codes and intellectual property rights.

To be considered an acceptable partner for a free trade agreement with the US an extensive list of eligibility criteria has to be met. Participation in the EAI, NAFTA, and the continuation of foreign aid is going to be contingent on pursuing this development strategy. Countries which choose another path are likely to find themselves ostracised by the US and excluded from trade arrangements such as. The following criteria which have been explicitly stated embody implicitly a particular development strategy:
(a) elimination of tariffs on substantially all the trade between the parties to the agreement — this would include trade from all other countries already included in the customs union;
(b) phase out of nontariff barriers;
(c) inclusion of services in the agreement;

(d) provision for standards for the treatment of investment, guaranteeing the principle of national treatment of investors — there should be no inclusion of 'trade-distorting performance requirements' on the part of investors;

(e) inclusion of a dispute settlement mechanism;

(f) assurance of the protection of intellectual property rights;

(g) inclusion of special provisions, if necessary, to handle trade in and access to natural resources and natural resource-based products; (h) inclusion of a variety of operational, technical, and security provisions such as rules of origin, public health safety exceptions and safeguards;

(i) monitoring of government actions that could undermine the basis of the agreement, such as provisions covering subsidies, state trading, trade restraints justified on balance-of-payment grounds and the use of foreign exchange restrictions and controls;

(j) a stable macro-economic environment and market oriented policies as certified by the IMF, World Bank, and IDB;

(k) a commitment must be displayed by these countries to a multilateral trading system, assessed by the extent to which their positions concur with those of the US in the GATT Round of negotiations.

Adverse Impact of NAFTA

The draft NAFTA could put Jamaica and other CBI countries at a disadvantage in terms of access to the US markets as it allows Mexico to remove tariffs and quotas over specified adjustment periods. This would inadvertently create a situation in which Mexico, which already has inexpensive labour, cheap energy, lower transportation cost, and economies of scale, would now have a further advantage over the CBI countries. What has already happened and is likely to continue and intensify is: (a) diversion of US demand from suppliers in CBI countries to firms in Mexico, thus reducing CBI exports; (b) diversion of investment which is already evident. For instance, in the last two years there has been a pause in investment in the region as investors waited to evaluate the NAFTA provisions. The US International Trade Commission's (ITC's) report entitled, *Potential Effects of a North American Free Trade Agreement on Apparel Investments in CBERA Countries,* has concluded that 'a NAFTA will introduce incentives that will tend to favor apparel investment shifts away from the CBERA countries to Mexico'; (c) there is danger of a transfer or closure of existing productive capacity, particularly in apparel and garments — a 'foot-loose' industry that can easily be relocated.

Is CARICOM Still Relevant?

Globalization, the emergence of trade blocs, in particular , and the divergence of economic policy and the differences in the pace of adjustment among CARICOM countries, raise the question of whether CARICOM is an idea who's time has come and gone. This is a question which very few Caribbean persons would dare to raise publicly because CARICOM is a 'sacred cow'. Anyone who has the temerity to raise the question of the benefits of CARICOM is viewed as inept (i.e. unable to see 'the Emperors new clothes'), or immediately becomes an intellectual pariah.

If the truth be told CARICOM is still far from becoming a genuine common market; the reason being that the corporate integration which drives the process of integration in Western Europe has not taken place in CARICOM, and what multinationalization of enterprise that is occurring involves the spread of Caribbean firms to countries outside of CARICOM (e.g. the US, Canada, Great Britain, Cuba, and Cayman). In addition, even if a common market is created it will still be insufficient in market size to provide economies of scale which would allow effective competition in the global market place.

The eminent creation of and the proposed expansion into a western hemisphere free trade area, raises the question of whether CARICOM is obsolete. It is more likely that CARICOM will be useful for functional integration and as a mechanism for a common front in negotiating with other trade groups and industrialized Caribbean countries, while to a diminishing extent providing a preparatory stage for firms moving from producing for the national market to export production.

Part III   Challenge And Policy Response

Jamaica requires urgent remedial action in order to adjust to and survive the impact of hemispheric developments. This must proceed on two interrelated fronts: (a) foreign policy initiatives to influence developments at the global level and in the western hemisphere, in particular US foreign and economic policy; (b) and the formulation and implementation of a new development strategy which will enable Jamaica to achieve high rates of growth on a sustainable basis in the new global and hemispheric circumstances.

Foreign Policy

Jamaica must pursue a foreign policy which realistically attempts to influence hemispheric developments which affect the economy and its prospects for growth. Given Jamaica's small size many of its objectives will have to be pursued in consort with other developing countries in the Caribbean, Central America, and Latin America. The priority in the immediate future will be to influence US policy towards the region, with particular emphasis on ameliorating NAFTA's impact.

Response to NAFTA

The governments of the CBI countries must make a collective response to the potential adverse implications of NAFTA by calling on the US to preserve CBI provisions by ensuring parity with NAFTA in terms of conditions governing access to the US markets.

Specifically, Jamaica and other CBI countries should press for the following (Bernal, 16 December 1992):

1. Parity with NAFTA as a transitional arrangement:
   The CBI should have parity with NAFTA. They should enjoy the same conditions of market access to the US which Mexico receives under NAFTA. Specifically, there should be simultaneous and equivalent treatment for CBI countries and Mexico in terms of tariffs, rules of origin, and quota elimination. This would involve upgrading CBI to cover those products which are exempted from duty free treatment, and those goods and services placed at a disadvantage vis-a-vis Mexico by NAFTA provisions. For example, the textile and apparel sector is a key CBI export industry and is currently subject to many restrictions. Unless legislative action is taken to ensure parity between CBI and NAFTA, CBI countries will have to compete for market share and for investment with a Mexican textile and apparel sector that will enjoy reduced restrictions in the US market, and no restrictions at all after 10 years.

   Parity as a transitional arrangement will enable the economies of the CBI region to complete their process of economic reform and structural adjustment, which will put them in a position to move towards full reciprocity. A premature attempt by the CBI countries to provide full reciprocity could be detrimental to the process of adjustment, since export-led growth is only possible with stable market access. The period of time necessary to attain a position where reciprocity can be provided will vary among economies depending on their size, level of development, and economic structure.

2. Phased Reciprocity Over a Suitable Adjustment Period:
Having utilized a transitional period based on similar market access to that provided to Mexico under NAFTA, CBI countries will be in a position to begin to phase in reciprocity over a suitable period. A suitable adjustment period will take account of the small size and undiversified structure of Caribbean economies. Furthermore, reciprocity should not be given a restrictive connotation; that is, reciprocity does not mean strict equivalence in tariff reduction or elimination of quantitative restrictions, but must reflect the range of issues encompassed in international economic relations, namely trade in goods and services, investment, and intellectual property rights.

3. Transparent Process Trade Liberalization:
If NAFTA is the first building block of the EAI, there must be a clearly demonstrated commitment to completing the structure, otherwise there will be uncertainty. This uncertainty is detrimental to private sector expansion and long term investment. The procedure and time table for expanding NAFTA beyond its current three members should be clearly set out. There should be specific provisions put in place through implementing legislation to allow accession of CBI and other countries to NAFTA. This process should be transparent and based on clearly defined criteria for eligibility. This will provide the kind of predictability that diminishes investment diversion and discourages private capital flows. It will also diminish unwarranted fears that an inaccessible North American trading bloc is emerging.

4. A Level Playing Field:
NAFTA would prove to be a watershed in hemispheric trading relations, particularly if the foregoing issues are resolved. Many Caribbean countries are implementing programmes of market oriented reforms and the success of this adjustment process will largely depend on increased investment and export growth. Jamaica and several CBI countries are well advanced in a process of economic adjustment which will enable them to compete more effectively in the global market. Domestic economic reforms can be enhanced and brought to fruition by improved market access for new and traditional exports. Legislative and other action should be taken to ensure that the CBI countries are not placed at a disadvantage in the short or medium term and that the full potential NAFTA offers the region is realised. Competing on a level economic playing field is vitally important to Jamaica and to other small, undiversified economies of the Caribbean.

Influence Through Collaboration

Jamaica and the Caribbean must not be passive participants but must be active in shaping US policy towards the region. The Caribbean must seize the opportunity afforded by the unique nature of the US political process and the consultative institutional mechanism of the Framework Agreement to articulate its views. It is incumbent on Caribbean governments to become active participants in the process of shaping US policy by their lobbying efforts and diplomatic initiatives. This could most effectively be done by collective action on the basis of the wider Caribbean; that is, the traditional Caribbean together with Central America. It is possible for small, vulnerable economies, which are a particular genre of economy with their own peculiar constraints and specific development problems, to argue successfully to receive special consideration and even priority treatment.

Regional Co-operation to promote trade and investment

Jamaica should be an active advocate and participant in establishing regional arrangements which promote growth, through liberalizing trade and capital flows. This process could take the form of expanding CARICOM through ever widening concentric circles of cooperation and, or, participating in regional arrangements originating in Latin America.

A New Development Strategy

The events and trends now taking place at the global level and in the hemisphere pose an unprecedented challenge to Jamaica. The difficulties are not insurmountable but a new development strategy will be required. The most important components are outlined below.

Abandoning the Traditional, Thinking The New

There must be both a recognition of the need to change and a willingness to innovate. This, like every process of adjustment begins with a change of mind, outlook and attitude. This process of adjustment will only commence in earnest when there is a change of mind in both the public and private sector and Jamaican entrepreneurs dare to think the new and adventurous. For example, succeeding governments since the early 1950s have been locked into a mind-set which sees the transition from underdevelopment to development, as industrialization. This is viewed as progressing from import 'sub-substitution industrialization' to the export of manufactured goods. Despite protection and other government support, this transition has not taken place. Perhaps this is no longer a viable strategy given developments in the world economy, and despite the success of the newly industrialized countries of Asia. Maybe Jamaica should skip the traditional development by industrialization, and pursue development by the export of services. The advantages of this are numerous, including the fact that services are the fastest growing items in world trade and in the US economy which is our largest trading partner. The jobs created would be relatively high-wage and environmentally safe. The prospects for the export of services, especially to the US, are very encouraging. The services sector will provide one-half of all new jobs in the US between now and the year 2005 (*Occupational Outlook Handbook*, 1992, p.10). Many of these 12.5 million jobs (e.g. data processing and accounting) can be undertaken in Jamaica given wage differentials and communications technology.

Exploring New Investment Opportunities

The prerequisite to taking advantage of new nontraditional investment opportunities is the capacity to dare to think of new ventures, and to attempt to supply goods and services which we have not done in the past. For example, the high cost of health care in the US makes it cheaper for someone to fly to Jamaica, receive treatment, have a holiday, and still save. All operations, other than open heart surgery, could be done in Jamaica at a fraction of the cost. The day is coming when there will be multinational hospitals. A hospital in Washington, D.C. may own a hospital in Jamaica to which it would refer all cases requiring certain types of surgery and certain forms of rehabilitative treatment.

There is also a huge market for retirement homes, where people require custodial care. This would have the additional benefit of permitting our doctors and nurses to earn foreign exchange, stemming the loss of medical personnel, and rebuilding the health service. Lower costs, climate, and the standard of health care in Jamaica will allow the provision of health care to visitors and retirement homes at a cost lower than that available in developed countries (Alleyne, 1990). Cuba for many years has exploited this opportunity, particularly the market in Europe. An increasing number of Americans are going to Mexico for treatment because the cost of a doctor's visit is as much as 80 per cent lower than the US cost and some drugs are up to 75 per cent cheaper (*Hilts, New York Times*, 13 October 1992).

Jamaica has the right factor mix — lower wages and close proximity
— to be the haven for back-office operations such as data processing
and accounting. This is already happening: for example, Swiss Air is
moving its accounting department from Switzerland to Bombay, India
(*Green, Financial Times*, 13 October 1992).

Focus On Tomorrow's Exports

There has to be a willingness to look beyond traditional economic
activities and to financial services and the new dynamic sectors in the
global economy such as micro-electronics, biotechnology, telecommunications, robotics, and information. The transition from low wage,
labour intensive activities to technology, and information intensive
activities will depend on the quality of human resources. The work
force will have to be more skilled, knowledge-oriented, and capable of
adopting new technology. Management, production, and decision
making will have to be 'informationalized'.[13] Export firms in Jamaica
will have to develop the capacity to respond quickly to changes in
demand in existing and new markets, in particular, that of the US. This
more than anything else is the secret of success of the newly industrialized export economies of Asia. If product 'X' is demanded today, it
will be manufactured by Japan tomorrow, and by these countries at a
lower price the following day. It is this ability to respond quickly to
changes in the market place which will determine the success of
exports.

Mobilizing the Inputs

Apart from infrastructure all other inputs in the process of production
— for example, technology, machinery, and raw materials — can be
purchased. Capital can be attracted and finance mobilized on international money markets. The most difficult and important determinant
of price and quality competitiveness and speedy response to changes
in demand, and efficient marketing and distribution is the quality of
human resources. There are three aspects of the human resource
dimension (1) entrepreneurship, (2) management and (3) the productivity of workers.

Entrepreneurship

In regard to entrepreneurship Jamaica is well served, as there has been
an explosion of entrepreneurship in recent years. Jamaicans have a
natural flare for enterprise and nearly everybody in Jamaica, even
those working nine to five, is involved in some type of business.

Jamaican entrepreneurs have displayed the audacity which is the hallmark of Jamaican culture. They are competing in the world market in every sector. They are creating multinational corporations by establishing overseas factories, insurance companies, banks, building societies, and hotels. Jamaican multinationals operate in Britain, Canada, the US, Puerto Rico, Cayman Islands, Cuba, Panama, Trinidad and Tobago, Barbados, Belize, Antigua, and St. Lucia. They have demonstrated the capability, innovativeness, technical sophistication, and informed risk-taking which is necessary.

Management

Management will have to become more sophisticated, be constantly in touch with developments in international markets, and constantly update itself on new technological innovations. Our managerial capacity has improved considerably, and professionalism has increased in recent years. However, there is still room for improvement and we should be willing to upgrade the private sector's management capacity by importing skilled managers and other professionals. This need not mean a completely open door policy where foreigners, unaware of our culture and traditions take over top managerial posts. In the short run there are more than enough skilled Jamaicans overseas, who, under the right circumstances, would be willing to return to Jamaica. We must think of Jamaica, not as a physical place, but as a nation without borders. In the long run we need to reorient our post secondary education away from an emphasis on the arts, and towards management, accounting, and computer programming.

Productivity of Labour

The productivity of labour in Jamaica needs to be upgraded. This has to be tackled both within the individual enterprise and in the society as a whole. Firms need to put more emphasis on vocational training and on-the-job education. For the society as a whole, education will have to become the first priority; that is, the financial requirements of what is needed for a well educated work force should be the first charge on the government's budget. Specifically, the education budget must be drawn up first and then what is left allocated to the other functions of government.

To have a well educated work force is not necessarily going to mean spending more money, but it will require that expenditure be allocated differently so that more can be achieved. The two requirements of this are:

1. a reordering of the curriculum to concentrate on english, math, and science, both at the primary and secondary levels. This can be achieved by increasing the number of classroom hours devoted to these subjects by a corresponding reduction in other subjects.
2. increasing the salaries of teachers to a level which encourages the retention and return of experienced and qualified teachers — teachers who are now selling everything from garments to life insurance. Better teachers mean not only a better educated nation but improved public knowledge about nutrition, hygiene, sanitation, birth control, preventative health care and so on.

The emphasis in education should be on a solid and sound primary education, up to the age of 12 or 13, and technical schools, with a reduced focus on grammar school education at the secondary level. The curriculum should include more practical job related subjects, since only a small fraction of the total high school population will go on to university. This kind of programme for education should create a technologically oriented work force with a sound educational foundation capable of high productivity, oriented to learning new technology, and adaptable to new job skills.

Mergers and Corporate Integration

Jamaica must understand that it is part of a global capital market in which capital has no nationality; indeed, bitter political differences and economic rivalry have been swept aside. For example, Mexico's largest construction firm, Empresas ICA, is now 49 per cent owned by Flour Daniel of California (Daniel, *Journal of Commerce*, 19 May 1993). A Nigerian trade delegation visited South Africa (*Journal of Commerce*, May 1993), while China and Taiwan will collaborate in building a petrochemical plant in Malaysia (*Journal of Commerce*, May 1993). Rivals Toshiba and Samsung (Korea) will collaborate on chips (*New York Times*, 22 December 1992).

Corporate integration, consolidation, and restructuring through cross border mergers and acquisitions is a world-wide phenomenon. This has resulted from: striving for increased size; enhanced market presence; consolidation and pruning forced by competition; easing of regulations governing mergers and; preparing for more intensive competition from US and Japanese firms in the global market place (*Business Week*, 18 May 1992, pp.64-65). Traditional rivals are now collaborating in Europe; for example, Air France and Lufthansa plan to merge their hotel chains and Meridian and Kempinski share marketing and reservation costs (pp.64-65). Nissan plans to buy auto parts from a Toyota affiliate (*Wall Street Journal*, 14 May 1993). This has been a well established pattern in Japan.

A merger movement between Jamaican multinational firms would make them more viable, and joint-venture partnership with foreign investors is critical for survival as many exporters are small compared to the firms and multinational corporations against which they have to compete especially in major export markets like the US and Europe. Small size puts CARICOM exporters at a severe disadvantage and, therefore, there is need for collaborative corporate alliances or mergers to provide a larger capital base and pool of resources and expertise.

Arms length international trade is being displaced by intra-firm trade (Helleiner, 1981) and global marketing networks. Jamaican exporters have suffered in the past from having to deal with middle men in penetrating the distribution chain in the US and other export markets. It is of paramount importance that this obstacle to effective marketing be removed as quickly as possible. The solution is for large exporters or groups of exporters to establish retail outlets in major export markets by strategic transnational alliances.

Transnational corporate alliances and multinational cooperation could enhance the obvious complementarity between Jamaica and the US, which derives from differences in wage levels and factor endowments. This complementarity takes the form of the location of different aspects of the production process in different places, allowing the product to be competitive in the global marketplace. For example, the CBI region is the largest supplier of garments and apparel to the US, 80 per cent of which are 807-type products in which US labour and raw materials constitute 80 per cent of the finished product. In the absence of this complementarity both the US textile and apparel sector would face a flood of 'cheap labour' imports. In order to preserve this complementarity a transition period of 15 years is required for the phase-in of the new arrangements, which integrate textiles and apparel into the GATT.

Part IV   Why Jamaica Can Make it

There is no need to panic because there are plenty of opportunities for earning foreign exchange and for providing employment for Jamaicans. Jamaica has several advantages. It is close to the US, English-speaking, has relatively inexpensive labour, a hard working labour force, if adequately remunerated, and a tradition of excellence.

(Jamaica has produced over a sustained period of many decades, products which are the finest in the world.The fact that we have produced the best rum, and the best coffee, over so many years is not accidental or fortuitous). Jamaica has a new entrepreneur whose business acumen has been honed by the adversity of the economic difficulties over the last two decades, an environment in which there is a new legitimacy of business, investment and profit, a government which has removed the constraints on private enterprise and the restrictions and regulations which inhibit the operations of the market, and a partnership between the private sector and the public sector. There is a proven managerial and entrepreneurial capacity which has produced goods and services which are competitive in price and quality in the global market-place. The achievements of the bauxite-alumina industry and the tourism sector demonstrate this capacity and there is no reason why similar competence should not be achieved in other sectors. Finally, Jamaica has a hospitable climate.

Jamaicans are a special people. We are hard working and enterprising and we have an audacity which allows us to survive in any system or situation. Our history demonstrates our capacity to overcome challenges. We have triumphed over colonialism, slavery, regulation, deregulation, liberalization, and devaluation. I am convinced that we will meet the challenge of the twenty-first century.

References

Alleyne, George, *Health and Tourism in the Caribbean; Bulletin of PAHO20, 3, 1990, pp.291-300.*

Edward, Balls,'Building Trade Blocs in East Asia and the Pacific, *Financial Times,* October 1991.

Bernal, Richard L., 'Impact of on the Economic Development of the Caribbean and U.S./Caribbean Trade', Statement at the Hearing Before the House Committee on Small Business, 16 December 1992, Washington, D.C.

Bernal, Richard L., 'Debt, Drugs and Development in the Caribbean', *Trans-Africa,* 9, 2, Summer 1992, pp. 83-92.

Bernal, Richard L., 'Regional Trade Arrangements in the Western Hemisphere', *American University Journal of International Policy and Law,* vol.8 no.4. Summer 1993.

Bhagwati, Jagdish, 'Aggressive Unilateralism', in Jagdish Bhagwati and Hugh T. Patrick (eds), *Aggressive Unilateralism,* Ann Arbor: University of Michegan Press, 1992, pp. 1-45.

Bradford, Colin, Jr., (ed.), *Strategic Options for Latin America in the 1990s*, Organization for Economic Cooperation and Development and Inter-American Development Bank, 1991.
Brzezinski, Zbigniew, 'Selective Global Commitment', *Foreign Affairs*, 70, 4, Fall 1991, pp. 1-20.
Business Week, 'Feeding Frenzy on the Continent', 18 May 1992, pp. 64-65.
Cardoso, Eliana,Helwege Ann, *Cuba After Communism*, Cambridge, Mass.: M.I.T. Press, 1992.
Preeg, Ernest H., *Cuba and the New Caribbean Economic Order* , Washington, D.C.: Center for Strategic and International Studies, 1993.
Caribbean Week, 'Is Belize now Belice?' 10 September, 2 October, 1992.
Davis, Stan, Davidson, Bill, *2020 Vision*, New York: Simon and Schuster, 1991.
Financial Times, Daniel Green, 'SIA considers moving department to India', 13 October 1992.
Fisher, Richard D., 'How Bush can prevent creation of an Asian Anti-U.S. Trade Bloc', *Heritage Foundation Backgrounder No. 169*, 31 October 1991.
Helleiner, Gerald K., *Intra-Firm Trade and the Developing Countries*, London: Macmillam Press, 1981.
Hills, Carla A., *Trade, the Americas, and the World: Addresses by Ambassador Carla A. Hills, U.S. Trade Representative before the Organization of American States Conference of Trade Ministers*, Washington, D.C., 29 October 1991.
Hoon, Lim Siong, 'ASEAN tables first step to regional customs grouping', *Financial Times*, October 1991.
Hufbauer, Gary Clyde, Jeffrey J. Schott, *North American Tree Trade: Issues and Recommendations*, Washington, D.C.: Institute for International Economics, 1992.
Johnson, Chalmers; Laura D'Andrea Tyson; John Zyman (eds), *Politics and Productivity*, New York: Harper, 1989.
The Journal of Commerce, 'China Joins Taiwan-Led Chemical Deal in Malaysia', 19 May 1993.
The Journal of Commerce, Flour Daniel, 'ICA Form Jointly Owned Company', 19 May 1993.
The Journal of Commerce, 'Nigeria Delegation's Visit is Boost for South Africa, 19 May 1993.
Kennedy, Paul, *The Rise and Fall of the Great Powers*, New York: Vintage Books, 1987.
Kotkin, Jol, *Tribes: How Race, Religion, and Identity Determine Success in the New Global Economy*, New York: Random House, 1993.
Kuathammer, Charles, 'The Lonely Superpower', *The New Republic*, 29 July 1991, pp. 23-27.
Moynihan, Daniel Patrick, *Pandemonium, Ethnicity in International Politics*, Oxford: Oxford University Press, 1993.
National Journal, 'Opinion Outlook: Views on Foreign Policy', 1 August 1992.
Nau, Henry R.,*The Myth of America's Decline*, Oxford: Oxford University Press, 1990.
New York Times, 'Toshiba to Work with Samsung on Flash Chips', 22 December 1992.
New York Times, Howard W. French, "U.S.Lures Dominicans, Too, to the Cruel Sea", 8 December 1992.

New York Times, Phillip J. Hilts, 'Quality and Low Cost of Medical Care Lure Americans on Border to Mexico', 23 November 1992.

Nye, Joseph S., *Bound to Lead*, New York Basic Books, 1990.

O'Brien, Richard, *Global Financial Integration, New York: The Royal Institute of International Affairs Council on Foreign Relations Press, 1992*.

Office of the United States Trade Representatives, *The United States-Canada Free Trade Agreement*, Washington, January 1991.

New York Times Book Review, Robert B. Reich, 'Is Japan Really out to Get Us', 9 February 1992.

Schlesinger, Arthur M., Jr., *The Disuniting of America: Reflections on a Multicultural Society*, New York: W.W. Norton, 1992.

Sullivan, Mark P., *Latin American Debt Characteristics: Trends and U.S. Policy*, Washington, D.C.: Congressional Research Service, 11 April, 1991.

The Atlantic Monthly, Alan Tondson , 'What is the National Interest', *July 1991, pp. 35-81.*

Tyson, Laura D'Andrea, *Trade Conflict in High Technology Industries*, Washington, D.C.: Institute for International Economics, 1992.

U.S. Department of Commerce, *U.S. exports to Latin America and the Caribbean: A State-by-State overview 1987-1990*, Washington D.C.: International Trade Administration, U.S. Agency for International Development, March 1992.

U.S. Department of Commerce, *1990 Caribbean Basin Investment Survey*, Washington, D.C.: Latin America/Caribbean Business Development Center, Caribbean Basin Division, February 1991.

U.S. Department of Commerce, *Enterprise for the Americas Initiative* (EAI), Fact Sheet, Washington D.C.: Office of Latin America, 30 August 1991.

U.S. Department of Labor, *Occupational Outlook Handbook: 1992-93*, Washington, D.C., May 1992.

The Wall Street Journal, 'Nissan to Buy Auto Parts From a Toyota Affiliate', 14 May 1993.

Washington Post, Patrick, Buchanan, 'Now that Red is Dead, Come Home America', 8 September 1991.

Washington Post, Don, Oberdirfer, 'Opinion Builds for Smaller U.S. Role Abroad, 27 October 1991.

Washington Post, Peter Maass, 'Flood of Foreign Investment Capitalizes on New Hungary, 10 November 1991.

World Bank, *World Development Report 1990*, Washington D.C., 1990.

World Bank, *World Bank Annual Report 1992*, Washington D.C., 1992.

Wriston, Walter B., *The Twilight of Sovereignty*, New York: Charles Scribner's Sons, 1992.

Zuboff, Shoshana, *In the Age of the Smart Machine*, New York Basic Books, 1988.

Notes

1. Wriston points out that instant global communications and computers have resulted in an 'information revolution', which makes national boundaries increasingly irrelevant, undermining 'sovereignty'. See Walter B. Wriston, The Twilight of Sovereignty.

2.There is apprehension in the US about the emergence of trade blocs which will portent an escalation of protectionism e.g. Richard D. Fisher, 'How Bush can prevent creation of an Asian Anti-U.S. Trade Bloc'. Heritate Foundation Backgrounder No. 169. There is also a current of opinion that views Japanese protectionism, exports and investment as a threat to the US. For a review of this literature see Robert B. Reich, 'Is Japan Really out to Get Us', New York Times Book Review.

3.In October 1991, the member countries of the Association of South East Asian Nations (ASEAN) formally announced their intention to form an Asean Free Trade Area (AFTA) with the objective of creating a single market in 15 years. See Lim Siong Hoon, 'Asean tables first step to regional customs grouping, Financial Times.

4.An East Asian Economic Group consisting of Japan, the Asean countries (Brunei, Indonesia, Malaysia, the Philippines, Singapore and Thailand) and the newly industrialized countries (South Korea, Hong Kong and Taiwan) would encompass 33.8 per cent of the exports of these countries. See Edward Balls, Building Trade Blocs in East Asia and the Pacific', Financial Times.

5.There is a raging debate over whether the US has declined or is declining and whether this decline is absolute or relative. See Paul Kennedy, The Rise and Fall of the Great Powers, who argues that there is decline and it is inevitable; Henry R. Nau, The Myth of America's Decline, who denies the decline of US power; and Joseph S. Nye, Jr., Bound to Lead, who suggests that US power has not declined but has changed.

6.In 1987, Latin America and the Caribbean accounted for 14 per cent of total US exports and 13.6 per cent in 1990. See US Exports to Latin America and the Caribbean: A State-by-State Overview 1987-1990, p. 7.

7.President Bush has stated that 'prosperous Latin America is a natural market for United States goods and services. Strengthening our neighbours' economies will result in more exports'. See Text of Remarks by the President in an address to the Council of Americas Dinner, Washington, D.C.: Office of the Press Secretary, White House, 23 April 1992, p. 4.

8.The impact of race and ethnicity may extend beyond politics to affect economic affairs. This intriguing proposition is mooted but not convincingly demonstrated by Jol Kotkin, Tribes: How Race, Religion, and Identity Determine Success in the New Global Economy.

9.Some observers date this as early as 1986. See 'Free Trade Areas, the Enterprise for the Americas Initiative and the Multilateral Trading System' in Colin J. Bradford Jr. (ed.), Strategic Options for Latin America in the 1990s, p. 259.

10.Ambassador Carla Hills has warned that 'The United States Congress will want to see the positive results of the North American Free Trade Agreement before authorizing the Administration to launch new free trade agreements with other trading partners in the region'. Trade, the American and the World: Addresses by Ambassador Carla A. Hills, U.S. Trade Representative before the Organization of American States Conference of Trade Ministers, p. 4.

11.One proposed agenda for US economic engagement and normalization includes the suggestion that the US should allocate $1 billion of aid per year for the next five years. Eliana Cardoso and Ann Helwege, Cuba After Communism, p. 114.

12. For an extended analysis of the implications for the Caribbean of Cuba's economic reintegration in the Western Hemisphere see Ernest H. Preeg, Cuba and the New Caribbean Economic Order.

13. Information technology has not merely added a new dimension to the way business is conducted, but has altered fundamentally the nature, management and organization of business. See Stan Davis and Bill Davidson, 2020 Vision; and Shoshana Zuboff, In the Age of the Smart Machine.

CHAPTER 14

The Future of CARICOM in the Global Economy

Alister McIntyre

Introduction

The subject on which I have been asked to speak requires me to comment on how the CARICOM countries, and CARICOM as an integration scheme, might fit into the evolving global economy. The first issue speaks to the performance of the world economy and to the new structural features that are unfolding. The second directs attention to developments in trade policies and in the trading system.

Global Economic Performance

It is well known that the growth of the world economy, which stayed at a level of about three per cent per annum for most of the 1980s, slipped in 1990 to 1.8 per cent, and then in 1991 to -0.4 per cent — which is the first occasion on which world GDP declined since the end of the second world war. Despite optimistic forecasts both by governments and the private sector in the major countries, the upturn from the recession has not yet taken hold. At best, growth this year is likely to be weak. The United Nations world economic survey predicts a one per cent rate, while most forecasts project no more than a return in 1993 and beyond to the three per cent growth of the 1980s.

It should be recalled that several commentators made the point at the time, that three per cent growth in the major countries was insufficient to generate satisfactory rates of growth in the developing countries.

It is true that in 1990 and 1991 developing countries, taken as a whole, grew faster than the world average at 4.7 per cent and 3.4 per cent respectively. However, this was largely due to the performance of Asian countries, especially China, which grew at the impressive rates of five and seven per cent respectively. A few Latin American countries — Mexico, Chile, and Argentina, in particular — recorded relatively high rates of growth, but this was not generally the case in the countries of the Caribbean.

We are facing a situation, therefore, where the global economic environment is unlikely to provide much general impetus to our growth. The rate of growth of world trade itself has declined from the peak of over eight per cent attained in 1988, to just over three per cent in 1991. In such a context of slow growth, the only way we can perform above average is to increase our market shares, both with respect to traditional and new products.

The Traditional Exports

There is very little to say about the traditional products. The bauxite and alumina market is unsettled and over-supplied at the present time. Petroleum production is declining in Trinidad and Tobago because of the depletion of reserves. In the case of the traditional agricultural exports — sugar and bananas — the challenge is to retain market shares. Given present costs and quality there is only limited hope of increasing them.

Tourism is probably the only product where some positive growth is taking place, but it is patchy. The all-inclusive hotels are doing well, as are some of the newer destinations in the Eastern Caribbean. But certain traditional destinations are in trouble. It would seem that major investments are called for to refurbish the hotel plant and to improve the quality of attractions and service. There is no doubt that international competition in tourism is intensifying, with new destinations coming on stream, and with the inroads being made by the cruise ships.

Developing New Exportables

It is already well understood that the CARICOM countries need to find new exportables, both of goods and services. The multilateral financial institutions and important bilateral donors have been pushing for institutional and policy reforms to make the economies more competitive and to remove export biases. The missing element has been a well-targeted effort to build up the knowledge base for exports. Experience elsewhere shows that this will not happen spontaneously. A deliberate government/private sector effort, backed up both by local and external resources, seems to be indicated.

We stand our best chance of improving our export performance through product development and innovation. In the agricultural field, despite long standing recognition of the need for it, insufficient attention is being paid to product development in areas such as fruit and vegetables, aquaculture, and marineculture. Individual countries lack the critical mass of expertise to do all of the research and development needed on their own. It has long been recognized that we need to organize regional research and development teams to undertake the investigative work, but action is slow in coming.

The same thing is true with respect to traditional manufactures, such as garments and furniture, where informed commentators have long made the point that our best bet may not lie in labour-intensive mass production, but rather in going up-market with smaller scale custom-tailored production. The point needs to be made here, again, that in tourism we need to work harder on product development and innovation, in areas such as local dishes and beverages, health and eco-tourism.

Services

A field of great promise for export development is services. Some banks, building societies, and insurance companies are already beginning to set up subsidiaries, affiliates, and offices abroad. At least one accounting firm is selling software services as far afield as Southeast Asia. There are opportunities, too, for exporting services in areas such as engineering and construction, design, medical diagnosis, legal advice, agricultural technology, and education, to name only a few.

If we are not careful, despite our potential in these fields, we may end up in the future as net importers, not net exporters, of these services. Subject to what I shall say later, it is not too fanciful to project the establishment of a world-wide regime for open multilateral trade in services, following the conclusion of the Uruguay round. If we do not make strenuous efforts now to improve our competitiveness in services trade, we shall find ourselves in a disadvantageous position when that time comes.

The Era of Knowledge

The points that I have been making can be summarized in the observation that we are living in an era where knowledge is increasingly becoming the key to economic progress. We have to take action now to develop much greater capability than ever before in knowledge-intensive production of both traditional and new exports of goods and services. As several people have argued, this requires unprecedented efforts to modernize the education system at all levels.

In their report entitled 'Time for Action,' the West Indian Commission has set out a number of areas where CARICOM countries can work together to their mutual advantage. Colleagues at the University of the West Indies (UWI) and, myself, have stressed repeatedly what needs to be done to increase access to the University and to improve the quality of its graduates. Today, I underscore the urgent need to improve access and the quality of tertiary education as a whole, by drawing attention to the grave situation with respect to intermediate level technicians and technologists.

The World Bank report on "Access, Quality and Efficiency in Caribbean Education" makes depressing reading on the subject. The report shows that the annual output of craft-level graduates in CARICOM as a whole, is between 1200 to 1500 technicians. This level of output means that improvements in the quality of the labour force are very slow. For example, as a percentage of the projected labour force by the year 2000, the annual addition of workers at this level ranges from 0.2 per cent in Barbados to 0.1 per cent in Trinidad and Tobago, 0.04 per cent in the OECS and 0.06 per cent in Jamaica. In other words, at present levels of output, it will take between five years in Barbados, 10 in Trinidad and Tobago, 25 in the OECS, and over 30 in Jamaica, to achieve a one per cent increase in the proportion of technicians in the labour force. This situation is clearly untenable.

The UWI cannot do the entire job of knowledge development, but it is ready to play its part in strengthening the knowledge base for exports. We have undertaken in our current development plan to achieve a 50 per cent increase in our enrolment by the year 2000, with an emphasis on science and technology. We have secured a US$66 million concessional loan to upgrade our facilities and staff in science and technology.

We hope to discuss with government and the private sector our plans for establishing a science park, and reorganizing and upgrading our consultancy services.

UWI is also working to become an export earner. We are embarking on a very substantial expansion of our summer programme, with international summer schools in Caribbean studies and multicultural education, to which we expect to attract students from many countries. We are looking at the feasibility of introducing summer programmes in English as a second language, targeted towards the non-English speaking Caribbean and Latin America. We are developing, with encouragement from the Commonwealth Fund for Technical Cooperation (CFTC), short courses for students from other developing countries, particularly in Africa and the Pacific. We are already making a start with courses in plant tissue culture, solid waste management, and gender studies.

CARICOM countries need to mobilize all of their companies, firms, and institutions, to work on export development. The world economy is in an anaemic state, but as the fast-growing developing countries are showing, there are still possibilities for expanding exports. Small countries, like our own, should be particularly favoured, since our needs are modest in global terms.

CARICOM as an Integration Scheme

I turn now to the second question: the future of CARICOM as an integration scheme in the light of trade policy developments in major countries, and the evolution of the international trading system itself.

There continues to be great controversy over whether regional and subregional groupings are building blocks or stumbling blocks to the reestablishment of an open system of multilateral trade. Article xxiv of the present GATT rules permits the formation of customs unions and free trade areas, and part iv of the agreement recognizes the value of economic integration to developing countries. However, GATT has never in its history approved an economic integration scheme, since in every case there was a division of opinion as to whether the scheme was on balance trade-creating rather than trade-diverting.

It is possible that the rules emanating from the Uruguay round would be stricter on integration schemes. This was foreshadowed in the Leutwiller report on the world trading system which was negative on the matter. The negotiating text of the GATT's Director General makes no mention of these schemes, except in relation to trade in services. Nevertheless, it is not realistic to suppose that given the many schemes around the world, especially the larger ones, such as the European single market and NAFTA, they could be completely excluded from consideration in any final negotiated text for a new world trading system. Accordingly, it is doubtful whether the continued existence of CARICOM will be in conflict with any future regime for international trade.

Integration and Export-led Growth

Nevertheless, the substantive point is whether an integration scheme is appropriate for countries following strategies of export-led growth. There is a point of view which sees integration schemes as essentially protectionist arrangements designed to support import-substitution strategies of development. Those who hold that view argue that countries pursuing strategies of export-led growth should liberalize their trade as much as possible since import tariffs are essentially export biased. In a fully liberalized economy exporters can identify sources for their imports from the cheapest suppliers without incurring a duty penalty. If other countries reciprocate, they can also export to them on an equal footing with other exporters and with their domestic producers.

This line of reasoning cannot be contested in conceptual terms, but, in reality, the world is very far from a regime of universal free and open trade, notwithstanding the genuine efforts being made in the Uruguay round to roll back protectionism. Some are even arguing that managed trade is gaining ground as major countries revert to protectionist devices to deal with their trade imbalances and disputes with other major countries. Agriculture is a particularly difficult sector where quite recently decisions have been taken to increase the sale of subsidized products.

Timing Trade Liberalization

In that scenario, the CARICOM countries will have to judge very carefully the extent and timing of trade liberalization. Advocates of unilateral trade liberalization by developing countries tend to say that even if developing countries get no reciprocity from such liberalization, their consumers will benefit from cheaper imports. But as a very distinguished economist used to say, it is cold comfort to an unemployed man to tell him that the cost of living has declined.

CARICOM agricultural producers have a problem competing with producers from other countries who enjoy producer-subsidy equivalents of 50 per cent and more. While cheaper food for the CARICOM consumer is an important consideration, this must be set against the need to sustain production in the region. It is quite possible that unilateral trade liberalization with respect to agricultural products could generate a wave of subsidized imports that would force regional producers to cut back production, if not to go out of business entirely.

Accordingly, tactical considerations alone suggest that an appropriate protective tariff be retained on a transitional basis, both for bargaining purposes and to provide temporary protection for sensitive products such as agriculture, until the process of liberalization has definitely taken hold.

A CARICOM Single Market and Economy

It is sometimes not appreciated that CARICOM is likely to become more than a scheme of market integration. CARICOM heads of government committed themselves in 1989 to establish a single market and a single economy by 1994. If that decision is implemented, CARICOM would go beyond the freeing of trade in goods to include: (i) freer trade in services; (ii) freer movement of people for purposes of work, starting with university and professional graduates and media personnel; (iii) freer movement of capital, including the development of a regional stock exchange, and the establishment of a caribbean investment fund for the mobilization of venture capital; (iv) steps towards the creation of a common currency; (v) more structured efforts to negotiate jointly on international economic matters and, where appropriate, joint external representation.

In other words, CARICOM would progressively become a single economic space within which not only goods and services, but also factors of production, will move freely. This could significantly improve the climate for investment and export development in all countries of the region. Entrepreneurs will be able to meet their requirements for management, highly skilled personnel, and finance from throughout the region.

Production Cooperation and Production Sharing

Companies and firms can enter into production cooperation and sharing whereby they can package large volumes for export and achieve critical mass in vital areas such as research and development, marketing, and market development.

A single economic space can also provide a solid base for reaching into the non English speaking Caribbean. Trade and economic cooperation with the non English speaking Caribbean can eventually represent a vast enlargement of the potential for production sharing, as well as the size of the market open to CARICOM producers. Jamaica will be exceptionally well placed to take advantage of such developments.

It is no accident that the Dominican republic and Venezuela have applied for membership of CARICOM, rather than sought bilateral trade and economic agreements with individual CARICOM member states. Neither is it an accident that under the Enterprise for the Americas Initiative, the US administration has pointedly indicated its willingness to negotiate with groups of countries rather than individual countries.

The fact of the matter is that it is easier for countries to deal with a group rather than negotiate separately with 13 mini- and micro-states. This has been the region's experience through the Lome Convention, to CARIBCAN, CBI, and now the EAI.

We have to be hard-headed about this. CARICOM is a starting point into a wider world. As the West Indian Commission has argued, we have the advantage of multiple entry points into that world. We must try to utilize all of them so that we can respond to opportunities as they arise.

NAFTA

NAFTA is perhaps the development to which we must give the keenest attention. The prospect of eventual hemispheric-wide free trade is breathtaking, but it will not happen overnight. Considerable time must necessarily elapse before over 20 countries and groupings can gain access to the free trade area, because of the protracted negotiating and legislative processes involved. This is not to argue for delay in opening a negotiating dialogue with the three NAFTA partners. To the contrary, it is to say that the earlier one starts, the better the chances of bringing an arrangement within reach.

The Complexity of International Economic Negotiations

International economic negotiations are by their very nature time-consuming, require substantial inputs of diplomatic and technical expertise, and are vulnerable to the ebbs and flows of politics, governmental changes, and the shifting influence of special interest groups. In charting a course for the future we have to be realistic and flexible, and prepared to adapt and fine-tune our strategies as developments unfold. We should not delude ourselves into thinking that substantial benefits are just around the corner. It is only through a sustained effort that success can ultimately be achieved.

To conclude: I do not have a crystal ball; I do not know what the future of CARICOM might be; but based upon the considerations I have outlined, I see nothing emerging in the global economy that would negatively affect its continuance as it moves towards a single market and economy.

What West Indians need to show is a determination and capacity to stay the course; to implement plans and decisions which have been agreed; to eschew delusions of grandeur which can lead us to misjudge our importance to other countries; and to work resolutely to transform our economies into high growth, internationally competitive countries that can take advantage of the many opportunities that are arising in different parts of the world for greater trade, investment, and production.

APPENDICES

APPENDIX 1

Speeces at the
Opening Session

Dennis Benn:
UNDP Resident Representative

It is a distinct privilege and a pleasure for me to bring greetings to this symposium. I think too, that it is very important that the UNDP should be involved in an event of this nature. Therefore, we are equally pleased that we were able to cosponsor this event. I think that the symposium is very timely, in that it provides us with an opportunity to look beyond the immediate preoccupations of stabilization and adjustment, which, in a way, have dominated the development vision of the 1980s. My own feeling is that while we have been preoccupied with establishing the broad macro-economic framework which will govern development in Jamaica for the next few years, that if we were to be honest — and I follow the lead given by Dr. Davies to say that we must in fact display some honesty in the analysis we present — I am not sure that we have always done justice in identifying the critical development equation that should in fact govern longer-term growth.

My own feeling, therefore, is that it is very timely to look beyond that immediate preoccupation and to try to identify that strategic vision Dr. Davies talked about. I believe, just as the East Asian NICs in the 1960s and the 1970s embarked on a very daring strategy to establish a competitive manufacturing base, and 30 years after are in fact competing with the might of western economies, that given the talent that is evident in Jamaica, and given the accomplishments of the past 30 years, there is a real possibility that Jamaica, with some creative vision, might be able to imitate the example of the NICs: not in the same form, but I think we are ready in Jamaica for an 'NIC' too. And what do I mean by that? It would seem to me, given the advent of technology, given the fact that we have moved through a different historical context and circumstance of change, that there is a real possibility for Jamaica to apply a strategic vision in terms of the application of technology to the development process: to apply technology to create competitive advantage in terms of the production, not only of goods, as Dr. Park said, but of services. And I think that that is a very important strategic vision. And let me say that the UNDP — and I am sure other members of the our community — would be prepared, based on the outcome of this symposium, to support a number of initiatives that might be identified in terms of moving us into the twenty-first century.

It is not often that one sees such an array of local and foreign experts, and I am indeed very impressed with the list of participants. I know at one time when we sat to discuss the form of the symposium, there was a fear that the 'economist' vision might dominate our thinking about the future. But I am happy to say that a number of perspectives have been brought to bear on the decision as to where Jamaica should go in the twenty-first century.

Keynote Address:
Hugh Small, Minister of Finance

I would like to thank Omar Davies for his generous comments in linking me with the idea of having the seminar. But I want to tell you exactly how it happened, the circumstance in which it happened, and why I was so haunted by the idea that we really had to have it this year. It was on the sixteenth of January this year, I had only been in office as minister of finance for two weeks, and as has been perhaps the practice for half of the 30 years of our independence, the most immediate preoccupation of newly appointed ministers of finance is to go to Washington and have discussions with the international financial institutions.

This, of course, was my second experience, and so I was concerned that we should bring this cycle to an end. We were having dinner at Richard Bernal's official residence, and Richard, Dr. Donald Harris, and Gladstone Bonnick were there. We were discussing the all too terrifying business of taking on the responsibility of being minister of finance and planning, and what we really needed to do as a country to ensure that we took our sights off all these short-term perspectives that have become so much a part of IMF programmes, and what we needed to do to try and influence the Jamaican society to start to look at the longer-term on what had to be done to take us out of this relationship with the International Monetary Fund.

We felt that one of the things that had to be done was to develop a better understanding among the Jamaican people as to how we got to where we are now; what is it that we have done that has led us to where we are; what are some of the opportunities that we had that we may have missed; what are some of the talents that we have that we may not have maximised. And as the night grew older we felt that having what we thought at the time of calling a 'futurology' seminar was what was required; and we wanted to make sure that it brought into discussion, not just policy makers, not just economists and theoreticians, but some of the people who have had practical experience in terms of the Jamaican experience in the last 30 years. We thought that in particular we needed to bring together trade union leaders; we needed to bring together educators; and we needed to stop and pause and take a look at ourselves and what is happening in the world.

And so I would like this morning to thank Gladstone Bonnick, Donald Harris, and Richard Bernal, who all participated in that very informal soul-searching, for the encouragement they gave me at the time to look at the task of being Minister of Finance and Planning, not just in terms of the immediate tests and the preoccupation which the media has with judging the success or failure of ministers in terms of passing or not passing tests.

I would also like to thank them and to say that these three distinguished scholars had a lot to do with what is happening here today. I would also like to thank the Planning Institute of Jamaica because once I had that second phone call with Omar, they have been very enthusiastic about the task and have really put together what I consider to be a very fine programme. Dennis Benn has a special interest in these matters. He has often written us memos and comments, sat down and spoken to me in the ministry — not only the Ministry of Finance and Planning but when I was at the Ministry of Industry and Commerce —

about the need for us to step back and look down the road at what we can do. And I want to thank Dennis for his contribution. This month of October is the month in which we look at our national heritage, and in a very real sense what we will be doing in the course of the next two days is looking at the important path of our national heritage. And it comes 30 years after we assumed responsibility for our own affairs, and I think that it is a very fitting time for us to take this look.

I want to emphasize something that both Omar and Dennis have said and that is that the seminar really is going to be of very little value if it does not have honesty as its absolute imperative. And we wanted to demonstrate the extent to which we want that honesty by involving not only members of the Administration in the presentation of papers and in the discussions; we have invited representatives of the Opposition and the trade unions; and we have invited people who have points of view which do not coincide with that of the Administration. We don't want anybody to come here on the basis that they are participating in something that is meant to aggrandize the government's view or the government's effort, because this must be really a soul-searching national exercise in which we can honestly answer some of the burning questions of the day: Where are we now? How did we get here? What are some of the perceptions which influence the choices which we made during the course of the last 30 years? And what is the difference between our achievements and the aspirations which we fostered when we became independent 30 years ago?

Last night when I was reflecting on some of what I thought I ought to say, I recognised that it would be quite superfluous to speak about the global economy and the new technologies because people who are more expert than anybody in public life could claim to be on these subjects will be participating and sharing their views with you. But there is a thought that kept coming back which I wanted to share with you — a thought that I think has influenced a lot of what has happened to Jamaica in the last 30 years — and it is that we who are 90 miles away from Cuba gained independence just three years after the Cuban Revolution and months after the missile crisis of 1961. We gained independence in the shadow of the Alliance for Progress. And maybe we started off with perceptions about the kind of provisions that would be made for us, and the kind of entitlement that we had because we came of age at that time. We, maybe, also felt that we were special, as the first English-speaking country of the Caribbean to gain independence. But, certainly, when we look at the world as it is now, we recognize that whether or not those were some of the perceptions that may have influenced how we approached our responsibilities as an independent people (as an independent nation) that none of that matters in the world of the 1990s. There is a very real sense in which we cannot prepare ourselves for the twenty-first century unless we are prepared to come to terms with the 1990s: and part of the reality of the 1990s is that we are no longer in a bipolar world. We are now in a world in which there is a greater consensus about how development should take place, and there is nothing to be gained from the conflict of ideology and the threat of military conflict that so much influenced development perspectives when we became independent 30 years ago.

And there is another thought that kept coming to my mind last night when I was thinking of what I should say in pleading for us to be honest and to really look at all of the subjects in a thorough way. There was a thought that came to my mind when I was so very concerned that we should entertain conflicting points of view here and it is this: That because we are a small nation in terms of the number of people who live in this country, on this island — sometimes I think we tend to feel that we are only like corks on a river being swept along by powerful forces that are too complex and overwhelming for us to influence. It is very easy for us to get that perspective. Then I began to remember some of the students who were in London with me in 1962 when we became independent, and particularly some of the students from Singapore who seemed to have come to London with a much more clearly defined objective of why they were there than so many others of us who were part of what in fact was a much greater invasion than just an academic invasion of the United Kingdom. I thought that they too are a small nation that have not accepted the concept that they are corks on a river, unable to influence the sweep of the currents of the river. It occurred to me that we need at this time, as we look at our problems, to recognize that although we are a small nation in a big and sometimes terrifying and threatening world, everything that we do in this country in terms of facing up to our own problems and designing solutions to our own problems matters. And it is more what we do that matters in the context of the 1990s than what other people do or design. Because, whether we like it or not, we are going to have to learn to exist and survive in this competitive environment. Everything we do can result in changes that will be of lasting impact on our country, and we have to reconcile that feeling that we are small and insignificant with the commitment to be responsible for the consequences of our own actions.

So we have to ask, what have we learned from this experience of 30 years? What is there to learn from the experiences of others? And in this respect I am very glad to see that we have been able to attract, not only some of our most distinguished scholars from the Caribbean, and from Jamaica, in particular, but we have also been able to get to come to this seminar people like Dr. Park of Korea, who has a distinguished career in moulding the economic planning that helped to move that country from a state that was no more advanced than where we are now or where we were when we became independent, to the state of which it is now — one of the new industrial forces in the world: one of the really strong economies that has made the transition from the third world into being on the stage where it can claim to be considered to be amongst the first world.

I am glad that we have been able to attract to the seminar Dr. Michael Best whose work on 'The New Competition' has been so important in influencing the thinking of people, not only in his country, but across the world.

I am particularly happy too that the trade unions have responded, and I am happy also that members of the private sector are here. But perhaps the thing that gives me most pleasure is that we have been able to include in some of what we have set aside for discussion the whole question of the Jamaican political culture and the challenge of the twenty-first century. Because I believe that if we honestly look back on what has happened in the last 30 years, there are many aspects of our political culture which require detailed examination, and that we may conclude that there are aspects of our political culture that have perhaps distracted us from having the single-mindedness of purpose that is necessary as a guiding force in the development of economies such as our own.

And we have at this time, not just because we are coming to the end of this century, not just because we are at our thirtieth year as an independent nation, especially because we are entering into that volatile period of our political cycle when reckless things are said and criticisms are made without any reference to the validity of the argu-ments, and when we hold forward and hold forth perspectives that may be unrealistic, it is particularly important — and I am not saying this in pointing a finger anywhere; I am saying it as much of my party as I am saying of the other parties that exist in the country — it is particu-larly important for us to stand back and look at the scene where the political culture of the country has led us and how relevant it is in leading us into the twenty-first century.

One of the experiences that I had recently at the World Bank and IMF meeting was the recognition of the fact that one of the consequences of living in a unipolar world is that we have to look around at the experiences of countries that are closer to our own state of development, and we have to examine more closely some of the things that people in our own hemisphere have been doing to conquer the problems of poverty and underdevelopment. There was a meeting that was put on by the president of the World Bank for Latin American Ministers of Finance — it was a luncheon meeting —and after he had spoken he invited a number of us to speak about out own experiences. And one of the things that came out was that a number of ministers were saying: 'We are convinced that the reforms that we are making, we have to make, not because the International Monetary Fund is advocating them, or the World Bank has been advocating them, but we are convinced from our own experiences that we have to do them for our own sakes.' Perhaps that is one of the aspects of our political culture that we need to face up to. We need to take responsibility for harsh decisions. We need to address the whole question of what is there to be gained by short-term political mileage in attacking things that are harsh now but which are necessary for the process of development.

I remember, in particular, that the Minister of Finance of Mexico spoke when the World Bank President invited comments. It was very informal, and he said: "Yes, we in Mexico have done a number of things which are bringing positive results now. And one of the experiences that we have learned is that although we have been able to stimulate confidence, it is very easy to blow that confidence". And he was saying that in the face of the fact that the United States of America had announced that they were ready to put the NAFTA Agreement to Congress for approval. He was saying: "Look, we have got that far, but this confidence is very easy to be blown." Then he said something which I think is very relevant to us and to the question of our political culture. He said "You know we have learned that you don't own confidence, (you) only rent it."

And I thought of the Jamaican situation and the fact that when I entered that room the first questions that I was asked of some of the representatives of the World Bank were in relation to the demonstrations that had taken place the week before, and they were a little perplexed to understand why in a country like ours that had means of democratic expression, that that particular kind of expression was used when it could have such a negative effect on us. And when the Mexican Minister spoke about renting confidence, I realized that renting it is not just simply that the government has to continually address the question of the appropriate policies, but the whole political culture has to recognize that if you don't continue to pay your dues you are going to lose in this competition for the scarce capital that there is in the world — the scarce capital that is now being sought, not just by those countries that have for years been trying to attract private capital, but those countries that have now newly joined the race.

And, so, I look forward to this seminar and hope that, as I said and others have said, we will be honest with ourselves. I ask us to consider in this quest for honesty that, whereas we in Jamaica are very much tired of the process of adjustment, the longer we delay it the more we are going to have to endure that adjustment fatigue. And I ask us to recognize that there is another development taking place which is of equal importance to the adjustment fatigue that we are facing, the adjustment fatigue that we are feeling. And it is that among the first world countries, among those countries that are taking decisions to form regional trading blocs in their own interest, in the interest of their people, in the interest of widening the economic space of opportunities for their people; among those countries that are going after the expansion of economic space through trading groups, not on the basis of sentiment but on the pure basis of the betterment of their people; among those countries there is developing an *aid fatigue*. Therefore we cannot count on the munificence of others for the development of our people. We can no longer count on mobilizing other people's savings while our savings are leaving to go elsewhere. We have to count on ourselves and our resources, and we have to count on being able to attract those savings here. We cannot count on PL 480 and Food Aid, because as this aid fatigue takes hold of the industrialized world they look at us and compare our relatively privileged position with the position of our brothers in Somalia, Ethiopia, and war torn regions of the world. So we prepare ourselves for the twenty-first century by trying to prepare ourselves for the reality and dealing with the realities of the 1990s. And I sincerely hope that everyone will feel free to speak freely, but to do so in an atmosphere of tolerance: and that out of this Seminar will come something of value that will be looked at as the beginning of a new dialogue in the Jamaican experience for making something worthwhile of being an independent nation.

APPENDIX 2

Summary of Discussions

Although the main text included only the major papers presented at the symposium, important and insightful contributions were made by many of the discussants. The comments on the papers reflected, in some cases, violent disagreements with views presented, but on others there was general consensus on approaches to the twenty-first century. This appendix presents a brief summary of the discussions.

Perhaps the most fertile discussion centred on the economic prescriptions for Jamaica. Owen Jefferson, commenting on Omar Davies' presentation, noted the absence of the word 'planning' which, he charged, had now become 'dirty'. He argued that although the days of the 'command economy' were over, even under a 'liberalized regime' there was room for indicative planning where government defined national goals and set out plans to achieve them. He called for a suitable 'mix' between public and private sector.

This position of a greater role for government was supported by Gladstone Taylor and Andre Gordon who focused on the development of technology. Taylor agreed with Ventura and Girvan that government was better able to perform this role than the private sector. He went beyond this to suggest new areas for government involvement in providing legal instruments, proper fiscal and financial instruments, and centralized services such as information collection and dissemination and the operation of patents and trademarks to facilitate technological development. He noted that in a situation where the ratio between professional and technical people was 90 to 10 as opposed to 50 to 50 in developed countries, the 'socio-cultural focus' had to be changed to emphasise technology. Professor Leslie Robinson supported this position by pointing out that at the University of the West Indies (UWI) registration for management studies exceeded all the registrations in the Arts Faculty, natural sciences, and in economics, sociology and government put together. Both he and Gordon called for greater remuneration for science graduates to address this imbalance. Taylor urged government to redirect some of its spending on foreign technology to local institutions. Here, he defined a role for the private sector of utilizing local institutions such as the Scientific Research Council and decreasing their reliance on foreign technology. Girvan added that there needed to be a consensus on determining key industries and activities crucial for economic development, with training for this made a priority. People in those areas should be rewarded more highly than those in relatively nonproductive activities. Martin Henry urged that the problem could be alleviated if scientists were trained as managers.

An area of dispute was on the role of services in economic development. Both Andre Gordon and Michael Best urged for a focus on the development of the productive sector as opposed to the service sector. Gordon disagreed with Bernal's focus on the development of the service industry. Development, he believed, should be focused on crucial areas such as agriculture to ensure linkages with farmers and to reduce reliance on importation. Best was stridently opposed to an initial focus on the service sector. While services were important, he warned that a development strategy should not start with services since they 'bled' other sectors. He was particularly critical of the banking and insurance sectors and the stock market. He called for a 'radical restructuring' of the banking sector since it posed 'a terrible barrier to the development of . . . industry and economic growth in Jamaica'. He was particularly critical of the stock market saying that the experience of the UK, which had the world's most efficient stock market, showed that it deterred long term investment in industry. He described it as a 'run-down industry'.

Gordon Shirley, discussing Harris' paper, was critical of his suggestions for solving Jamaica's problems, in particular, what he saw as his basic prescription: the need to focus on industrial programming and planning to attract foreign direct investments to increase economic growth. He was less optimistic that Jamaica, in attempting to attract expatriate Jamaicans to keep their money in local banks, was likely to be more successful than other Latin American countries in attracting investment and savings from immigrant groups in the UK and US. He also did not accept Harris' view that Jamaica had a sustainable competitive advantage in the industrial segments he identified. He argued that sectors for emphasis must be chosen carefully and strategies to handle them developed. This required trying to increase the level of direct foreign investment in these sectors in a situation where Jamaica had come late to the game in trying to attract foreign investment and where its supply was diminishing. He warned that increased competition for foreign investment, which involved government trying to outbid its competitors with attractive incentive packages, may impose greater social costs than the benefits they brought. On Harris' prescription for developing a new entrepreneurial spirit, Shirley commented that 'the million dollar question is how do we go about developing such an entrepreneurial group.' He noted that the UWI was trying to develop 'that precise set of skills' Harris identified.

The discussions on appropriate responses to the North American Free Trade Area (NAFTA) revealed the lack of consensus on how Jamaica should respond to NAFTA and what its relations with CARICOM should be. William Demas, a key player in the regional integration movement, disagreed with the urgency with which Richard Bernal viewed NAFTA urging, on the contrary, caution. Byron Blake, a CARICOM functionary, supported this position warning the Caribbean to consider the consequences of membership in NAFTA to our relations with Europe. Both men, supported by Norman Girvan, saw CARICOM as continuing to play a crucial role in addressing common problems, and as a platform for guiding relations with NAFTA. Demas and Paul Chen Young both argued that the Caribbean needed to focus, not on access to more trade blocs, but on putting structures in place to enable the utilization of opportunities already provided by existing blocs such as CARICOM, CBI, and Lome. The problem lay, not in the existence of such blocs, but in our ability to make use of what they offered. A more critical view of CARICOM was also expressed. Finance Minister, Hugh Small, argued that CARICOM was too small an economic space for Jamaica's development so it had to look beyond this. He warned that if Jamaica could not get a consensus within CARICOM in addressing its structural weaknesses, then its 'relevance' to Jamaica would have to be questioned. Chen Young echoed this sentiment by suggesting that Jamaica should see whether its programmes coincided with CARICOM's and to determine the extent to which there could be 'collaboration under CARICOM'. 'Jamaica ... needs to ask itself what is in its interest . . . and to see how we can pull CARICOM along with us'.

Gladstone Bonnick's paper on crime and economic development was heavily criticised by Don Robotham on the basis of the approach to crime taken, its failure to analyse the causes of crime, and the 'extremely thin data base' on which it tries to draw solutions. He described Bonnick's approach which, in his words was 'akin to marshal law' as punitive and based on the 'very dubious assumption' that economic development could not work unless the problem of crime was solved. He criticized what he saw as Bonnick's failure to comment on Stone's assertion that the most important cause of crime was 'the maldistribution of income ... the opening up of the gap between rich and poor which creates a sense of injustice in society and fosters a framework in which crime has become an acceptable thing, certainly at the community level.' This analysis, he pointed out, requires an economic policy which addresses the question of the maldistribution of income. A strategy focusing on strong central authority, for instance the police and army, was not going to work. He dismissed Bonnick's reference to the strong authority system in Asia, pointing out that this was focused on the community rather than central authority. This approach would be difficult in Jamaica because the community structures had been eroded and destroyed by political tribalism. Consequently, resources should be directed at the community since the problem existed at that level.

Robotham presented some data of his own to show that the single largest source of murders was domestic disputes which, he concluded, raised the issue of the quality of family and community life and 'the question of the strategy of economic development that we are pursuing'. Moreover, the fastest growing type of crime was burglary, which further suggested an economic connection. He noted that there was an increased rate of incarceration of women which indicated 'that there is an erosion at the value level in that same zone of interpersonal relations'. He also noted a tendency for the age of offenders to 'edge downwards' into lower age groups.

Peter Phillips called for a social consensus on development, involving parties and nonparty institutions, to decide on where to concentrate limited resources and to deal with questions of crime and security. He questioned the extent to which the 'culture of violence' was the role of the media or changes in communications technology.

Robotham's focus on the gap between rich and poor was echoed by Bruce Golding in his comment on Stone's paper. He suggested that Jamaica was entering an era of 'violent conflict' between the interest of 'one segment of the society and the other'. He criticized what he saw as a tendency to blame the political parties for the violence and expressed disappointment that Stone did not place sufficient emphasis on the question of political culture, in terms of presenting his perspectives on its deficiencies and offering suggestions for its reformation. Peter Phillips echoed Golding's concern with the focus on the political system but suggested that 'the political climate' was not the whole story. Other variables such as the cold war environment needed to be analysed to determine their influence on the institutionalisation of the political system and, consequently, what the implications of a change in that environment meant. Other questions needed to be asked about the consequences to the political parties of the relative decline in the resources at the state's disposal and what were the implications of that for the structure of 'clientelized politics'. Golding argued for the relevance of politicians by suggesting that they had to be responsible for change to the political system since they were the interlocutors between the state and the people.

Neville Ying called for a new approach to politics where it is treated as a profession and public management as a business. Politicians should be trained as managers, and politics will operate along the lines of quality management with quality planning, control and improvements. Furthermore, if politics was to be run as a business, the reward system should reflect this.

Peter Phillips, commenting on Trevor Munroe's presentation, raised the question of the relationship between the new forms of industrial relations concentrated in particular sectors of the economy and the old forms concentrated in others. For instance, how did sugar relate to new service industries and what was the role of the union? He extolled the unions to assume greater responsibility in shaping social policy rather than pursuing a narrow focus on wage negotiations. He posited that the dominance of the political parties could be partly attributed to the inactivity of other critical social institutions such as the trade unions.

Discussion on Beverley Anderson-Manley's presentation revealed contending views on the position of women. One questioner, Morin Seymour, charged that both JLP and PNP governments had 'given away the top jobs to women' but were, nevertheless, still being criticized. Another, Norma Newman, wanted to know how would the women's movement guard against committing some of the 'very sins that they complain about'. She argued that men were 'at great risk' and this required some balance in looking at the problems. Lynette Vassel linked what she saw as the 'crisis' facing the country with the quality of existing male leadership. This leadership, she contended, fails to consider issues of quality of life, human relationships, and vision.

Professor Elsa Leo-Rhynie called for urgency in addressing the inadequacies of the National Policy Statement on women. She urged women's group to lobby to ensure that it was translated to action.

John Maxwell, discussing Henry-Wilson's presentation, warned that there was a tendency to use citizen participation as a means of manipulation rather than giving them real power. The challenge was to broaden the democratic process by sharing power with community groups. This required attracting a higher calibre of community worker competent to make comprehensive sociological analyses of the community, identify community needs and resources to address these, as well as organizational and management skills. Janos Beyer, who worked with community groups to develop community tourism on the North Coast, intervening from the floor, identified a contradiction between policy and action. While the concept of eco-tourism as 'the only possible path for tourism diversification' was accepted, the reality was that large parcels of land were being sold for traditional type development, which was in opposition to eco-tourism.

APPENDIX 3

Summary of Debate

The symposium ended with a panel discussion which allowed some broader commentary on the proceedings. It was chaired by Omar Davies. This appendix provides a brief summary of the key points made by each panelist.

Archbishop Neville DeSouza mentioned the need to question how such a small nation as Jamaica had been able to spawn so many violent people. He suggested that violence was a reaction to the deprivation of basic needs such as love, acceptance and affirmation. In Jamaica's case, he argued, it says something about the society's inability to create and sustain in many citizens a sense of inclusion and creative participation in social life. He believed that the violence in Jamaica, which was endemic, was the method by which the 'marginalized' in society were seeking to take political action in a situation in which government had abdicated the responsibility, vested in them in the 1938 uprisings and subsequent Universal Adult Suffrage, to address their problems. This violence would continue until they were included in the 'reality of the nation' and its economic life — things which they would have regarded as a promise following independence.

Norman Girvan said that while he was excited by the symposium, he was disappointed at the omission of any discussion on the questions of population and the environment. Determining population trends and characteristics was important in any discussion on the twenty-first century in order to address such questions as the needs of that population and the skills and capabilities required for development. Population and environment were interconnected because Jamaica's limited resource base meant that the environment had to be carefully managed in order to sustain its population.

He was impressed at the interconnectedness of the presentations but called for a national consensus to provide a strategic vision for Jamaica in the twenty-first century. This should involve political parties, trade unions, the private sector, churches, women's organisations, *inter alia*, furnished with 'hard information about the kinds of trends we are going to have to deal with' which, hopefully, would result in a document to which all major social and political forces would have to subscribe. The political parties would have to base their campaign on how they intended to implement this document.

Donald Harris called for a focus on what he saw as the key issue of how to orient the financial system to investment for production and innovation. He argued that current discussion on the issue was misguided and highly polarised because it focused exclusively on interest rate policy. It was polarised between the 'production theorists' who advocated a focus on production and who viewed the financiers as 'a bunch of parasites', and the financial theorists who believed that finance drives the system. This polarisation obfuscated the real problem which Harris defined as organising a proper system of credit rationing to ensure that credit was properly directed. This called for a questioning of the institutional framework within which the banking system operated. He identified three models for such a system: the British model in which finance was essentially an autonomous sector — from both business and the state — and left to operate by its own rules; the German system which has an intimate relationship between the banks and the business sector where the banks sit on the board of directors of companies and intervene directly in the allocation of credit to the business sector; and the Asian model which has elements of the other two, where business, banks and the state play a direct role in the workings of the banking system and in the allocation of credit to different sectors in accordance with a predetermined plan. A system of financing must be designed for Jamaica to achieve the objective of promoting production and innovation and define a proper role for government.

In approaching the twenty-first century Maxine Henry-Wilson suggested that we should focus on human capital and its development as opposed to narrowly focusing on the economic question. Any development strategy required human capital of a high calibre. She suggested that discussion on the correct approach to the twenty-first century should involve as much participation as possible and not be left to the government or policy makers. Towards this end she called for papers to be 'disaggregated into operational forms' indicating what needed to be done and who must do it. She urged the 'demystifying' of economic issues, particularly the symposium papers, by translating them into simple terms and making them widely available.

Minister of Finance, Hugh Small, expressed disappointment at the low level of participation in the symposium. This, he felt, reflected the 'disjuncture' in the society and the lack of linkage between important sectors. In particular, 'the public sector people, the policy makers at the political level (both on the government and opposition side) have not given it the kind of support that it deserves'; neither did 'business leaders' who were often critical of government. This was particularly worrying, he believed, in a political culture which did not have 'the facilities for research and reflection'. He said he intended to identify the policy issues and recommendations from the presentations and put it before Parliament for discussion. He also wanted to put them in a form which could be disseminated widely.

INDEX